Religion and Critical Psychology

Religious Experience in the Knowledge Economy

Jeremy Carrette

Routledge
Taylor & Francis Group

LONDON AND NEW YORK

First published 2007
by Routledge
2 Park Square, Milton Park, Abingdon, Oxon OX14 4RN

Simultaneously published in the USA and Canada
by Routledge
270 Madison Ave, New York, NY 10016

Routledge is an imprint of the Taylor & Francis Group, an informa business

© 2007 Jeremy Carrette

Typeset in Sabon by
HWA Text and Data Management, Tunbridge Wells
Printed and bound in Great Britain by
TJ International Ltd, Padstow, Cornwall

British Library Cataloguing in Publication Data
A catalogue record for this book is available from the British Library

Library of Congress Cataloging-in-Publication Data
Carrette, Jeremy R.
  Religion and critical psychology : religious experience in the
  knowledge economy / Jeremy Carrette.
     p.   cm.
  Includes bibliographical references and index.
  1. Psychology and religion. 2. Critical psychology 3. Ethics.
  4. Knowledge, Theory of. 5. Knowledge management.
  6. Information technology. I. Title.
BF51.C37 2007
200.1´9--dc22   2007012708

ISBN10: 0–415–42305–8 (hbk)
ISBN10: 0–415–42306–6 (pbk)
ISBN10: 0–203–93467–9 (ebk)

ISBN13: 978–0–415–42305–2 (hbk)
ISBN13: 978–0–415–42306–9 (pbk)
ISBN13: 978–0–203–93467–8 (ebk)

For Cécile

Contents

Preface

When William James circumscribed his psychological analysis of religious experience, in his second Gifford Lecture at Edinburgh in 1901, he made it clear that he proposed 'to ignore the institutional branch entirely' (James [1902] 1960: 49). James has rightly been critiqued[1] for the limitations of his approach, but he did not quite make the error of explaining social phenomena in terms of psychological phenomena, which Durkheim ([1895] 1982: 125–35), so ardently, regarded as a false explanation. James rather tried to isolate psychological processes and set up the terms for exploring so-called 'religious' experience within the psychological method of individual 'feelings, acts and experiences' (James [1902] 1960: 50). Cognitive science of religion, likewise, seeks to privilege and isolate the 'mind' as a category prior to institutional and social factors (Sperber 1985b: 79). However, the question remains as to whether the psychological method can so easily and coherently isolate 'experience' and 'mind' from the representational orders of knowledge established within institutional discourses; not simply in terms of including the social dimensions of religion and considering the social-institutional aspects of psychological knowledge (Danziger 1990), but in terms of the implicit values of knowledge and, more precisely, the ethics of the disciplinary division of knowledge and the way systems of knowledge protect and isolate their primary categories from external accountability.

This ethical approach to the subject is to follow the French biologist and 1965 Nobel Prize winner Jacques Monod (1972: 161) in seeing how 'values and knowledge are always and necessarily associated in action as in discourse', even within the study of science. Such an ethical attitude raises questions about how ideas are strategically excluded, privileged and ordered within the scientific or humanities enterprise. It raises important questions about the material context of all statements about the self and the mind and their ethical constitution within different regimes of knowledge. Such questions turn the modernist project of the study of religion towards a critical reading of its once cherished – *scientific* – methods, which sustain the category of religion and make it an object of analysis through an uncritical preservation of the method and its inter-disciplinary alliances. It enables us to read the interfaces of different forms of disciplinary knowledge as ethical registers in the constitution of a subject of knowledge. The problem of inter-disciplinary knowledge, as it is articulated in the socio-political reading of psychology and religion, is therefore a way to understand the orientating values of knowledge about the world and the self. In this book, the complexity of ethical values within knowledge will be brought to the surface by examining – what for some, at this stage at least, will be a rather bizarre association – the interface of the history of economics and the study of psychology and religion.

Unfortunately, in the endeavour to assess the values operating at the juncture of inter-disciplinary knowledge, we are faced with the problem that previous attempts to integrate the psychological with the socio-political world of institutions in the theory of religion have remained limited; although feminist and cultural readings did offer some important redirection on this front.[2] The lack of engagement is, however, itself an important historical register of value. This division in the order of knowledge is established in the very formation of nineteenth-century disciplines, along the individual-social divide, that continues to plague the ways we think in the late modern world of academic study. The problem is not resolved by balancing different perspectives, but rather by finding ways to think through the binary divisions and institutional frameworks that shape modern forms of thinking. The solution is, therefore, to think in, through and beyond such frameworks in order to resist the disciplinary isolationism of modernity and reveal the values behind such knowledge.

One way to understand the values behind the individual-social binary at the heart of nineteenth-century subject formation is to follow twentieth-century post-structuralist accounts of discourse (statements within social systems) and read psychological discourse as a socio-political reality; a central characteristic of what has become known as critical psychology. In this scenario, statements, to follow Foucault (1969), occur within a 'field of use' and become bound by rules of formation and coherence. They operate according to a power-knowledge regime and function within the social order. However, while all of these views offer important questions for establishing some social justice within our models of self, they can easily become submerged in a 'Cold War' framework, as Gregory Alles's (2001) incisive reading of Foucault and my previous study of Foucault reveal. Although distinct and in some ways counter to Marx, post-structuralist social models carry much of the same analytic of power and post-war European political discourse into a critical reading of psychology. While I am sympathetic to some of these readings, critique in a post-Cold War world can no longer be framed effectively in the same terms.

Critique was once, according to Terry Eagleton ([1984] 2005: 9), 'a struggle against the absolute state', but now, in world where Left and Right collapse as meaningful terms in globalization and identity politics, the focus shifts; critique must now become a more dynamic struggle against absolute economy and its related absolute knowledge, wherever these emerge in thought and practice. Thus, to address the ethical problematic of the exclusion of the 'institutional branch' requires thinking through and beyond the industrial inter-disciplinary model of the nineteenth century and the post-structural model of the twentieth century (even as we carry these points of reference and critique forward). To think about psychology and religion with the 'institutional branch' today demands thinking through the politics of the present dominant institutions (financial and global corporations) and the ethical forms of knowledge they generate. It requires trying to follow the emerging patterns of inter-disciplinary thinking within a new socio-political environment of what has become known as the 'knowledge economy'; the situation where knowledge (not information) becomes an economic good and where technology reframes how knowledge is both transmitted and used within the socio-economic order. The old industrial discipline of the psychology of religion, as it emerged from the 1890s, is now – like psychology, religion, politics and economics – a specific form of knowledge production saturated by wider economically driven institutions and markets. This is not a reduction of thought to economics or institutions, but rather a recognition that the Western systems of knowledge are now unable to think outside the present economic conditions, which have politically reshaped our lives through their financial and technological domination. Knowledge and thought are bigger than the discourse of 'economics', but all thought occurs within the material conditions of our social and intellectual exchange, especially in the present order of economic hegemony. Specialist disciplinary knowledge, far from challenging the contemporary social order, becomes part of the knowledge production of a market-generating world. We need then to think through the ethical problem of inter-disciplinary knowledge in psychology and religion according to the values of the knowledge economy and its concealed influences on how we think, order and know the world.

Over 100 years after James's reflections on religious experience, we are faced with the fact that inter-disciplinary thinking occurs within the institutional politics of the knowledge economy. This work, therefore, seeks to read the individual-social binary of psychological knowledge, within the context of the knowledge economy, in order to reveal the ethical foundation of knowledge. The problem of knowledge must now become an ethical task, rather than simply a problem of ideology or power, it must become a question of the values behind how we know and understand the world and ourselves, in, through and beyond our ideological aspirations. Central to this ethic of knowledge is the limitations of all knowing, especially within and across our disciplinary constructions. As Monod (1972: 178) makes clear, the 'ethic of knowledge' is appreciating the 'limitations' not just of one's biological being, but also of our knowledge. Being aware of ethics within scientific knowledge, within the categories of knowing, is to establish some ethical account of the formation of knowledge. In making the psychology of religion an object of the political-economic conditions, I am not returning to some Marxist order, those days are behind us, I am also not entertaining some post-modern subversion, those days were only the mistaken tricks of the non-reader, we need therefore to go beyond ideology and social construction to the new ground of ethics. This work thus turns disciplines inside-out to imagine new forms of thinking. Indeed, the theoretical manoeuvres between different subject areas will form unfamiliar combinations of knowledge that will be challenging to many working in a narrow epistemology.[3]

The paradox today is that the rigid rules of modernist discourse are being challenged not by enlightened intellectual engagements from the political Left, but rather from the 'invisible hand' of technological and socio-economic forces that are redefining the nature of our intellectual practices, institutional funding, and forms of knowledge dissemination. Modern industrial forms of knowing and subject division are being transformed in a new knowledge environment. The industrial disciplines were formed for very different scientific and imperial ambitions than are found in the new economic and technologically driven environment (even if the same ambitions are carried forward in new forms). Knowledge is now 'networked', not 'manufactured', across traditional disciplines and reordered according to the 'use-value' and 'technological-economic' benefits. Non-technologically useful knowledge (Mokyr 2005: 2–27), becomes useful within small educational and interest-related retail markets. In this space, knowledge becomes both reinforced along traditional industrial lines as market viability and reconstituted in the new knowledge economy.

In the past inter-disciplinary thinking meant a binary dialogue between different sets of disciplines, but now the production of knowledge in late capitalism allows for the possibility of what I will call, borrowing from the economist Hayek (1973–6: 34–35, 108), 'knowledge catalaxy', self-regulating and decentralised knowledge productions in the free market of knowledge.[4] Knowledge use and knowledge transmission allow for new networks of inter-disciplinary knowledge, overlapping and duplicating, and above all creating – even with the unsettling neo-liberal ideology behind it – ruptures within old industrial disciplinary systems. The knowledge economy is thus both the realisation and mutation of industrial Left and Right critique and it now brings critique to the absolute economy of knowledge production. The implications of this new environment of thinking are still unclear. In the new constellations of institutional power, the industrial model of the psychology of religion is now altered unrecognisably in the collision of disciplines (becoming psychology and religion) and pushed towards its new political and economic frames in late capitalism (the cultural studies of religion and psychology). Critique now tells us something about the end of our political innocence, the end of our dis-connected knowledge and the end of our confused yearnings for certainty. This move beyond the positivity of modern knowledge is not nihilism, reductionism or social determinism, it is recognition that all knowledge 'constitutes an ethical choice' (Monod 1972: 163).

If, as Althusser and Balibar ([1968] 1979: 158) argue, critique of political economy 'means to confront it with a new problematic and a new object; i.e. to question the very object of Political Economy', then we can critique the objects of our 'fragile sciences' – to echo James ([1892] 1985: 334) and extend Wilson's (2004: 8) terminology – by confronting them with new objects and by making the methods themselves the objects of our study and in turn rethinking political economy, psychology and religion. The fragile sciences of religion, psychology and economics are thus ordered by a hidden ethics of knowledge (by which I mean the hidden and debatable values within knowledge and the philosophical ground through which we assert a certain way of shaping what we know). Putting the institutional into the psychological study of religion means confronting the subject with a new ethical object of concern. I will, thus, read political economy through the problem of its foundational philosophical-politic of what it is to be human – something hidden by neo-classical economics – and read psychology according to the new object of political-economic institutions in order to reveal its central values of knowing the world and the self. The ethical order of knowledge occurs at the point of cross-fertilization in imagining ourselves as human beings through the ways we live.

The remaining concealed object in my study is the 'religious', which, following William James ([1902] 1960: 46), I see not as 'any single principle or essence' but rather as a taxonomical order formed by various institutional and ethical investments in the order of knowledge. It is thus part, to follow James again, of the philosophical discourse of the 'more', that which is outside of human empirical enquiry (statements of value not fact). I am thus arguing that 'religion' is a parasitical object created – in part at least – by, and inside, the hidden values of the method of analysis. The methodology stabilizes the object inside the politics of modern social institutional arrangements. In this sense, I see the taxonomical order of religion (disseminated by various institutional powers) as formed in relation to other precarious objects of study, such as 'economy' and 'politics', in the management of knowledge. The study of 'religion' is therefore inseparable from its inter-disciplinary formations. In this respect, the critical study of religion requires a critical study of its methodological disciplinary practices in order to see how the religious object functions at the intersections of its related discourses. By contesting the object of psychology we can extend critique of the category of religion to those discourses that make the religious object a possible subject.

I should add at this point that I am concerned with the 'fragile sciences', rather than the so-called 'hard sciences', because I am shifting psychology away from its physiology components (biology) into the philosophical ground of its statements in the human sciences and a different set of ethical concerns emerge within these two locations of knowledge. As James makes clear, psychology holds an unstable object at the point where philosophy meets physiology and here the science becomes very fragile and value-laden. As James ([1892] 1985: 334) clearly articulated:

> When, then, we talk of 'psychology as natural science' we must not assume that means a sort of psychology that stands at last on solid ground. It means just the reverse; it means a psychology particularly fragile, and into which the waters of metaphysical criticism leak at every joint …

The error of the 'science' of religion is to imagine its methods are without political, economic and philosophical values. In many ways this book is concerned with the theoretical issues before the possibility of a science and extends science to a wider rational canopy of knowledge in the social world. While it is true that the conditions of all sciences are politically and economically driven, in terms of the questions asked, types of project funded, choices of theory and forms of application at any particular point of history, there is no sense in questioning such things as physical laws of gravity, the travel of light and sound and chemical compositions as parts of a cultural-political environment (except at some extreme points of scientific enquiry where natural objects change through methods of observation). Where as I accept, in line with Williams's (2000) discussion, that what constitutes science changes historically and that one strategy can be to develop a wider view of 'science' to include social and ethical dynamics, I prefer Wilson's (2004) idea of 'fragile' sciences, as an echo of James ([1892] 1985: 334), to focus a different set of ethical concerns. I maintain a working distinction between the 'natural' and 'human' sciences in order to differentiate the philosophical object of study and the interference of *a priori* models of knowledge in the study of being human.[5] I have therefore no need to replay tired old debates between religion and science, because these debates subvert the importance of the ethics of knowledge.

This book is, therefore, following a line of critical thinking 'in, through and beyond' the disciplines of religion, psychology, politics and economics by creating a new ground in the ethics of knowledge, which reads the interfaces of those competing ideologues within the sociology of knowledge and the scientific positivity of knowledge in terms of a wider ethical critique. The introduction of the ethics of knowledge, in order to think about old forms of disciplinary knowledge, is a reordering of the subject of knowledge itself. My concern, as will be become evident in the conclusion, is to uncover a disturbing philosophical ground behind all our knowing – the ethics of closure and control in the ways we think. I will, therefore, attempt to read 'knowledge' according to an 'instinct/attitude' of openness or closure at the base of the human sciences, but particularly as it is read across the binary logic of the individual-social. Such an ethic humbles the imaginative possibility of what we might be in the face of not only the limits of knowing, but also in the desire to control knowledge as it becomes manifest in the knowledge economy.

I seek to confront the objects of the absolute economy and absolute knowledge as they frame the creative capacities of imagining human life. In our present era, the discourse of economics is the mask and betrayal of knowing, a mask and betrayal of not only the values through which we live and make the world, but of how we know the world in which we live. Reading economy within the realm of the ethics of knowledge is, as Monod (1972: 165) recognised, the 'knowledge of ethics'; it is being aware of our values and choices. In our present era, critique must become the search for an ethics of knowledge, which will perhaps mean that in the absolute knowledge of the knowledge economy we find the importance of the ethics of not-knowing in order that we may know again.

Acknowledgements

This book began as the 2002 Cunningham Lectures delivered at the Faculty of Divinity, University of Edinburgh, Scotland, in November 2002. The original six lectures at the University of Edinburgh were developed and expanded, and sections were omitted and new chapters included, as the argument of the book evolved during a period of change from the University of Stirling to the University of Kent in September 2004. After a period of transitional hibernation and rethinking, the book was finally completed in Paris during the autumn semester 2006, following an HEFCE-funded research initiative from the University of Kent. I am grateful to the University for supporting me in this way and enabling me to finish the project. The invitation to give the Cunningham Lectures in 2002, the centenary year of William James's Gifford Lectures, *The Varieties of Religious Experience*, was to reflect on the contemporary situation of the psychology of religion. The book differs from my original lectures through extensive revision, updating and rewriting; to the extent that parts of some lectures and one complete lecture were omitted from the final book.

I published, in revised form, the omitted lecture 'Religion and Mestrovic's Post-Emotional Society' in the journal *Religion* ((2004) Vol. 34, pp. 271–89) as a separate study, but retain some references to Mestrovic's work in the completed text. Chapter 4 originally appeared in a somewhat different form as 'Psychology, Spirituality and Capitalism: the case of Abraham Maslow' ((2003) *International Journal of Critical Psychology*, Issue 8, *Spirituality*, pp. 73–95). I am grateful to Lisa Blackman for her interest and support in publishing this article. Two new chapters were included from my subsequent research at the University of Kent. However, the original direction and critique of the lectures remains the same.

My original aim had been to bring the question of the psychology of 'religious experience', which James had explored, into the critical perspectives of contemporary inter-disciplinary thought, particularly following my work on Michel Foucault, economic history and critical theory. The work, therefore, is a critical reading of the psychology of religion, according to its strategies of excluding and privileging certain forms of knowledge. It became increasingly a reflection on the ethics of knowledge and an attempt to resolve a number of concerns presented during my research and teaching at the University of Kent on globalization, the knowledge economy and my engagement with the Lacanian world in Paris, which gave me an increased sense of the different cultural and political readings of psychology and religion in Europe and America. I also included a chapter from new research material I had been developing on a critical reading of cognitive neuroscience and religion; I am grateful to Kelly Buckeley for his interest and publication of other aspects of this research on cognitive science. For the final realisation of this book, I thank Lesley Riddle for her interest and support in publishing the work, and Gemma Dunn and the team at Routledge, Taylor & Francis, for supporting the work through its various stages of publication.

I wish to thank Alister Kee and Marcella Althaus-Reid for originally inviting me to the University of Edinburgh to give the Cunningham Lectures and for their courage to think and support work that challenges dominant trends of thinking in the academy and beyond. I have enormous admiration for them both. I only wish we had longer to develop our conversations while I was living in Edinburgh. I am also grateful to many rich discussions following the lectures with those who attended, especially from those outside the fields of religion and theology, who provided useful inter-disciplinary debates. In particular, I thank Kerry Jacobs, from the Department of Management Studies, at Edinburgh, for his comments.

The later stages of this book are very much part of a new adventure of working at the University of Kent. I am, therefore, grateful to my colleagues in the School of European Culture and Languages for engaging with my ethical-political mapping of knowledge. I am particularly grateful to Karl Leydecker for both his friendship and professional support, which are too great to mention, Robin Gill for creating the possibility to teach at Kent, for his extremely useful comments on the book and for his continuing support for my research and my family, Chris Deacy for his friendship and laughter in the department and Jeremy Worthen for his unique support and creative insight. I am also grateful to the wider community of scholars at the University of Kent, both in the Department and in the School, who are too great to mention, but special mention should be given to Laurence Goldstein for some useful comments on Wittgenstein, Jeff Harrison for some fine editorial comments on the cognitive science chapter and Shane Weller for enriching intellectual exchange.

This book is a response to 20 years of working as both student and teacher in the psychology of religion and it marks my own attempt to speak to one part of my intellectual formation (standing alongside my other formative areas in the philosophy of religion and Christian ethics). I am very grateful therefore to a long line of intellectual voices in my formation and understanding of the field; even though, as they say, I am entirely responsible for the critical views contained in this book. I wish to thank John Hinnells and pay tribute to the late Tony Dyson and the late Robert Hobson, my first teachers of psychological themes in religion and theology at Manchester University in the mid-1980s. I thank Adrian Cunningham, who taught me much about the philosophical displacement of the field during my research on psychoanalysis at Lancaster University, and pay special tribute to my greatest mentor, the late Grace Jantzen, who helped to sharpen my critical philosophical mind, at King's College, London and Manchester. Her death is a great personal and professional loss. During my time in London, I also had the pleasure of meeting Sonu Shamdasani, whose friendship and insights continue to nourish my thinking about the history of psychology.

I have been fortunate to develop some very valuable conversations at various international forums over the years the ideas of this book developed. I am grateful, not least, to Naomi Goldenberg and James Jones for initially inviting me to speak at the American Academy of Religion (AAR) in 1998 and for developing a special AAR panel in 2002 to extend debate on a paper I gave at the 2001 AAR, which formed the basis of one early lecture and now chapter. I have appreciated their honest and open disagreements and their passion for thinking. Naomi's own critical thinking has been an inspiration since I first read her work *Changing of the Gods* (1979) as an undergraduate in the mid-1980s and it is now a privilege to know her in my academic life. I am deeply indebted to her for all her insights and editorial comments as the Routledge reviewer and reader for this book, especially for her clarification of my thinking on the ethics of knowledge and highlighting my own moments of desire for stable objects within thought. I have responded to most, but not all, of her concerns. Nonetheless, the book is very much improved with her own energy for fluid and ethical thinking.

I am also grateful to Diane Jonte-Pace for all those brief moments taken at conferences to wrestle over issues and Bill Barnard for his witness and contributions to these conversations. I know they will not be satisfied with the ideas, but I look forward to the continuing conversations this book may initiate. I also thank Diane Jonte-Pace and William Parsons for publishing one of my earlier papers on critical psychology and religion. I am grateful for the continuing support, friendship and conversations with Richard Fox and

Jude Fox, not least for invitations to deliver parts of this work at Williams College in autumn 2005, and James Bernauer for continuing intellectual engagement and friendship.

I am particularly grateful to Gregory Alles for many informative conversations on various developing issues in this book, not least over a glass or two of Scottish whisky, during his visit to Scotland. His published comments on my first study of Foucault have been invaluable points of intellectual reorientation. During my last years at the University of Stirling, I was grateful to a wonderful team of colleagues including Tim Fitzgerald, Gavin Flood, Alison Jasper, Andrew Hass, Richard Roberts, Vicki Clifford and John I'Anson. I thank them for indulging me in many useful conversations and for their support, especially during a turbulent time as head of department. I have also appreciated various creative conversations in the area of this work with Robert Segal and my first doctoral student in the area of critical psychology of religion, Ewen Miller. I thank Sheila Dow in the Department of Economics at the University of Stirling for introductions to many economists as they visited Scotland and to our joint doctoral student Iara Onate for useful reflections on the history of economics.

As ever, I am indebted to my friend and intellectual collaborator Richard King, who always sees the margins of my thinking and with whom my thought is constantly transformed, not least in the writing of our joint work *Selling Spirituality* (2005), which was written during the research for this book. Thanks also to Flo Faucher-King for keeping me aware of the politics of everyday life and activism; and, of course, for all those life-changing suggestions it took me so long to hear. I am also grateful to Anne-Marie Bourrelly and my wife for introductions to the Lacanian world, for useful textual references and for those early morning seminars in Paris explaining the Borromean knot! Thanks also to Oppie, our neighbour's cat, who moved in for the final writing of this book and provided comforting distractions walking over my desk.

Last, but certainly not least, this book owes its greatest debt to my wife Cécile for grounding me in the embodied world and transforming my life in so many extraordinary ways. Many of the ideas in this book have been nourished through our conversations and I am deeply indebted to her for her creative engagements and encouragement. Her patience, love and affection supported me every day in the final writing of the book and she is the new reader for whom I write. Finally, it is in the meeting of cultures that we have the potential to see things differently and I am grateful to Cécile and Célia for their transforming love.

Introduction

The politics of religious experience

Many people make believe what they experience. Few are made to believe by their experience.

R.D. Laing [1967] (1984) *The Politics of Experience*,
Penguin, p. 118

In the age of the 'knowledge economy' (Drucker [1968] 1969),[1] experience has been returned to its central paradox of knowing between the inner and outer worlds. It has been drawn out of the safe territory of modern interiority into the perplexing world of late modern social uncertainty. It is for this reason that the idea of experience requires constant re-evaluation, because the context and ground of its articulation marks out the complex relation between knowledge, truth and power in each different social, political and historical situation. The framing of experience, both in its theoretical use and its practice in everyday language, provides the mechanisms for both empowerment and disenfranchisement. Indeed, the semantic territory of experience and its philosophical analysis is contested precisely because it offers the possibility of facilitating and restricting individual and social action and related forms of knowledge.

To understand the discourse of experience is to understand something of the very quality of human consciousness and its embodied and lived realities in the social and political world. What makes this idea even more fascinating is that its very epistemological ambiguity opens up the politics of knowledge itself. Reading experience is reading the self, society and environment inside the very categories we have constructed to know the world. Experience, as has been well documented, is therefore never isolated from the theoretical models we have for the experience. Experience thus becomes the process of the ongoing imagining and re-imagining of ourselves and the world. Even the very theoretical articulations or pronouncements about experience carry a qualitative judgement about the conditions of experience; such that discourses about experience are themselves involved in the political mapping of experience. How discourses of sensory data, embodied codes, institutions, culture and language are modelled in the discourse of experience contributes to the will-to-power of experience.

More importantly, the theoretical dependency of experience means that it is the so-called experts in theory that seek to offer claims for the truth about experience. It also means that social groups appeal to the primacy of experience as a device to convince people about who they are and the nature of the world they live within. At the same time the contemporary shifting discourses about experience move in and out of the strained language of modernity and the even more thwart language of post-modern relativism. This predicament of experience means that Martin Jay ends his history, or archaeology of experience, with an invitation to join the interactive journey of making experience rather than making a claim to have captured experience (Jay 2005: 409). Jay's appeal to Blake's poetic imagining of the 'songs of experience', which frames his work and creates the title of his book, reflects his intellectual sensitivity to the academic limits of 'knowing' experience in its cognitive, linguistic, embodied and social formation.

Martin Jay's (2005) work on the concept of experience in American and European culture recognises that it is difficult to eradicate experience because, following Joan Scott's insight, he realises that it is 'so much part of everyday language, so imbricated in our narratives that it seems futile to argue for its expulsion' (Scott quoted in Jay 2005: 4). Instead, Jay focused his work on the different 'modalities' of experience, linking experience and language and holding 'the productive quality of discourse' (Scott in Jay 2005: 6). Experience for Jay becomes the 'nodal point' of 'public language and private subjectivity', the space between 'expressible commonalities and the ineffability of the individual interiority', even as this carries a certain Jamesian psychologism (Jay 2005: 6–7). The constant basis of 'otherness', as Jay indicates, within experience and the constant transformation of consciousness means that he and others are led into a hall of mirrors and distorting points of reflection. However, Jay does attempt to navigate the subject-object dialectic by showing how experience functions in religious, aesthetic, political and historical discourses and in so doing he creatively appreciates the 'volatility' of the concept.

Unfortunately, in Jay's admirably democratic attempt, as cultural historian, to avoid the 'claim to exclusive ownership of an experience' and the 'stigma of conservative essentialism', there is something of an ethical impasse that the 'struggle' to live certain lives requires. Even as we need to create space for the conversation of experience we also need to make some ethical judgement in our will-to-experience. Making choices about the experiences and the social orders we wish to construct for those experiences requires some assessment of the disciplines we use to evaluate the category of experience itself – not least the disciplines of economics, psychology and religion, which we can loosely capture under the human sciences. These discourses impinge on the making of experience, and the meta-representational thinking *about* the making of experience, through the institutional validations of our material order and the practices of everyday living. While not all experience is institutional, the discourses of psychology, economics and religion are all grounded in institutional practice and these social orders interface with innate predispositions to determine the articulations of embodied life.

As the sociologist Georg Simmel (1908a: 37) rightly identified, the problems of the category of experience relate to the binary problem of the individual and the social, which will become the central theoretical concern of this book and the platform for understanding the ethical ground of knowledge. Experience is a mediating category between interiority and exteriority and one that is framed by the fluctuations of time. It allows one to validate events and it marks out both autonomy and dependency. This place between individual and social reality, and between autonomy and dependency, locates experience inside the ethics of knowledge, because the very fluidity of its mediation means that the point of closure or openness draws a boundary of operation and encloses the known against the unknown. Experience is located at this ethical point between knowing and not-knowing. It is here that the forms and ways of knowing determine the utterance of experience. The individual-social binary thus becomes the dividing line of knowledge and experience; it constitutes one of the central ethical fields of knowledge that in turn makes experience.

The important idea within Simmel's analysis is that the individual-social is never closed, but rather becomes a dynamic 'relation', 'an interactionally determined pattern of development among forms of association' (Simmel 1908b: 252).[2] There is always an inverse relationship between the two variables:

[T]here is, as it were, an unalterable ratio between individual and social factors that changes only in form. The narrower the circle to which we commit ourselves, the less freedom of individuality we possess; however, this narrower circle is itself something individual, and it cuts itself off sharply from all other circles precisely because it is small. Correspondingly, if the circle in which we are active and in which our interest hold sway enlarges, there is more room in it for the development of our individuality; but *as parts of this whole*, we have less uniqueness: the larger whole is less individual as a social group ... Expressed in a very terse schema, the elements of a distinctive social circle are undifferentiated, and the elements of a circle that is not distinctive are differentiated.

(Simmel 1908b: 257)

Simmel reveals the difficult politic of freedom in experience in so far as the conversations about experience are becoming fewer and fewer as the theoretical models for thinking about experience become ever more restricted. If experience and the beliefs sustaining experiencing are held within ever fewer institutions then the public space for articulating alternative experiences becomes restricted; something that becomes even more pertinent when the economic institutions increasingly dictate our experience. Experience and thinking about experience constantly evolve, but the direction and the shaping of experience requires scrutiny.

The problem is that the options to think and imagine experience become limited when social and political systems and their corresponding institutional structures reduce the forms of knowledge. The question of experience thus also becomes an ethical question of the types of discourse that are available for experience and the existing institutions that sustain such discourses. Resistance is possible in an oppressive world precisely because of the plurality of discourses that are available for making and unmaking experience inside each specific historical struggle, but this requires a continuation of the plurality of discourses and institutions for corrective encounters. This diversity of associations and interest was important for the economist Friedrich Hayek (1944, 1945) in the overcoming of totalitarian systems through the market, but his own solution now returns us to the same problem in the new conditions of restriction in the neo-liberal economic hegemony. The ethical task before us is always to ascertain the forces of absolute knowledge, especially when so-called freedom unwittingly reduces the institutional orders that can provide alternative discourses.

Politics, the locus of experience and late modernity

In the light of the complex politic of experience and the discourses about experience, writing a book about a particular *type* of experience and the *disciplinary* modelling of experience raises all sorts of problems, especially when we locate these discussions inside the problems of late modern society. It returns us to the celebrations and suspicions of experience Jay (2005) has so carefully documented. Experience is problematized in the present age – and creates a new intellectual enigma – because of the instability between the individual and social worlds. There is a volatility and paradoxical reversal between inner and outer and public and private, as the locus of self is both limited to the body and simultaneously understood through the external enactment of the body on the public screen; resulting in a disembodied-embodiment. Experience is multiple, without constancy and without certainty, it is entirely self-determined and entirely other-determined. It has become the impossible because the orders of the knowledge economy require competition not coherence. To consider the constant re-inventing of experience in a technological and globalized world opens up the question of the impossibility of experience in a so-called post-modern reality. As the cultural theorist Terry Eagleton remarked, in an article concerned about academic practice and reflection in the contemporary university:

> According to one modernist theory, the problem was not having experiences but communicating them … For a postmodern culture, the situation is the exact reverse. Now it is communication that is easy and experience that is difficult. Instead of experiencing the world, we now experience the experience of it.
>
> (Eagleton 2006: 18)

Eagleton's comment pertains to the political problem of experience and Eagleton's own debate with E.P. Thompson, which Jay (2005: 190ff) identified in British Marxism. It raises the question of how experience is related to the ideological superstructure and the 'romantic' appeals in Leftist literature, including the works of R.D. Laing (noted at the beginning of this chapter), to an empirical experience – in the tradition of Hume – to escape the modern political order (see Jay 2005: 172, 200). However, Eagleton's recent comments also register the problem of how to understand such discourses of experience in a technological world of mediated experience and how academic thinking about experience may itself be implicated in the process. The very simulation of experience and the alteration of time and space in the 'network society' (Castells 1999) prevent the possibility of certain types of 'reflective' experience; or at the very least the conditions of human reflection about experience are changing as the locus of experience is dispersed. Good 'old time' reflective experience may be a privilege not of the capitalist bourgeois, but rather of those outside of the capitalist driven technological world. Experience and the ability to think about experience become problematic when individuals are faced with 'the unprecedented expansion of theoretical and practical perspectives' (Simmel 1957: 217). We are so overwhelmed by the multiple systems of knowledge for making experience that experience becomes indecipherable. Giorgio Agamben ([1978] 1993: 13–14) expresses such a predicament poignantly when he writes:

> The question of experience can be approached nowadays only with an acknowledgement that it is no longer accessible to us ... For modern man's average day contains virtually nothing that can still be translated into experience ... Modern man makes his way home in the evening wearied by a jumble of events, but harrowing or pleasurable as they are, none of them will have become experience ... It is this non-translatability into experience that now makes everyday existence intolerable – as never before – rather than an alleged poor quality of life or its meaninglessness compared with the past (on the contrary, perhaps, everyday existence has never been so replete with meaningful events).

Attempts to clear experience and thought – romantically or not – from the debris of modernity may be becoming increasing impossible because we lose the ability to think about experience without the conviction and passion of a community of experience. In such an atmosphere the ability to think is no longer, as Sartre (1948) believed, a 'privilege', but rather a professionally strained economic repackaging of nineteenth century disciplinary formations for the service of the new skills-based economy, where knowledge becomes *techne* (Drucker 1993: 24; Mokyr 2002: 4).[3] The very possibility of individuals being linked together by experience is undermined by the refusal to see the present economic orders of truth as themselves implicated in the making and unmaking of experience. We face a complex situation where the strategy of ordering experience and the knowledge of experience is hidden in the sheer force of dis-integrating experience in the market. Knowledge as *techne* removes the capacity for critique of knowledge, because knowledge is applied to the known rationality of economy rather than to the unknown rationality of values.

The future of experience will be determined by the theories and beliefs we hold and our ability to unmask the hidden values of knowledge about experience. As we have seen, the question of experience becomes a question of what types of discourse we wish to sustain and support for our narratives of experience. It becomes a question of the institutions and discourses that support such ways of living in the world. The resulting cacophony of circulating discourses of modernity increases the individual need for 'a fixed and unambiguous point of reference' (Simmel 1957: 223), which can only be established by drawing back knowledge to the philosophical ground of how we imagine what it is to be human and interrogating the discourses and institutions that inform such an imagination. However, the common error, as Jerrold Seigel (2005: 43) argues, in a challenge to Charles Taylor's (1989) history of the self, is to think that, because the individual stabilizes the experience of the self, it is *only* the self that is making such experience, rather than the languages and institutions in which that person is embedded. The politic of experience and the self returns us again to the moral register of the individual-social binary problem and the values that unify this dynamic relation. Only at this point can we discover the will-to-power of our experience and the ethical force that draws the line in the shifting sands of change.

Critique and religious experience

The theoretical tension in the discussion so far rests on the interaction of three orientating concepts, *experience, knowledge* and *institutions* and the way they are read ethically in relation to each other and across the 'artificial unities' of the individual and the social (Beer 2002: 102). The weight of this problem is at the heart of James's *The Varieties of Religious Experience* (1902), where experience mediates a certain arrangement of knowledge and operates upon a strategic omission of the institutional. The binary politic, however, unravels at the very point of the negotiated arrangement of knowledge in the inverse relation of the two variables, such that when James seeks to ignore the social-institutional it returns in the operations of the institutional religious language used to mark out the experience of the individual. The inverse relation is also seen at the point at which the emerging institutional apparatus of psychological knowledge employs individualism as a defining method. This can be seen in James 'arbitrary' classificatory schema of religion, organised as it is around *individual* religion (James 1902: 50). While James recognises there is 'no one essence' to religion, he is unable to theorise the knowledge and institutions that allow him to make his own 'religious object' and the implicit values he asserts in the making of such psychological-religious objects (James 1902: 46–7). Late modern scholars have usefully picked up many of these problems surrounding James's text in a wider critical analysis of religious experience, but the critical approach avoids sufficient analysis of the psychological.

The specific analysis of religious experience since the 1980s, for example, embraces important lines of critical and cultural theory, in relation to the respective waves of philosophical critique, from Wittgenstein's work on language to post-structuralist and post-colonial inspired readings of Foucault. In these debates, 'religious experience' has been explored as rhetorical and ideological (Proudfoot 1985; Jantzen 1989; Sharf 1998; King 1999; Fitzgerald 2000; McCutcheon 2003) in accordance with the politic of representation between theological and 'secular' scholarly allegiance.[4] However, while James's own philosophical concerns with the category of 'religion' and 'religious' experience have been brought under greater critical scrutiny,[5] the supporting discourse of the psychological 'science' of religion remains seriously insulated from such critical reflection at the point of inter-disciplinary engagement.[6] One of the reasons for this hesitation is that the wider traditions of the subject of religion are caught in the modernist politic of distinguishing a 'science of religion' from the assertions of theology, rather than developing a critique of the contributing disciplinary knowledge. There is an odd collusion of knowledge to achieve a certain political objective. This means there is yet to be full appreciation of the related inter-disciplinary politics and the supporting institutional apparatus of psychological knowledge, especially in its contribution to the making and unmaking of the religious object and religious experience.[7]

While all modern disciplines of knowledge have faced independent critical analysis of their objects and discourses in the post-1968 reconfiguration of knowledge, the psychological subject is preserved at the point of its inter-disciplinary differentiation. This is not simply a question of whether psychological knowledge is reductive of religion (a well-rehearsed debate), but rather what order of political knowledge is sustained in the appeals to the discourse by scholars of the 'science' of religion and psychologists. The modern discipline of psychology that informs the study of religion is thus implicated in the political shaping of 'religious experience' *and* the critique of 'religious experience'. It is therefore necessary to establish a critique of the political structures of psychological knowledge in its encounter with religion in order to break the illusions of a value free knowledge.

Russel McCutcheon (2003: 261) rightly argues, from the 'discipline of religion', that 'future scholarship in our (sic) field will investigate *how it is that this particular socio-rhetoric makes selves (a.k.a., citizens) appropriate to the needs of those whose material interests dominate the modern, liberal-democratic nation-state*'.[8] In the same wave of critical thinking, 'critical psychology' attempts to bring psychological knowledge to political account, but in the inter-disciplinary points of connection these critical values of knowledge are concealed and largely undeveloped; not least in an alliance of amnesia to preserve the imagined object of 'religion' and the imagined neutral object of psychology. Ironically, the critique of the category of 'religion' is caught in the deployment of methods that preserve and make the category of 'religion' possible. The critical amnesia can be seen in McCutcheon's focus on the problem of 'religion' without drawing sufficient attention to the problem of the objects of the related fields of study. He, for example, assumes psychologists have the benefit of 'knowing precisely what constitutes their field' (McCutcheon 2001: 119).

I hope to show the psychological object is as unstable, and as obscure, as the religious object and that there is an important ideological link set up in the inter-disciplinary work, which is masked inside the politics of isolating subjects of knowledge. The making of 'selves' for 'nations' is also profoundly linked to the alliance of the 'religious' subject with the orders of psychological and economic knowledge. Future reading in the history of the discipline of religion will also, therefore, need to bring all the detailed suspicion of 'socio-rhetoric' and 'material interests' to the intersections of disciplines and the collusions with the human sciences – something this study attempts to do in relation to economics and psychology. The making and unmaking of the 'religious' object has been the historical practice of the 'sciences' of religion, but if the socio-political interests are to be seen clearly there needs also to be some understanding of the making and unmaking of the 'methods' of religion and their adoption of the material interests of the old industrial economy and the new knowledge economy of corporate culture. The act of stabilising the object of 'religion' is an inter-disciplinary exercise and the critique of 'religion' is the beginning of the critique of those forms of knowledge used in the critique of 'religion'.

In order to reveal its own investments in the knowledge economy, the psychological study of religion, as a key marker in the discourse of religious experience, has to be re-examined according to the new objects of knowledge; not with the aim of returning knowledge to pre-modern belief, but to place all knowledge inside the late modern context of the economy of knowledge – the present dominant regime that informs all subjects of knowing. If we assume that living institutions and communities always sustain discourses then it is always important to identify the related institutions and communities that require the discourse and the object of study, which must certainly be more complex than any one-dimensional reading of the social order. It is my contention that the discourse of psychology is caught in a specific ethical-political ordering of experience, knowledge and institutions along the axis of the individual-social divide, which reflects the values that make and unmake the religious object.

Proudfoot's hidden politic of experience

In order to anchor my position and identify more clearly the ground from which I write, I want to engage with Wayne Proudfoot's now classic study of 'religious experience' as a conversational partner in the debate. I wish to begin by engaging Proudfoot's position because his own strategic closures of discussion enables me to draw out more clearly my specific critical contribution and to show how a will-to-power of experience requires new forms of classification about not only religious experience but the disciplinary reading of such experience in the psychology of religion. I want to do this in order to show how the ethical-politics of knowledge implicates 'psychology' and 'religion' as overlapping sites of critique. Proudfoot's study is thus representative of an important intellectual watershed in the reading of religious experience, but I wish to show how it – along with subsequent studies of its nature – is a *modernist* 'placeholder' for the 'material interests' of the social-apparatus, established in and through its allegiance to psychological knowledge. I do *not* question its central insights, but rather note its theoretical restrictions and limits. What I wish to show is how psychological knowledge functions as a support inside the critique and reflects a hidden ideological value.

My concern is not to increase the value of religion against modernity (although that is often a strategic trope), but rather to show how the practices of modernity in the study of religion are implicated in the political closure of representations for understanding human beings. I thus take the critical project of religion seriously enough to be suspicious of the emperor's new clothes and push the critical platform to those old industrial and neo-liberally transformed supporting fields of the discipline of religion. I am seeking therefore to appreciate some of the central contributions made by Proudfoot, but recognise the need to push his thinking further into a new political concern with psychology. Because my wider ethical-political positioning of psychology and religion may appear too far-fetched at this stage in my argument, I will appeal to the shared ground of the philosophy of discourse to engage Proudfoot's work and only later will I show how psychology holds an ethical-political structure, not only in its encounter with the discourses of 'religion' but as a cultural practice.

Wayne Proudfoot's incisive 1985 study offers philosophical 'scrutiny', using insights from Wittgenstein's language games (Proudfoot 1985: 84, 90, 133, 171, 28–30, 209–10, 214), psychological theory and philosophy of mind, to explore the concept of religious experience in Schleiermacher, James and Otto. His central contribution is to question the appeals to religious experience as the ground of belief by illustrating the 'ambiguity' within the term and its function within language. Proudfoot seeks to show how the 'concepts, beliefs, grammatical rules, and practices' (1985: 228) shape an understanding of an experience as religious. In his engagement with the theological piety of Schleiermacher he shows that experience is never prior to the concepts and beliefs, but rather formed by them through a hermeneutic of experience. Proudfoot shows that there is no 'uninterpreted given' in experience or some irreducible ground of experience. As he convincingly argues: 'Religious beliefs and practices are interpretations of experience, and they are themselves fit objects of interpretation' (1985: 41).

Following two lines of interpretation in the hermeneutical and pragmatic tradition, he correctly shows the different 'interests' (1985: 67) involved in interpretation. He thus marks out the difference between an 'understanding of the description under which the experience is identified by the subject or in the culture in which it is embedded, and an attempt to arrive at the best explanation of the experience' (1985: 71). The middle sections of the work explore the ideas of emotion and mysticism to show, following cognitive theory, that belief is 'constitutive of the experience' (1985: 154). Responding to questions of reductionism, Proudfoot usefully concludes by differentiating 'descriptive' (subjective explication) and 'explanatory' (theoretical) accounts of religious experience and also recognises the 'explanatory commitment' within the identification of experience as religious.

In the process of mapping out the respective types of claims about religious experience, Proudfoot is also able to show how the rhetoric of experience operates in religious discourse as 'protective strategies' for 'apologetic purposes' and to avoid contestation; such that Schleiermacher appeals to religious experience as if it constitutes a primary God-consciousness that cannot be questioned (it seeks to close the discussion through the rhetoric). This mapping out of the cognitive and strategic nature of thought holds fascinating links to the 'rules of formation' in Foucault's archaeology, just as the links to Wittgenstein's language games parallel with Foucault's idea of the statement and discursive practice. However, the central difference between these two is located in the appreciation of language as discursive practice and language as ontological rules.[9] This distinction reveals precisely the theoretical problem at stake in Proudfoot's work. He limits his work to rhetorical analysis and only infers indirectly that discourse operates within institutional contexts and social struggles of power. For example, Proudfoot (1985: 232) is aware of the tensions between religious discourse and science:

The concept of religion and the idea of religious experience were both shaped by the conflict between religion and the growth of scientific knowledge.

However, this conflict remains at a generalised level of concern as a backdrop to his unease with the use of religious experience in the writings of Schleiermacher and James. What never appears fully under his critical gaze is the 'science' within his own philosophical discussion and the strategic significance this holds for his own 'protective strategy'. What is extraordinary is that the signifiers *religion* and *experience* come under extensive critical examination – and rightly so – but then the philosophical discourse solidifies other terms to stabilize this critique without comment (he rhetorically closes the debate with appeals to a secondary order discourse). In my view, the 'most important ambiguity' in 'religious experience' is not religion or experience as such, but the *apparatus of modernity* that makes such terms function, namely the discourse of psychology which carries such authority in Proudfoot's work. We can thus see that *psychology* functions in the work, as in so much so-called 'science-of-religion' critical discussion, as a 'placeholder' of truth or authority. The reason for this authority is that the prevailing discourse of psychology has an institutional support (read economic and political validity) to displace the 'placeholder' of religious experience.

I am *not* seeking to re-instigate religion over science, but rather expose the hidden political and economic entanglement of those inter-disciplinary discourses operating in relation to the discourses of religion. Proudfoot, and other such critical thinkers, have done a good job problematizing the categories, but what I want to develop is a certain awareness of the critiques in order to show their own political operations in the theoretical leakages of modern knowledge. If the discourse of *religious experience* is formed in the conflict of science and religion, my contention is to show that the psychology of religion was formed in the historical shift within state-organisations of power (business, education, medicine and social welfare) to create new 'subjects' of political order.[10]

There are two aspects of Proudfoot's work that I want specifically to examine; first, the place of psychology as philosophical 'placeholder' and, second, the key concern for 'context' and 'conditions'. I will inter-relate these aspects to establish the critical focus of my own work. These two aspects are the most under-theorized (but vitally important) aspects of his work and ones that are important for a critical reading of the psychology of religion and inter-disciplinary thinking. The introduction of psychology, to be fair, is something he follows up outside his particular expertise and from a later vantage point it is easier to critically contextualise, but they nonetheless need to be given some treatment. What I am trying to establish in this book is the hidden ideological assertion in an argument. I want to reveal what a discipline does not want to see in its logic – the will-to-truth of a position. This is an ethical-political assertion subsequently justified according to a disciplinary logic or the 'available evidence'. As Proudfoot (1985: 110) establishes for us:

> We must employ whatever evidence is available to us in order to ascribe emotions, attitudes, and even beliefs to ourselves or other.

Such a move must entail a working blindness to the disciplinary logic. Indeed, I agree with Proudfoot that there is a need to explore the 'logical placeholder' which seeks to 'guarantee' the system of knowledge, but where Proudfoot applies his thinking to theological systems of 'religious experience' I want to apply such thinking to the apparatus of inter-disciplinary knowledge (Proudfoot 1985: 148). My argument in relation to Proudfoot and throughout this book is that there is – what I will call – a 'critical myopia' in inter-disciplinary studies of 'religion', which involves the same 'protective strategies' that occur in theological readings of experience. In the end what this means is that we cannot escape the political will-to-power that frames our knowledge – the ethical-political context. Let me show how I see this operating in Proudfoot in his use of psychology and then locate this in his discussion of context.

Proudfoot notes a series of experimental pieces of work, largely from 1970s social psychology (notably the period when social psychology went through a 'crisis' in thinking).[11] The point of introduction comes during a discussion of emotion, in which he has already appealed to Aristotle's idea on emotion in the *Rhetoric*, to show that cognitive processes shape bodily emotion. I fully endorse the complex model of emotions put forward by Proudfoot to include cognitive and physical aspects, but my concern is one of method and critique.[12] Following the introduction of theories of emotion, Proudfoot explores philosophical and psychological critiques of 'the traditional view' (*vis-à-vis* the view of Hume and James-Lange minus Aristotle).[13] In the psychological critique, we are introduced to an 'ingenious set of experiments', 'controversial experiments' and 'a more comprehensive research program' (Proudfoot 1985: 98, 105, 108, 109) to confirm – with 'evidence' – what Aristotle had already deduced through careful reflection; that cognitive factors influence emotion (Proudfoot 1985: 98).

Proudfoot then outlines a range of social psychology experiments to show the link between 'physiological arousal and contextually determined cognitive labels'. For example, 'attribution theory' shows how people 'perceive the causes of their bodily states and behaviour' and this adds useful narratives to enhance the thesis that the perception and explanation of events draws on the available cognitive evidence to construct an experience (Proudfoot 1985: 108–10). Proudfoot also outlines an experiment from Pahnke (1970) attempting to create a 'constant cognitive context' (with a Christian Good Friday service) for a drug induced (physiological) event. The aim is to show how the attribution is determined by the contextual data in order to make sense of the physical sensation (Proudfoot 1985: 105–7). Later in this discussion, Proudfoot turns towards religious communities and conversion to reveal the methods of cognitive persuasion in a circular logic that shows involvement, in this case with chanting, is given justification by later belief about the action (Proudfoot 1985: 112–14). However, in a psychological world, we are persuaded by being immersed in psychological *use*, we become convinced of psychological truth because it dominates the politics of everyday life and is sustained by the dominant institutional orders.

At one level, these are all useful additional illustrations of the central theoretical problem, but through a critical self-reflexive reading we can see how they work as 'placeholders' (to protect against exposure of the hidden ideological belief). 'Religion' and 'experience' are given detailed discursive analysis, but social psychological theory is never critically explored (although we do find a critical discussion of psychological verbs in relation to Wittgenstein earlier in the work).[14] The reason for the lack of critical reading of psychology is that it already exists in the academic culture as 'available evidence'. Even the qualification 'controversial' experimentation is seen to require no further explanation or political concern. The social psychological narrative (although certainly not all the psychological referents) are imported into this 1980s text with a cultural aura of 'ineffability' that he rightly interrogates in James's model of mysticism (Proudfoot 1985: 148). Of course, Proudfoot is doing no more than he recognises in his own study. He is offering 'the best explanation for what is happening' and using the 'concepts and beliefs employed' from his 'immediate context' (Proudfoot 1985: 146–7). His own 'critical myopia' is the failure to see how the 'rules' of his own discourse operate inside his critical reading of religious experience. It is to his credit that Proudfoot sees the 'rules' of engagement, but what he does not see is that he is inside the process of the 'rules that govern the employment of the terms by which a religious experience is identified' (Proudfoot 1985: 119).

The problem he does not see is that the critical insight he makes about 'religious experience' is true of all language games. The second order language of the science or philosophy of religion is not exempt from the rules or the political structures governing such rules. Critical myopia is a strategy employed to gain authority. The tragedy is that it is not possible to create a position of imperial truth outside the discourses and institutions that create such truth. I would not at this point wish to suggest we drift into the quagmire of relativism, but I do wish to show how our discourses follow rules of argumentation that reflect ethical and political values. It is here that we touch on the second aspect of Proudfoot's work that I think remains under-theorized; and, as we shall see throughout this study, it is precisely at the points of under-theorized knowledge that we reveal our hidden values.

Proudfoot's under-theorizing of psychology is linked to his restrictions around the discussion of the 'conditions' and the 'context' of experience.[15] Proudfoot, in a similar vain to Wittgenstein, understands the rules of language taking place within social processes, but never spells out the institutional location. What Proudfoot is unable to do is move from a cognitive theory to a critical social theory, even though he shows full awareness of this dimension. When analysis of discourse remains at the rhetorical level it never sufficiently marks out the ethical and political nature of thought. We find here a desire for a modernist 'science' of language and a restraint to follow through the implications of the wider social conditions and what this might mean for the order of knowledge that supports the argument. The anxiety within knowledge, once it leaves the assertions of positivity, is the vacuum it creates for stable authority. It is because of this situation that much 'science' of religion can appeal to psychology as a guarantee of knowledge without following through the fact that psychological knowledge might itself be open to the flux of language games and a will-to-power. The elision around context and conditions and the attempt to create an ontological cover over such questions is the crisis of modern knowledge.

Proudfoot maps the problem of context and the conditions of knowledge extremely well, but ends his study at this point. To be fair to Proudfoot, his work does not seek to demonstrate more than the shift in thinking from the essentialism of religious experience to the cognitive and rhetorical play of language, but he cannot but face the fact that as Wittgenstein argues language is 'public':

> [T]he concepts and beliefs are constitutive of the experience, careful study of the concepts available in a particular culture, the rules that govern them, and the practices that are informed by them will provide

access to the variety of experiences available to persons in that culture. Though it may be difficult to reconstruct, the evidence required for understanding the experience is public evidence about linguistic forms of practice.

(Proudfoot 1985: 219)

The rules of language do not appear from nowhere, they are part of the 'culture' and although Proudfoot is caught in explaining 'explanation' in the study of religious experience and marking out the problem of reductionism he is led towards the need for 'historical' circumstances (Proudfoot 1985: 225). As Proudfoot has already made clear:

People understand and identify their experience in terms of the concepts and beliefs available to them.

(1985: 184)

Unfortunately, the critical limit of Proudfoot's project does not allow him to see the cultural context of his thinking, which allows his import of the psychological. Although he does recognise that James 'could only have written in a culture in which there was some meaning to the concept of religious experience' (Proudfoot 1985: 184). Proudfoot's key insight is to see both 'descriptive' and 'explanatory' accounts as 'cultural'. However, what is lacking in the inter-disciplinary construction of the discipline of religion is to see how fields such as psychology and sociology, which carry intellectual authority, are themselves vulnerable to the same strategies that believers themselves assume. Could it be that we are all subject to a will-to-power? Such claims hide themselves behind the institutional validity prevailing at the time. What we need is to free knowledge from its certainty in order to make reality. It is not just 'seeing-as' or 'experiencing-as' as Wittgenstein and Hick reveal to Proudfoot, but 'theorizing-as' (Proudfoot 1985: 171).

What Proudfoot so usefully unravels is the 'explanatory commitments', but there is more 'evidence' to account for than is put forward on the table for analysis. What should be considered in the 'conditions' of 'explanation'? If thought is 'strategic' as Proudfoot argues – and Foucault before him had articulated so clearly – then it might be that it is 'not the relations of meaning but the relations of power' that become significant (Foucault [1976] 1980). When Proudfoot offers suggestions of the kind of explanation that could be offered for religious experience he includes the 'cultural patterns of thought, action, and feeling' (Proudfoot 1985: 226), but the 'cultural' is never given sufficient critical exploration. Proudfoot is aware that the *cultural, religious* and *economic*, despite their philological problems, still have what I would like to call a 'use-value' – their non-essential nature gives them strategic power in their deployment within institutional practice. As Proudfoot (1985: 198) recognised:

> The fact that it cannot accurately be ascribed to people in many societies does not require that it be excluded from the accounts we give of those societies.

It is indeed the 'habits of interpretation' (Proudfoot 1985: 226) within the study of 'religion' that we need to explore and this requires extending the evidence to the apparatus of knowledge that allows the 'explanatory commitment' to have a purchase in the social world. We can extend the rational platform of enquiry and see that is not only important to map the concepts and beliefs of those using the discourse of 'religious experience', but the related forms of knowledge that allow the very explanation itself. The discursive strategies of religious experience are political because they too arise from the 'contextual conditions' (Proudfoot 1985: 226). They are indeed difficult to identify but cognition is always a social processes of language-users living within political institutions. It is the institutions that support and service a discourse and turning our attention to such institutions – the political and economic infrastructure of our thought –might reveal more of our own 'explanatory commitments' in the theory and method of religion; and, in this instance, the psychology of religion.

In some ways, Proudfoot might argue that I have hijacked his work and attempted to pull lines of argument beyond his domain of use in the philosophy of religion. However, his thought contains such openings by the very nature of the mobility of language and we can perhaps see my reading as an acknowledgement of how he has shifted the debate to account for the conditions of knowledge and strategies of thought. It is at the edges of his work that I have tried to extend his thinking to what he does not think – to his unfinished thinking – and it is here I wish to begin my own study. The theoretical difference is between Wittgenstein and Foucault and the difference between language-games and discourse in the two writers. Wittgenstein is more specific in his analysis, because he wishes to reside at the level of language-users in a less ambitious manner than Foucault.[16] Foucault attempts to explore the 'conditions of thought' in the network of social relations and while this creates more uncertainty it reveals the heart of knowledge within social relations.

The idea of discourse takes us into the ethical-politics of experience. It raises a question about the kind of value commitment involved in using psychology – or any other method – to explain our practices in the social world. The scholar of religion draws on a field of study like psychology with a set of assumptions about the kind of work this disciplinary discourse can have for his or her reading of an equally ambiguous discourse called 'religion', but why suspend one category and not the other? What would it be like if we questioned the conditions of psychological thinking inside religion and exposed its strategies and relations of power? Perhaps, we might see that all our knowledge is a temporary process, dynamic and evolving. We may also have to face the fact that we can no longer build empires without some honest articulation of our values and acknowledgement of who benefits from such thinking. Knowledge might be the social apparatus through which we order the world in a new economy of power, not that of industrial imperialism but global networks, which requires a new ethic of thought as disciplines are reshaped for a new knowledge environment. This book is an attempt to map the discourse of psychology in such a knowledge environment and to examine the ethical ground of such forms of knowledge.

The twilight of modernist experience

By extending the discussion of religious experience inside the ethical-politic of the psychology of religion, I am trying to map the social orders and macro-politic of knowledge behind such thinking. I am attempting to shift the discussion away from modernist 'experience' to what I see as a new set of strategies of formation emerging in the contemporary social world. I am not suggesting that the category of religious experience or experience more generally is no longer valid, because discourses from different historical moments continue to oscillate in the public imagination for transformation and reconfiguration. I am suggesting that the conditions of formation are no longer appeals to modernist *experience*, but rather collective mediations in late modern orders of the knowledge economy. Individual *experience* is not a private event but a collective imagining, so that where *experience* once provided a space for resistance it now functions as a collective organising drive. *Individualism is the new collectivism and individuals are the new orders of social persuasion.* The individual-social binary has shifted according to its own paradoxical law of inversion as new constellations of knowledge appear inside the emerging dominant institutions.

Collective-individualism can therefore be seen to arise out of and rest upon a new constellation of knowledge management. The sense of the present impossibility of *experience* results from this new arrangement of values inside the individual-social binary as it forms a different set of associations between experience, knowledge and institutional order inside the knowledge economy. The present political economy restricts knowledge in its multiplication by establishing specific forms of selective transmission through its institutional base; all forms of knowledge are generated and permitted, but only those forms accessible to the conditions of the knowledge economy are 'translated', to recall Agamben's reading of experience, for use and value. Psychological individualism is translatable in the knowledge economy because it allows a certain collective codification of the self. At this moment, when individualism becomes collective, the narrative of psychological experience is returned to its formative errors and its disciplinary attempts to eradicate the social. The politic of individualism in the knowledge economy throws psychological knowledge back to its own political-theoretical values of the individual-social.

My concern in this study is to establish a critique of psychology in the framing of religious experience through a wider critique of knowledge in the political environment of the knowledge economy; a term I have so far repeatedly employed, but which will be explored in more detail in Chapter 1. In the new political economy of knowledge, scholars of economics, psychology and religion can no longer remain innocent of their assumed neutral categories. They may even have to give up the comfort zones of their inherited industrial disciplinary formations. These are strange times, but they are ones that need articulating, because the present strategy of knowledge is to restrict knowledge and hide the ethical values behind our binary thinking.

Critical method: the ethics of knowledge

The contested space of the category of experience illustrates that the conditions of utterance are as important as the utterance in the making of experience. If experience is shaped by interpretation and interpretation by the social conditions, then the social agencies or institutions that have the power to provide the model of interpretation always shape experience, even as they form spirals of inter-dependence with other institutions. While recognising that experience, knowledge and institutions are linked together, it is important to register that knowledge is never a transparent one-dimensional system of propaganda and social control – as our conspiracy fantasies may wish to dream – but rather a social network of complex interactions across mobile lines of engagement. Nonetheless, there are always attempts to exert an influence, even if in the end it may be a kaleidoscope of half-revealed notions that inform our lived-embodied reality. We are, of course, always trapped in the hermeneutical circle in our attempts to disentangle the social history of institutions and the deployment of discourses, which is why appeals to a higher discourse or an original ground are attractive. The desire to think we know is more reassuring to our incoherent living; such is the nature of those fractional adjustments of statistics to conform and confirm our knowing.

It is also the case that we are caught inside our own necessary strategic arrangement of knowledge in a sophisticated, survival-equilibrium to 'make-believe' our experience and cope with the constant onslaught of networked information and the overwhelming orchestration of media. It is through these complex folds of human limits, social living and survival that groups assert and impose a will-to-truth. The very 'habits of interpretation' follow long lines of social investment and politically ordered values. In such plural worlds we cannot escape from the flux of historical discourses, change and provisionality and our will-to-truth, because there is no Archimedean point outside ourselves to offer us a different fantasy. Our knowledge is caught in the conditions of our measurement and the illusion of thought is to imagine that everything is measurable. It is however our very capacity to 'imagine' what we are which defies the measurable.

Kant rightly questioned, in his *Metaphysical Foundations of Natural Science* ([1796] 1903) and his *Anthropology* ([1798] 1974), the possibility of an empirical science of psychology, because he recognised humans defied the criteria of a natural science object. Indeed, the later developments of 'scientific' psychology were a complex hybrid of physiological, philosophical and political discourses, which allowed a certain social will-to-power to emerge in the elisions between these discourses (see Teo 2005). The testable hypothesis of biology is conviction enough to credit a discourse as it moves into the unmeasurable uncertainty of consciousness. The powerful desire to know so easily hides our not knowing and creates opportunity for those who desire the power of knowing. In this sense, knowing and not-knowing are ethically determined. As Jacques Monod (1972: 163) has so insightfully argued:

> True knowledge is ignorant of values, but it has to be grounded on a value judgement, or rather on an *axiomatic* value. It is obvious that the positing of the principle of objectivity as the condition of true knowledge *constitutes an ethical choice and not a judgement reached from knowledge, since, according to the postulate's own terms, there cannot have been any 'true' knowledge prior to this arbitral choice.* In

order to establish the norm for knowledge the objectivity principle defines a value: that value is objective knowledge itself. To assent to the principle of objectivity is thus, to state the basic proposition of an ethical system: *the ethic of knowledge.*

In this book I seek to explore some of the lines of knowing and not-knowing as an ethic of knowledge. In the attempt to create humility as practice in thought, I wish to establish a critical method in the ethics of knowledge to reveal the lacunae in thought which hide the fragility of thinking, not least within disciplinary thought. Disciplines, as Monod (1972: 163) hints, are 'moral rules' of discourses and thus need to be ethically assessed. *This study is an ethics of knowledge in so far it seeks to (dis)locate disciplines in a dynamic of knowing and not-knowing across the binary values of the individual-social divide.* In many ways this book is, to follow Josef Bleicher (1982: 146), a kind of 'hermeneutic imagination', where 'the ongoing formation of a consensus among practitioners in which criteria for valid knowledge, worth-while objects of research, etc, are developed and applied'. Although, we might go further in giving the historically determined spontaneous imagination greater emphasis in the making and unmaking of our worlds.

The frames of representation for experience, psychology and religion in this book are built on the establishment of a philosophical critical method that follows a Nietzschean tradition of 'will-to-power', where knowledge is the 'raw energy' of change and imposition (Nietzsche [1883–8] 1968: 1067), but I qualify such an innate structure with recognition of choice and value. Such a tradition of thinking was developed by Foucault to incorporate a strategic and institutional understanding of knowledge and I follow this understanding to show how knowledge works in social networks, but I also go beyond Foucault. I do not follow a model of 'power' without 'interest' or 'ethical choice'; rather 'power' is always modelled according to the symbolic system of interest and value. Power, to slightly shift Foucault's emphasis, is always power through networks of meaning and, in this sense, values and power are not distinct or mutually exclusive but work in unity. Knowledge is ethical in the sense of advancing certain 'interests' and 'values' of networked individuals and groups in a society for the advance of their power, which is why collaboration is important and why intellectuals become ineffective in their muted and isolated disciplinary spaces. They simply mirror external interests and internally compete to undermine the significance and political force of their knowledge, which in turn undermines effective resistance. I am thus locating knowledge within an ethics of knowing in order to expose the categories through which we hide and protect our values.

My critique is a critique of knowing and not-knowing as an ethic of knowledge and in this process I want to employ a series of strategies to read disciplinary thought in the human sciences. In order to show knowledge as provisional and reveal the assertion of values we need to expose the political logic of certainty. This requires displacing disciplinary thought along the lines of its fragile construction and bringing thought into engagement with its uncomfortable edges. Indeed, it requires a strategy of thinking within and outside disciplines – disciplines sustained and created by the political logic of institutional power. The arrogance of thought is to build a community – with its departments, conferences and journals – around its articulations so it never has to think otherwise or other-wisdom and never has to think its objects are ethical choices in the making of the subject. The strategies that I employ are therefore openings at the interfaces, or ways out of the closed logic, of a disciplinary order that only has the desire to preserve its existence and self-importance. Beware the borderlines of thought least someone from outside stumbles into your labyrinth and realises the ethical choices of your knowledge. And so I create another labyrinth for others to wrestle with my own ethical choices in the making of the subject of knowledge.

My first strategy is *to read across inter-disciplinary spaces*. In order to reshape domains of knowledge and show the leakages between the discourses of economics, psychology and religion as systems of thought, it is necessary to discover how disciplines close down certain unresolved questions to preserve a certain truth-formation. Disciplines, like dysfunctional family relations, require collusion in order to function as a living entity. Thus when we read across disciplines or bodies of knowledge we see a wider inter-dependency hidden in the isolated unit of knowledge. The collusion of the disciplinary family is seen when meeting with other family units, which expose the secrets of (en)closed thinking and living. Difference allows recognition of the provisional thought and wider social links, which sustain multiple disciplines.

The second strategy is *to examine the nature of binary knowledge and the values it holds* in the disciplinary formation of psychological thinking. The distinctions within thought depend on maintaining divisions within thought as fixed rather than temporary operations. This solidification or reification within thinking is a central practice in assuming authority in knowledge, even as the lived practice may reveal other silenced truth. A third strategy is *to show the operation of disciplinary amnesia* and how this form of forgetting the history of the discipline prevents recognising the lived errors of thought.

Disciplinary amnesia, as I have shown elsewhere, is the art of suppressing those features of a discipline that undermine the logic and coherence of a disciplinary practice (Carrette 2001a; 2002).[17] This practice is employed by projects claiming the rhetoric of science, because it does not wish to make its own historical assertions vulnerable to the past statements, contradictions and errors. I specifically apply the above three strategies in the first part of the book, which seeks to provide a rationale for thinking about how the psychology of religion can be read as political-economy. In the second part, I employ a fourth and fifth strategy in the examination of specific 'case studies' (read as ethical-political formations) of the subject.

The fourth strategy that I employ is that already mentioned of *critical myopia*. This is the restriction of critical thought to an object or process outside one's own position. This closure of thought prevents the self-reflexive fear of critical thought and prevents us from facing the shameful acts of acknowledging our will-to-truth and the raw assertion of our chosen hermeneutical position. The final strategy is to read *thought as ethical-political practice*, by which I mean the assertion of a desired way to live. The link between conceptual thought and lived practice is difficult to mark out in specific detail and I do not seek to discover specific practice, but rather types of knowing and not-knowing as ethical-political orders linked to socio-economic patterns. This strategy follows the assumption of the inter-connected nature of thought and seeks to show that what happens at the conceptual level interacts with an embodied social reality, such that a will-to-power requires a symbolic framework to assert its values.[18]

My understanding of the ethics of knowledge will become clearer in my reading of the psychology of religion and in my conclusion about the ethics of knowing and not-knowing. In carrying out these above strategies, I have consciously adopted three forms of approach: broad historical overview (to link different areas of thought); detailed corrective reading of texts (to build critique and position the specific historical examples in my argument); and philosophical provocation and playfulness (to reveal my own values). Each strand will hopefully carry the limits of the other and return the study of religion and psychology to their primary philosophical analysis and, in turn, to the ethics of knowledge.

Critical psychology: the beginning and end of the subject

Before I outline the specific stages of my argument in each respective chapter, some explanation is required of the term 'critical psychology' and how it reflects my method. The first thing to establish is that there is no such thing as 'critical psychology' as such.[19] It is rather a loose collection of writings, or an 'umbrella term' (Walkerdine 2001: 9; Blackman 2001: 6), for a group of works providing a politic reading of psychological knowledge (including a whole diverse range of critical perspectives from feminism to post-colonialism); although it now takes on a professional and market formation of its own.[20] Born out of the 'crisis' in 1970s social psychology, and engaging with the politics of the subject in post-structuralist theory, critical psychology attempts in different ways to make psychology a political object of knowledge (see, for example, Shotter 1975; Westland 1978; Henriques *et al.* [1984] 1998; Parker 1992). The ideological critique of psychology is the driving force of critical psychology, as seen in Fox and Prilleltensky's (1997) seminal collection of essays. Fox and Prilleltensky (1997: xiii) called for the end of 'political innocence' in psychology. They were concerned with what Esquicie (2000: 214) later saw as the 'false neutrality of official psychology' and much of the early understanding of critical psychology operated on this political critique of so-called 'mainstream' psychology (Fox and Prilleltensky 1997: 4). The critical space is nevertheless extremely divergent and reflects a range of positions that allow individuals to make certain statements of 'disenchantment' (Ussher 2000: 7).

The poly-vocality of critical psychology allows us, as Parker (1999) has indicated, to make a distinction between those voices 'inside' the professional discipline and those 'outside' or on the edges of the discipline. The distinction reveals the important nature and types of critique and enables us to see the nature of such critique as reflecting a different set of debates about methodology, ethical practice, political and historical-philosophical concerns, which may or may not seek to challenge the discipline of psychology as such. Thinking within critical psychology operates along a spectrum (Figure 0.1) that opens the field to an inter-disciplinary dynamic where knowledge of the subject is reconstituted within a new set of terms.

The danger of critical psychology is that it can become a sub-disciplinary space and a market category that covers the philosophical and political construction of knowledge it attempts to question.[21] There is a problem, as John Morss (2000: 105) notes, of keeping critical psychology continuously

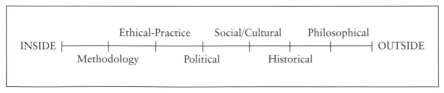

Figure 0.1 Spectrum of themes in critical psychology

attentive to its own project and a constant anxiety about how its message is diluted when it is 'incorporated into the academy'. Parker even goes as far to suggest that critical psychology 'is part of the problem rather than part of the solution and that radical work needs to turn against it' (Parker 2001: 127). The fact that critical psychology is now part of a wider disciplinary and marketing enterprise easily hides its silent assimilation into the ideologies it seeks to oppose, even as such avenues become necessary for transmitting critical debate and the problems of knowledge (there are no pure realms of mediation in a market world). The term should therefore hold a strategic temporality for critical intervention.[22] As Esquicie (2000: 212) notes:

> Our general sense is that we should probably emphasize the *critique of psychology* rather than develop a *critical psychology*, in the sense that we should not want to stay trapped in the illusion of a possible partial reform of a discipline that appears to be situated as an apparatus for control and social normalisation, as Michel Foucault and others have already explained.

The importance of giving emphasis to the 'critique of psychology' rather than 'critical psychology' is given support by Thomas Teo (2005) in his historical overview of critical accounts of psychology from Kant to post-colonial theory. Teo (2005: 28, 149) rightly argues that 'critical psychology is part of the history of psychology' and that 'critique of psychology' is part of modern not just 'post-modern' thinking. While Teo's analysis could have developed a more nuanced reading of the 'post-modern' and appreciated thinkers such as Foucault within the context of post-structuralist thought and thus working within modern critical paradigms, he nonetheless appreciates the wider epistemological, ontological and, what he somewhat obscurely calls, 'relevance' critical perspectives (Teo 2005: 32–3). This latter categorization to cover *ethical-political*[23] themes illustrates how Teo's work is caught – and thus restricted – inside a set of disciplinary assumptions and subject-specific theoretical concerns, even as he identifies longer philosophical traditions.[24] He is thus concerned with questions of ethical *practice within psychology* in relation to so-called post-modern themes, rather than ethics as a wider philosophical problem of knowledge about the individual-social.

By taking psychological knowledge to its inter-disciplinary edges we can dissolve the subject-specific restriction and return the question of the human subject to philosophical questions of knowledge, which involves some account of the history of religions and economics. This necessarily entails transforming the intellectual domain and questioning the very constitution of

'Psychology'[25] as a disciplinary form. The psychology of religion is thus one site of knowledge for demonstrating the ethics of knowledge surrounding the discursive and political making of the human subject; it displaces the frame of reference. Such inter-disciplinary thinking allows critique to emerge more clearly in the disjunction of disciplines and in the displacement of knowledge.

In my view, following Shamdasani (2005), critical psychology takes us to the beginning and end of the subject, in so far as it reveals the fault lines of the formation of the discipline. In this sense, Teo (2005: 28) is right to see critique as ever-present in the subject of psychology, but what he does not appreciate is that this reflects central foundational problems, or persistent faults, in the very constitution of such disciplinary knowledge. He does not see how it reveals an ethical problem of knowledge formation as opposed to an ethical problem within psychological practice (something to which I will return in Chapter 2). This ethic of knowledge returns us to the question of subject formation and enables us to widen the philosophical and ethical analysis to the kinds of knowledge used to form what it is to be human, something that determines the contours of this book.

In this respect, Maritza Montero's (2001) paradigm for 'critical construction and transformation' in psychology rightly places 'critical psychology' within an ontological and epistemological context (questions of the nature of reality and the construction of knowledge that Teo (2005) explores before the advent of the discipline psychology) – to which we might also add hermeneutics (Browning 1998: 40).[26] In such a space the basic assumptions of 'psychology' are challenged and 'psychological' knowledge is opened to the outside of the discipline, it is opened to an ethical question about the nature of how we think about ourselves in the present world. The fault lines of the subject of 'Psychology' mean that we have an ethical responsibility to re-examine such knowledge.

Critical psychology is therefore the key to returning us to the primary philosophical questions before the formation of 'Psychology' as a discipline, even as the return is always a move through the existing space of thought, rather than an impossible return to the past as such. It is rather the creation of a new philosophical ordering of inter-disciplinary thought in the age of the knowledge economy that demands the introduction of new ethical categories of knowledge outside 'Psychology'; it is thinking about being human with the edges of other systems of knowledge, such as religion and political economy, to expose the values behind how we are thinking and dividing knowledge (see Chapter 1 in this book). Parker (1997b: 298) sees this opening when he writes: 'A critical psychology has to be constructed from theoretical resources, life experiences and political identities *outside* the discipline. Only then does it make sense to deconstruct what the discipline does to us and to its other subjects'. By thinking in the wider context we can unravel the ethic of all forms of knowledge in the way we think about the world and the self.

In the present study, 'critical psychology' acts as a useful theoretical space of thinking from which to reconfigure knowledge in the human sciences; it takes us to a critical hermeneutics of the imagination about being human, but I am not bound or limited by this frame other than as focusing a set of critical questions. I take a hermeneutic of political-economy and the taxonomical tool of 'religion' inside my central critique of psychology in order to bring all these forms of thought back to the critical philosophical task of the ethics of knowledge. This critical imagination becomes a practice of living and takes us to the place of 'not-knowing who we are' (Caputo 2004) in the hope of becoming ethically responsible about how we think and know the world. Critique is the ability to push thought to its limits and imagine frameworks of interpretation that bring us to an ethical space of thinking about experience, knowledge and social institutions. As Foucault ([1978] 1997: 36) observed in his reading of Kant's *Aufklärung*, 'critique's primordial responsibility' is to 'know knowledge'; to know the material conditions by which we know and understand ourselves and the world at any one point of time. It is this form of critique that constitutes my understanding of an ethic of knowledge. Critique is thus the basis of an ethical account of knowledge.

This work can be seen to include ever-increasing circles of knowledge to address the problem of experience, mind and institutions in the study of religion and psychology. It is most immediately a critique of the psychology of religion, second, a discussion of economic knowledge in relation to psychology as a way to reveal the ethics of knowledge and, at its most outer edges – or rather at the heart of the turning spiral – it is a wider philosophy of the ethics of knowledge in the human sciences. In bringing these different levels of thinking together, knowing and not-knowing who we are is seen to take on a different intensity in the new knowledge economy. If knowledge has a material benefit to the exchange of goods, services and information then it might be that knowledge of who we are has an even greater purchase on the order of our embodied living. To claim to know who we are in a knowledge economy is to make human beings into the greatest commodity. It is also to control production of who we are for the new economy. The link between images of being human and the economic system is at the heart of my ethic of knowing and not-knowing.

The imagining of who we are, or rather the shocking ability we have as individuals and groups, to hand-over who we are to a unquestioned philosophical logic is now fed into a greater system of control. The types of knowing inside the traditions of psychology and religion are some of the most dangerous forms of knowing because they provide the models of being human to justify and support absolute forms of knowing and absolute forms of economy. Indeed, in the knowledge economy, asserting that we do not-know who are may very well be the best form of resistance, because knowledge is always more than we can yet imagine and this requires more of us than we yet know. As Foucault (1980: 181) argued in relation to the hermeneutics of the self:

> Maybe the problem of the self is not to discover what it is in its positivity, maybe the problem is not to discover a positive self or the positive foundation of the self. Maybe our problem is now to discover that the self is nothing else than the historical correlation of the technology built in our history. Maybe the problem is to change those technologies.

However, to follow Alles's (2001) critical sense of the limits of Foucault, maybe it is time to update Foucault's critique of Cold War knowledge and establish a critique of the representation of human experience, mind and institutions in the emerging knowledge economy, with all its new forms of knowledge management and binary logic of self and other.

In the world of the knowledge economy we need to examine 'economy' not as some old Marxist determinism or a new neo-liberal freedom, but rather as a space to think through how knowledge is shaped by the binary ethical framework of the individual-social. By marking out how 'economy' frames knowledge we can see the values implicit within different forms of knowledge. We can also see not only how knowledge is managed for economy but how economy becomes a central register of value. Once knowledge is constituted and framed in and through the institutions of economy, it displaces other forms of knowing and allows an opening to the values of all knowing by locating its excluded categories and privileged concepts at the points across the irreconcilable binary forms. It is the inherent ambivalence of the discourse of economy in its binary constructions and inter-disciplinary edges that enable it to mask and, at the same time, reveal an ethic of knowledge. I will thus use the economic register of the individual-social binary as a way to read the ethics of knowledge in psychology and religion.

Outline of the book

The two parts of the book are based on two stages in my argument that the methods of psychology in the study of religion need to be critically assessed according to an ethics of knowledge in the age of the knowledge economy. What is at stake in this argument is the problem of absolute, or totalitarian, forms of knowledge and related forms of absolute economy that close down the capacity of human beings to recognise aspects of ethical choice and selection at the points at which knowledge faces its irresolvable binary tensions and ordering of knowledge. Drawing out the values implicit with disciplinary systems becomes a vital ethical task and this study brings these to the surface through a variety of hermeneutical and epistemological strategies. The first part lays down the theoretical ground for an ethics of knowledge in the human sciences by considering the boundaries of economics and psychology and the individual-social binary axis as a way to read ethical values within a system of knowledge. The second part seeks to think through the values of knowledge in three specific traditions of the psychology of religion using the economic context to read the ethical-political dimension.

The two theoretical chapters in Part I establish the ethical-politic of disciplinary knowledge. Chapter 1 links psychological knowledge to the history of economics and the history of economics to psychological models. The concern of economists with 'non-economic factors', which make economics possible, is uncovered and the idea of a certain ideology of the self beneath economic processes is developed. The result of this examination reveals the 'leakage' between disciplinary systems in the nineteenth century and the ethical-political constraints around knowledge formations. Chapter 2 unfolds the central conceptual dilemma at the heart of disciplinary knowledge in psychology, sociology and economics, which I have already touched upon in the discussion of the politics of religious experience. It examines the nature of how the binary politic of the individual-social operates in psychological and economic discourse. It is argued that psychology sets up a deliberate form of 'disciplinary amnesia' around this problem, because it reveals the historical fault lines of the subject. Following the work of Andrew Abbots on disciplinary knowledge, it is argued that disciplinary knowledge replicates the 'axis of cohesion' of a subject throughout its history. The chapter then shows how the fault line of the individual and social is replicated in four key historical moments in the work of Le Bon and McDougall, Freud, Fromm and Hayek. It is argued that the binary politic of the individual-social reveals a set of philosophical assumptions about knowledge formation and a hidden set of values. It is from this established base of binary politics and disciplinary leakage that psychological knowledge is evaluated in Part II of the book, according to a new object of political economy as a register of human value.

Part II takes examples from psychoanalysis, humanist psychology and cognitive science to show how the values of psychological knowledge can be read at the point of political economy. It reveals how the protected and privileged categories of knowledge reveal the underlying ethical-political values. Chapter 3 begins by exploring the notion of the 'economic' in Freud and then shows how psychoanalytical theory of religion suppresses the economic question through the appeal to science and an appeal to culture. The work of the so-called 'Freudian Left' is taken to illustrate this point, using examples from Reich, Fromm and Lacan. The tension between European and American psychology is developed to draw out the political nature of psychological theory and how such theory is transformed under different cultural conditions. Chapter 4 continues the exploration of the relation between psychology, economics and religion by exploring how Abraham Maslow's psychology carried aspects of the ideology of American capitalism and how his use of the category 'religion' facilitated this process. It explores how the economic conditions in the USA provided a platform for privatising experience. Maslow's psychology is shown to model 'religious' experience through psychological discourse and in turn reshape introspection for a new political ideology. Chapter 5 follows on from the two previous critical readings by showing the links between cognitive psychology and the politics of the knowledge economy. It focuses on the work of cognitive anthropologist Harvey Whitehouse to reveal the hidden political nature of cognitive thinking about religion. After establishing a critical reading of cognitive theory and Whitehouse's otherwise insightful works, the chapter goes on to argue that cognitive theories of religion are restricted to 'codified' models and that more dynamic models of mind are marginalised by the demands for specific forms of knowledge product in the knowledge economy.

The work concludes by offering a model for the ethics of knowledge according to different types of knowing explored in the previous chapters. The ethics of knowledge is then diagrammatically related to the formation of ideas in the disciplinary constructions of economics, psychology and religion along the two central axes of individual-social and closed-open forms of knowing. It is the aim of the book to show how knowledge is ethically framed by hidden philosophical values and the conclusion offers 'not-knowing' as a strategic form of critique and corrective to the knowledge economy, which returns the question to James's and Hayek's own knowledge constructions and their own forms of 'not-knowing' at the limits of knowing. In the end we reach the paradox of knowledge and experience, but also the liberation of our critical imagination through an ethic of knowledge.

Part I

The ethics of knowledge in the human sciences

1 The ethical veil of the knowledge economy

[T]he study of the economy contains premises and value judgements of which it is itself unaware.

> Robert Heilbroner (1988) *Behind the Veil of Economics*,
> W.W. Norton & Company, p. 13

Psychologists generally proceed with their work without stopping to reflect on the basic assumptions that underlie what they are doing.

> Charles W. Tolman (1994) *Psychology, Society and Subjectivity*,
> Routledge, p. 23

Adam Smith and William James both gave definitive public lectures in Edinburgh that were to shape the western intellectual landscape for centuries. The founder of modern economics speaking in 1748–50, sponsored by Lord Kames, and the founder of modern psychology speaking in 1901–2 sponsored by the Gifford Foundation. Defenders of disciplinary divisions might speculate that it is only through such broad historical correlations that we can find parallels between Smith and James. However, work in the sociology of emotions has established a more important thematic connection in their work (Barbalet [1998] 2001; Evans 2001). Although Smith is famous for his 1776 treatise *The Wealth of Nations*, it is his earlier 1759 study, *The Theory of Moral Sentiments*, that has attracted attention in the theory of emotions. *The Wealth of Nations* explored the idea of how self-interest could benefit society (grounded as it was in social concern),[1] but his *Theory of Moral Sentiments* explored how society dominated by self-interest could form moral judgements; according to Smith this was established through an emotional sympathy. H.T. Buckle in his 1861 *History of Civilization in England* captures the underlying focus of Smith's two major works:

> In the *Moral Sentiments*, he investigates the sympathetic part of human nature; in the *Wealth of Nations*, he investigates its selfish part. And as

all of us are sympathetic as well as selfish ... and as this classification is a primary and exhaustive division of our motives to action, it is evident, that if Adam Smith had completely accomplished his vast design, he would have at once have raised the study of human nature to a science

(quoted in Raphael and Macfie 1976: 21)

Smith's concern with human nature is the key correlation with James's later work on emotion, but the conception of emotion in these two writers hold very different epistemological concerns. Smith's 'sentiments' and 'passions' and James's 'sentiments', 'feelings' and 'emotions' are written within different orders of representation and within a different politic of the individual and the social. The sociologist Jack Barbalet can establish the importance of Smith for a 'macrosociological approach' to emotion because the different historical frameworks of knowledge allow the category of emotion to function in the social space and for collective purposes (Barbalet [1998] (2001): 188–9). The central question, as Barbalet has so usefully identified, is not that emotions were once social and are now private, but that emotions are 'represented' differently. As Barbalet states, there is a 'narrowing, in wider society, of what is referred to by the term emotion' (Barbalet [1998] (2001): 171). Emotion, or the passions in the eighteenth century, had a wider meaning than it does today. According to Barbalet, there is a 'shrinking of the phenomenal world of the self', which occurs as a result of the market and what Macpherson called 'possessive individualism' (Barbalet [1998] (2001): 172–3).

Barbalet, following Theodore Kemper's social interactional theory, is trying to present the 'social–structural components' of emotion by using Smith's work to challenge the representational order of contemporary individualistic theory (Barbalet [1998] (2001): 174; Kemper 1978). Smith's moral philosophy explores a 'natural' disposition of the pursuit of individual happiness 'as it may affect that of other people' and this opens the individual to the social (Smith [1759] 1976: 212). Barbalet's reading of James reflects a similar concern to problematize the order of the individual representation of emotion, showing how James was not restricted to a somatic model of emotion and how in his 1897 work 'The Sentiment of Rationality' he offers useful insights for understanding emotion in practical rationality (Barbalet [1998] (2001): 45–8).

Barablet's useful rescuing of James's model of emotion and the attempt to overcome the restricted individualism of psychological models, could have been developed even more extensively if he had considered James's *The Varieties of Religious Experience*, which allows for a wider social, as well cognitive, model (see Carrette 2005b, 2007).[2] Nonetheless, the tension between Smith offering a theory socially positioning emotion and James's attempt to hold a tension between the social and the individual in his reading of emotion is crucial in terms of the changing patterns of knowledge between 1759 and 1902. The nineteenth century is witness to a shift in the locus of knowledge from the social to the individual, even if in James this split has not yet taken the full force it assumes in later psychology. It would however be wrong to think that emotion resides in any form of simple individualism in contemporary theory.

The social theory of emotion becomes more complex in the Durkheimian influenced work of Stejpan Mestrovic (1997), who in coining the term 'post-emotionalism' shows how emotions can be recycled from past memories of emotion in contemporary politics and the media (see Carrette 2004a). According to Mestrovic (1997: 71, 149, 162), there is a 'rational control of emotional life' in the 'displacement' of past emotion, the 'mechanization' of emotion in social control and the rational 'marketing' of emotion for political and social ends. The shift in thinking about emotion – from social sentiment to media manipulation – reveals how this category can disrupt the discourses of economics, psychology and sociology through a leakage into other disciplinary concerns across the individual-social binary and how different historical regimes of knowledge allow different questions to emerge.[3] The category of emotion illustrates the problem of the politics of knowledge that grounds my discussion. My aim, however, is not to develop a discussion of emotion, but rather to show the inter-dependency of knowledge and identify the points of philosophical closure within types of knowledge. I will first outline my approach to the ethical-politic of knowledge in the human sciences as a methodological context for my argument.

Categories and classifications of knowledge

Barbalet's 'contribution' to a 'conversation' opens the space in which to conceptualise human emotion in a wider disciplinary landscape, but it also allows us to question 'conventional' disciplinary ways of exploring a problem. Referring to Smith and James, Barbalet writes:

> [T]hese writers proved to be not only inspirational, but their work constitutive of a number of particular discussions, and frequently corrective of conventional distortions of the role and outcome of emotions in social processes and social structures.
>
> (Barbalet [1998] (2001): 188)

Barbalet challenges the ways of thinking about a problem by returning to a different historical context to question present constraints. He can return to Smith, working in the area of eighteenth century 'moral philosophy', and James, thinking in terms of nineteenth century 'natural theology' (as James subtitled his project), in order to show how we limit our intellectual questions in a climate of individualism and disciplinary isolationism. The categories of knowledge employed by Smith and James offer a different scope for intellectual enquiry and provide a way to unsettle twentieth century assumptions about, in this instance, emotion within political economy and social processes. The containment of Smith and James in the later modern disciplinary spaces of economics, psychology and religion – in what Foucault (1966: 262) called a 'new arrangement of knowledge' in nineteenth century disciplines – encloses their thinking in a different set of rules and hermeneutical strictures. They become transformed and reshaped by a new order of reading. This ordering of intellectual categories of knowledge, or subject constellation, is the concern of this book and it returns us to the complex ways we order our world through categories.

Thinking about the way we categorize and classify knowledge is fractured across the discourses of philosophy, ethnography and linguistics and – to follow Mary Douglas – is also debated in terms of naturalism, idealism and constructivism (see Allen 2000: 92; Ellen 2006: 2). According to Allen (2000: 94), quoting Michel Bourdeau, the notion of category in philosophy is 'notoriously and perhaps irremediably obscure'. The obscurity reflects what is at stake in this issue and the way categories and classifications not only root the social order of the world, but also conceal different political configurations of knowledge. As Vinay Lal (Lal 2002: 122) makes clear: '[S]ome of the most intense battles in the 21st century will be fought over the shape of knowledge, and inconsequence a more politically informed ethnography of disciplinary structures of modern knowledge will be required'. Lal goes on to point out, in the context of globalization, that 'nothing is more spectacularly global than the formal frameworks of knowledge', linked as they are to the interests of colonial expansion and western economic orders of knowledge (Lal 2002: 122). The act of transgressing disciplinary limits and reordering the categories of economics, psychology and religion is a vital ethical activity in the critical re-imagining of human life, because behind it is a hidden order of the values of knowledge that silently shape our living.

My own reading of the categories of knowledge is concerned with the politics of disciplinary knowledge (the institutional and social ordering of knowledge). All knowledge, given or constructed, is used within the social order to the benefit of the dominant social regime and the frameworks of thinking mirror this domination; such that theology is the 'queen of sciences' in the age of medieval church power, the physical and human sciences dominate in the modern era of industrial state power and now the global knowledge economy dominates in an age of economic corporate and technological power. Although this should not be seen as an evolutionary development, but rather as a shifting and overlapping pattern of complex forms of institutional co-existence and levels of social domination. In each of these phases of knowledge, subjects are constelled in different ways and in those areas most vulnerable to ontological speculation, such as the 'human' sciences, modelling of the self becomes exposed to a new order of knowledge.

The nature of the human is based on a prior set of philosophical values and premises resting behind the different disciplinary forms of economics, psychology and religion, which are often concealed in the positivity of discourse. In different historical orders, knowledge is shaped by a different set of ethical values hidden in the assumptions of theological belief, empirical justification and, presently, efficiency value. The philosophical ground shifts the statements of value. By focusing on disciplinary knowledge, I am seeking to resist pure essentialism and simple constructionist models, because the object of study in the human sciences (as I frame my three subjects of concern) is caught between these dynamics of knowing. It is in the space between these disciplines that the social power of representational order marks the given and the constructed.

Disciplines operate according to rules and classifications that make a discourse possible (Foucault 1970), but by showing how disciplines collapse into each other we can begin to open knowledge to its own vulnerability – to its limits and exploitations. Here I follow Foucault (1966: 348) in recognising the 'essential instability' of the human sciences, 'their precariousness, their uncertainty as sciences, their dangerous familiarity with philosophy, their ill-defined reliance upon other domains of knowledge, their perpetually secondary and derived character, and also their claim to universality', formed as they are inside the 'complexity of the epistemological configuration' that constitutes them as knowledge. However, my reading of the human sciences is not limited to Foucault's (1966) schema for three reasons: first, the historical location of his work does not read the conditions of the new knowledge economy; second, I do not restrict my reading of economics, psychology and religion to his model of language, life and production (Foucault 1966: 347); third, I do not accept his thesis of the 'retreat of mathesis' (the science of calculable order), but rather see a reconfiguration of 'mathesis' inside the binary and auditing logic of global technology and finance. Foucault is, nonetheless, correct to see knowledge of the human sciences as precariously formed inside the three dimensions of mathematical and physical sciences, a field of application, and philosophical reflection. There is an aspirational appeal to the first dimension, a conceptual construction in the second and an ontological hope in the third dimension. Working within this context, I will, however, set up a more specific focus and consider the emergence and development of the psychology of religion according to an ethics of knowledge constituted by three related factors:[4] knowledge economy (*networked* mathesis), individual-social binary (field of application) and the hidden *a priori* values (philosophical reflection). These forms of knowledge begin in the nineteenth century and are mutated in the knowledge economy. They provide the basis for rethinking disciplinary knowledge, especially in fields of knowledge that never question the categories upon which they think.

Disciplinary knowledge is a distinct kind of classification linked to social institutions and the economic power that orders that knowledge. Modern forms of knowledge are shaped by the economic utility of nineteenth century disciplinary formations under the forces of mass urbanization, but, as I have indicated, the new knowledge economy is displacing these older constellations in ways we have yet to fully appreciate. Foucault (1966: 342–3) believed that anthropology (the question of *man*) 'governed and controlled the path of philosophical thought from Kant until our own day', but he believed that this was 'disintegrating before our eyes' and that those who continued to think in this way could only be greeted with 'a philosophical laugh'. But behind the so-called 'void' and silent laugh is the creation of a new order, which Foucault could not yet see. It is the birth of a *new* mathesis. What makes it *new* from Foucault's description of seventeenth century knowledge is the order of technology and globalization in the knowledge economy.

I call the present order of knowledge the order of *networked mathesis*, because the process of calculative logic is applied to all levels of thought and practice in the economy of the information age. This is more than electronic networks, which extend the range of the apparatus and the dissemination of knowledge, it is rather the control of the object of study and the subject of knowledge for its economic *containment*. We no longer 'think' in *networked mathesis*, but rather replicate systems of knowledge that are networked for control. Measurement is reasserting itself with increased technological application as the language of truth in the human sciences and critical thought is suspended in the networking of *mathesis* for economic benefit. Disturbingly, knowledge is now no longer interiorized into the subject of 'man', but *exteriorized* in the apparent removal of 'man' and 'experience' by locating knowledge and value in the calculus of efficiency and profit (Drucker 1993: 42). The inefficiency of 'man' has been removed by the 'supraterritoriality' of binary logic and the technology of finance (Scholte 2000).

In this process knowledge has lost its dynamic unknowing quality in the pathological quest to know and control the environment of knowing for efficiency. In this sense, disciplines stabilise the object of knowledge for its utilisation and exploitation. Networks can, of course, be dynamic, but when postulated according to calculative logic, they become mechanisms for copying and pasting rather than reading and thinking. We lose the value of thought in the process of controlled transmission. In postulating a new *mathesis*, I am not wishing to support uncritically Foucault's notion of the epistemic structures of knowledge, but rather to recognise the nature of calculative logic in our time in terms of Foucault's language of the classification of the human sciences, carried forward by specific institutional powers. The human sciences of economics, psychology and religion are subjects grounded on the vulnerability of philosophical speculation hidden in the unsaid of each time and the order of domination.

The exposure of subjects to different orders of *networked mathesis* rests on economics as a 'cyborg science', as Philip Mirowski's (2002) searching analysis reveals. It creates a situation where 'computational economics' closes out other criteria for the re-imagining of the human sciences. 'With increased dependence on the computer to carry out all manner of economic activities, it has and will rebound back upon the very meaning and referent of the term "economic" as well' (Mirowski 2002: 520). The transformation of economics in the knowledge economy will be seen later, but this also, as Mirowski (2002: 277–9) recognises, results in a situation where the modern scientific approach of statistics and cognitive science creates complex new orders where there is 'no clean separation' between psychology and economics. This contemporary bridging of subjects in *networked mathesis* will be seen in greater detail in Chapter 5, but it also returns us to the formation of these subjects and their permeable boundaries. If we are to establish some critical understanding of what is involved in setting up a project of the 'psychology of religion' we need first to mark out the vulnerable formative nature of those overlapping forms of historical disciplines that today reduce all knowledge to the logic of *networked mathesis*, but which begin as industrial units of knowledge in the nineteenth century.

In this chapter I want to explore a number of different ways of thinking about economics and psychology as a preliminary theoretical exercise in my framing of the psychology of religion in terms of my critical ethics of knowledge. I will, first, attempt to speak about the problem of the domination of the economic in reading contemporary knowledge and then explore concerns by critical historians from the respective fields to show the limits of disciplinary thought. This will entail showing the non-economic basis of economics and the social foundations of psychological knowledge. Building on the idea of historical leakages between the human science disciplines, I will then locate these strands of thinking within the idea of the 'knowledge economy' to show how nineteenth century knowledge is reconfigured according to a radical extension of individualism and *mathesis*. What is at stake is the very question of who we might be and what we might become, and identifying the links between the categories of economic institutions and the human sciences is going to be vital in this task. This chapter will reflect on some broad historical trends, which I will detail in various closer textual readings in the next chapter. At the very least they raise theoretical problems. My attempts here can only be a preliminary mapping of the hidden terrains of knowledge in the attempt to end the political innocence of one field of enquiry, but understanding the wider political implications will require a greater collaboration of critical thinkers who can reach beyond their intellectual and professional isolationism.

Orders of economy and reductionism

In an informative reading of economics in post-structuralism, Nick Mansfield (2003: 132), recognising how economics is the 'last remaining grand narrative', notes the use of the term 'economics' by writers such as Foucault, Derrida and Lyotard; not least recalling Foucault's call for a 'new economy of bodies and pleasures' (Foucault 1976: 159). He makes the important point that the use of the term 'economy' shows how post-structuralism is a 'significant cultural artefact in its own right', one that acts out the 'broader economics at the same time that it tries to describe it' (Mansfield 2003: 134; see also Peters 2001: 1–23). This is not say, as Mansfield makes clear, that employing the concept of economics cannot also be a legitimate questioning of the economic order, especially in the metaphorical use of the term, but that the persistence of the term reflects a cultural domination of this language.

It is, however, important to recognise that highlighting the economic is not a turn to economic reductionism, a prioritising of the economic as the central register of value. Knowledge is always greater than economy, but economy – particularly in the present order of power – is determining the means of representing knowledge and thus the rules of reading its own logic. The use of economics, as metaphor or material order, in a range of discourses requires a deeper understanding of the values and interests involved in its deployment. More importantly, the domination of economic institutions distorts the language by reducing the frameworks of what constitutes the economic realm.

The central problem is that the modern academic field of economics operates without understanding its own object – it operates like psychology unaware of its vulnerable formation and its hidden philosophical values, as the quotation from Robert Heilbroner at the beginning of this chapter indicates. However, the dangers of economic reductionism are no less present by appreciating its metaphorical or contextual use. Pierre Bourdieu, for example, challenges 'economism' as a form of ethnocentrism (that is applying categories and concepts which show no other forms of interest and value than found in capitalism). As Bourdieu states in his *The Logic of Practice* in 1980:

> Economism recognises no other form of interest than that which capitalism has produced, through a kind of real operation of abstraction, by setting up a universe of relations between man and man based, as Marx says, on 'callous cash payment' and more generally by favouring the creation of relatively autonomous fields, capable of establishing their own axiomatics (through the fundamental tautology 'business in for business', on which 'the economy' is based). It can therefore find no place in its analyses, still less in its calculations, for any form of 'non-economic' interest.
>
> (Bourdieu [1980] 1990: 113)

Economism appropriates a territory, like psychology, for calculation (measurement) rather than appreciating the 'social representation of production and exchange' (Bourdieu [1980] 1990: 113).[5] In response to 'economism', Bourdieu develops the idea of symbolic capital, alongside religious capital, as a form of credit and ritual significance. According to Bourdieu, economic and symbolic capital are 'inextricably intertwined', as can be seen in the way accumulating capital may offer 'honour and prestige' (Bourdieu [1980] 1990: 118–19). The relationship between so-called 'real' material economics ('real' only in so far that our thought is marked by the late nineteenth century) and the cultural economy, in Bourdieu, is examined by Scott Lash, who argues, following Piore and Sabel in *The Second Industrial Divide* (1984), that post-Fordist (mass production and consumption) is characterised by 'flexible specialization' – flexible production and specialised consumption as a response to niche markets. This means that supply and demand fluctuate in an ever-changing market due to the new branding of products and a changeable consumption due to marketing (that is cultural) devices. As Lash indicates: 'the material economy is increasingly driven by the cultural economy in the sphere of consumption' (Lash 1993: 206). This drawing together of different forms of economy is fascinating as it means, according to Lash, that the 'economic sphere is coming increasingly to resemble the cultural sphere' (Lash 1993: 207). This is an extraordinary moment in Western capitalism and one that allows us to find the fault line of modern 'economics' and open the space of the cultural, as well as psychological and religious practice. As Lash continues:

> [T]he crucial point is that whereas previously the production of culture was trapped in the logic of the commodification of the manufacturing sector, now the increased levels of innovation necessitated for post-Fordist accumulation in manufacturing itself necessitates that it must follow the design-intensive logic of the culture sector.
>
> (Lash 1993: 207)

Rescuing 'economics' from the plight of modern economics means that we can attempt to bring economics back to the human subject. This also means that we are no longer driven simply by economic determinism – as one reading of Marx might suggest – but rather, as Lash suggests, by cultural agency (Lash 1993: 208). As cultural agents, with imaginative possibility, we can influence the cultural symbolic and in turn change the material conditions – the way we think impacts the types of exchanges that are possible in the world. What I want to establish here is the multi-layered operation of economics as entangled with psychology and psychology entangled with forms of economics. The resulting knot is one that scholars of religion cannot afford to ignore for all that it reveals about the ethical foundations of our knowing and not-knowing.

Economics and psychology

With a rare sensitivity to Smith's language, Samuel Fleischacker (2004: 32), in his reading of the *Wealth of Nations*, shows how Smith's thinking remains much more an 'imagination to solve problems' and that his model of human nature is more open and fluid than later commentators assume. 'Smith', according to Fleischacker (2004: 62), 'does not share the bias toward "expressed preferences" of his contemporary heirs in economics. Human nature always includes what people aspire to, for Smith; it is never reduced to the desires they merely happen to have'. In recognising the tension between the empirical and the normative in Smith's work on human nature we see how the construction of a theory of human nature, or psychology, is easily lost in the 'science' of economics. Economics always holds a model of human nature, but the desire of empirical authority silences the philosophical imagination.

Karl Marx, likewise, recognised the anthropological ground of economics in a comment in his 'Economic and Philosophical Manuscript' (1844), when he states that the 'history of industry' has not grasped its connection to the 'nature of man' (Marx 1967). The fact that human thought and behaviour determine economic activity is not new in the theory of market prediction of human behaviour, but what is perhaps not appreciated is how models of 'man' influence economic theory and vice-versa, not least because it takes neo-classical economics (a mathematical calculus of variables) back to uncertain philosophical premises that its calculative logic wants to stabilize. Modern forms of psychology that offer a mathematical calculation of human cognition and behaviour are welcomed within such neo-classical economic speculations, because they operate on the same ideology of human nature. Such that Robert Lane, appreciating human needs in a return to Smith's question of happiness through a notion of complex cognition, seeks 'to discover how psychological and social principles govern the thinking, feeling, and behaviour of participants in a market economy' (Lane 1991: 4, cf. 116ff). Lane attempts to link cognitive and economic patterns by showing that it is not just work and wealth that contribute to a change of cognition, but also how markets can determine self-esteem, freedom and personal control:

> [T]he market contributes in its ways to both happiness and human development, principally through the *affluence effect* providing the material resources on which education, leisure, and moral development depend. By relieving poverty, the market takes a large step forward both in contributing to cognitive development and in making salient a variety of nonmaterial, or as Inglehart says, 'post-material,' values.
>
> (Lane 1991: 610)

Putting aside the problematic construction of 'cognition' and 'market' values in Lane's work, what we can see is how reflections about political economy and markets operate according to series of philosophical models of human nature. This can also be seen in the use of humans – and their emotions – for the market.

In Arlie Hochschild's (1983) illuminating work *The Managed Heart: Commercialisation of Human Feeling*, for example, she presents a sociological discussion of Delta Airline stewardesses and stewards. According to Hoschchild, the airline stewardess is required to manage her feelings for commercial reasons, where surface and deep acting become a resource (1983: 55). So that the phrases: 'Is there anything else madam?', 'Have a nice flight' and the obligatory smile become part of resource allocation.[6] According to Hoschchild, following Marx's assessment of an instrument of labour, air stewards and those in the service industry are offering 'emotional labour'. She defines emotional labour as 'the management of feeling to create a publicly observable facial and bodily display; emotional labour is sold for a wage and therefore has *exchange* value' (Hoschchild 1983: 7fn).[7] The category 'emotional labour' may not be a firm category for critiquing capitalism, but it opens the conceptually complex issue of psychology and the market.[8] Something Robert Lane recognises in his own cognitive examination of the market and emotion, when he states:

> Market behaviour is saturated with emotions. The consumer market arouses affects and constrains them through budgetary processes; the labour market constrains affects through performance criteria and arouses them through the desire for achievement and self-rewarding or self-punishing demands for excellence.
>
> (1991:77)

The idea of emotion once again reveals how models of human nature and psychology interact in the formation of political economy, whether in models of economic motivation (Smith) or the emotional market (Lane), but while psychologists are happily put to work in shaping minds and markets *the philosophical values of knowledge are never questioned*. The desire to calculate human feeling can be seen to go back to the roots of neo-classical economics, 1870 to 1914, and the period of industrial disciplinary formations.

Among the texts that historians see as marking the shift from political economy to economics and one that establishes part of the ground for neo-classical thinking – in the British tradition at least – is William Stanley Jevons's *The Theory of Political Economy* ([1871] 1970). This work carried forward the Benthamite tradition of the hedonistic calculus text to a new level of *mathesis* and influenced Alfred Marhsall's classic *Principles of Economics*, which appeared in the same year as James's *Principles of Psychology* in 1890; showing the new empirical mapping of disciplinary formations in the late nineteenth century. In the realm of economics, Jevons sets up a theory of pleasure and pain, and introduced a theory of utility and exchange that roots pleasure in consumption. What is striking in the text for our purposes is how he builds economics as a mathematical science and how it hides within it an aspiration of calculating human pleasure and pain. He argues that the making of the science of economics is precisely at the point of its *mathesis*, which he defends in his introduction by trying to argue that from Smith onwards this approach was necessary. In his introduction, he states, 'the mathematical treatment of economics is coeval with the science itself' (Jevons [1871] 1970: 66). Later the ground becomes even clearer: 'My theory of economics, however, is purely mathematical in character' (Jevons [1871] 1970: 78). The human emotions of pleasure and pain are thus reduced to *mathesis*. At the outset of his work we are also clearly presented with the economic-mathematical statement – that hides the philosophical ground – when he states his 'novel opinion' that *'value depends entirely upon utility'* (Jevons [1871] 1970: 77). These aspects are extended in the expansion of neo-classical economics when the market becomes deregulated and globalized in the neo-liberal context of the 1980s, but here the roots of the economic calculus of human life become clear, even if in 1871 Jevons ([1871] 1970: 83) had some initial reservation:

> I hesitate to say that men will ever have the means of measuring directly the feelings of the human heart. A unit of pleasure or of pain is difficult even to conceive; but it is the amount of these feelings which is continually prompting us to buying and selling, borrowing and lending, labouring and resting, producing and consuming; and *it is from the quantitative effects of the feelings that we must estimate their comparative amounts* … In the absence of complete statistics, the science will not be less mathematical, though it will be immensely less useful than if it were, comparatively speaking, exact. A correct theory is the first step towards improvement, by showing what we need and what we might accomplish. (original emphasis)

The successive waves of economic theory would sweep away Jevons' hesitations, because even if a *mathesis* of human emotion were impossible the apparatus of economic knowledge would elicit psychology to provide a model of being human that would sustain the calculus. The required units of the human mind would be found in the modelling of the mind on the very technology that would carry the new economy into the twenty-first century. If human nature resisted economics the easy solution is to shape humans in terms of the calculating machines through a codified logic. The human being becomes stabilized in the logic required for measurement, enforced by total practical application. Psychology and economics find useful alliances at this point of stabilization. The philosophical shifts and values would be concealed by the very utility of ideas in the social order of institutional life. Jevons ([1871] 1970: 119) himself was already shifting the calculus by shifting feeling into *intensity*:

> Now, the only dimension belonging properly to feeling seems to be intensity, and this intensity must be independent of time and of the quantity of commodity enjoyed. *The intensity of feeling must mean, then, the instantaneous state produced by an elementary or infinitesimal quantity of commodity consumed.* (original emphasis)

The phrase 'seems to be' carries a lot in this statement and it will soon become 'fact' with no further discussion, such are the philosophical blind spots within empirical thinking in both economics and psychology; *those subtle shifts where values become facts by blurring the logic out of demand* (what we might call the 'Jevons philosophical jump'). And it is then easy to make the next shift of renaming entities to hide the philosophical shifts:

> Intensity of feeling, however, is only another name for degree of utility, which represents the favourable effect produced upon the human frame by the consumption of commodity, that is by an elementary or infinitesimal quantity of commodity.

Jevons goes on repeating such phrases as 'must be' and eventually constructs a mathematical model for utility and human happiness, even as he notes that the difficulty for economics is 'conceiving clearly and fully the conditions of utility' (Jevons [1871] 1970: 122). Even though economists will express concerns and offer hesitations, the power of the economic drive aspires to control and grasp the reality through equation and calculus and the sheer force of institutional practice ignores any philosophical and historical leakages (Mokyr 2005: 228). Jevons was, of course, part of a wider set of epistemological shifts in the neo-classical school of economics.

Much of the wider influence comes from the traditions of the Austrian school, with Carl Menger (1840–1921), who, in the same year as Jevons's text, published his *Principles of Economics* (Grundsätze der Volkswirtschaftslehre). Here Menger ([1871] 1950: 108) locates the ground of economics in human needs: '[M]an, with his needs and his commands of the means to satisfy them, is himself the point at which human economic life both begins and ends'. However, he also, somewhat unwittingly, realised that it was causally linked to 'human knowledge' about such needs and their satisfaction (Menger [1871] 1950: 52). There was no philosophical question about the nature of being human posed in his text, which rather moved economics to questions of price and utility (as opposed to labour in Marx). In his later 1883 work *Investigations into the Method of the Social Sciences* (Untersuchungen über die Methode der Socialwissenschaften), he adopted a methodological individualism; which according to Hayek ([1976] 2004), in his own introduction to the *Principles*, was a deliberate 'polemic' against the Historical School (the nineteenth century German view that history not mathematical theorems were the basis of economics).[9] Menger's isolation of the individual as the basic unit of analysis, in his attempt to identify the 'essential' from the 'accidental', was yet another move that hides the philosophical ground of selection criteria and choice (Hodgson 2001: 82).

The Austrian school of economics championed the freedom of the individual, which evolved in the economic theories of those like Friedrich Hayek (1899–1992), one of the voices behind liberalism and the free market.[10] Hayek marked out the important post-war shifts against ideologies of collectivism, but the extensions of his work would go beyond his concerns for justice and he could never have envisioned the full extent of how individualism could itself become a form of collectivism, as I will examine in the next chapter (see Hayek 1944). Nonetheless, there is an important modelling of both psychology and economics within a new ideology of the individual from the nineteenth century that couples with a calculative logic. The contemporary economic shift to the neo-liberal extension of the *mathesis* of economics would embrace a specific narrowing of the psychological in the same terms. As the dead corpse anchored medicine for Foucault (1963), so forms of atomistic individualism would be the anchor for a new *mathesis* within the human sciences. The problem of knowledge was that what was measurable (the empirical) became the only mark of truth, but, significantly, critical voices of resistance to these models of being human emerge in both disciplines.

One challenge to the assumptions of neo-classical economics can be seen in the protest by a group of French economic students, who formed under the title of 'post-autistic' economics (autisme-économie) in 2000; developing into a reform movement and a subsequent wide-ranging discussion of teaching in the field of economics (Fullbrook 2003). While, as James Devine (2003: 212–19) makes clear, there are difficulties in comparing a human neurobiological condition to a reductive form of mathematical modelling in economics, it confirms how economic theory corresponds to human characteristics, even disturbing conditions. Responding to the post-autistic 'crisis' in economics, Sheila Dow (2003: 132) makes it clear that examinations of economics should be presented as a series of 'controversies instead of as an agreed body of thought'. Other pluralistic voices in the field of economics, such as Deirdre McCloskey (2003: 125, 127; see also [1985] 1998), challenged the rhetoric of science and the 'imagining' of what constitutes a science in economics, which she sees as detached from 'inquiry' in a broader sense. In a later polemical essay, McCloskey (2002: 41) was not so much critical of quantification, mathematics, the free market, or even the historical and philosophical ignorance of economics, but rather the detached nature of the subject:

> Economics in its most prestigious and academically published versions engages in two activities, *qualitative theorems* and *statistical significance*, which *look* like theorizing and observing, and have (apparently) the same tough math and tough statistics that actual theorizing and actual observing would have. *But neither of them is what it claims to be.* Qualitative theorems are not theorizing in a sense that would have to do with double-virtued inquiry into the world. In the same sense, statistical significance is not observing. *This is the double-formed and secret sin* [of economics].

The 'imagining' of a science of economics is what hides its historical and philosophical values. It is precisely these aspects that return us to the primary questions of psychology and economics or, in its more classical and gendered frame, 'models of man' and political economy. Returning to the past is one strategy of exposing the philosophical leakages behind the 'imagining' of the human sciences. It brings the subject back to the open question of 'inquiry' and not to the closed assumptions of *mathesis*. It could even mean unearthing in the past a more complex imagining of such 'science'; with a radical new equation of the values behind empirical objects and the limits of knowledge. Alas, the frightened, narrow minds are already closing thought to its complexity.

Economics of the past

According to Waterman (2004: 121–2), there was a 'sudden separation' of economics from Christian theology in the nineteenth century in the struggle to form a political science. Richard Whately (1786–1863) reflected on this situation before taking the Chair in Political Economy at Oxford in 1831 and stated, in a letter to a friend in 1829:

> that there is a sort of crisis for the science in this place, such, that occupying of it by one of my profession and station may rescue it permanently from disrepute. Religious truth ... appears to me to be intimately connected, at this time especially, with the subject in question. For it seems to me that before too long, political economists, of some sort or other, must govern the world; ... now the anti-Christians are striving hard to have this science to themselves, and to interweave it with their own notions.

The separation of theology from the discourse of political economy in the nineteenth century reveals the shift in the 'economy' of knowledge itself, in a similar way to how religion separates from the discourse of spirituality under neo-liberalism (Carrette and King 2005). What is striking at this moment of separation is the way economics separates from the 'divine' economy of the passions.[11] We have already seen the relationship between the passions and economics in Adam Smith's *Theory of Moral Sentiments*, but rather than reiterate Smith's thesis, which I have already touched upon, I want to explore the work of economic historian Albert Hirschman and his study *The Passions and the Interests: Political Arguments for Capitalism Before Its Triumph* ([1977] 1997). This is a fascinating study for its examination of seventeenth and eighteenth century justifications for capitalism and accumulation of capital. Hirschman shows that through Christian history, from Augustine onwards, we find the notion of checking or overcoming one vice or sin through another in the creation of a hierarchy of sins (Hirschman [1977] 1997: 10). In this sense, he argues that in seventeenth and eighteenth century economics, which was concerned with the whole of life, the idea was that one passion would harness another (Hirschman [1977] 1997: 16). We find these ideas running through David Hume and in Adam Smith's 'invisible hand', passions controlling one derive by another. As Hume wrote: 'There is no passion, therefore, capable of controlling the interested affection, but the very affection itself, by an alteration of its direction' (Hume quoted in Hirschman [1977] 1997: 25).

According to Hirschman, once the strategy of opposing one passion against another was set in place a distinction between which passions were the 'tamers' and which were the '"wild" passions that required taming' started to develop (Hirschman [1977] 1997: 31). The answer to this question, arising in response to Thomas Hobbes's suggestion in *Leviathan* (1651) that human beings were fundamentally selfish – which, according to Hirschman, set up the two concepts – was that the 'interests' were opposed to the 'passions'. As Hirschman indicates: 'When the term "interest" in the sense of concerns, aspirations, and advantage gained currency in Western Europe during the late sixteenth century, its meaning was by no means limited to the material aspects of a person's welfare ...' (Hirschman [1977] 1997: 32).

Interests included conscience, honour, and health, as well as wealth, but narrowed its meaning to Smith's 'augmentation of fortune' (Hirschman [1977] 1997: 40). Interests (money making) is then placed over against other, mainly bodily passions (which no doubt caused an interesting dilemma when money-making was linked to the body). If Hirschman's analysis is correct, by the time we get to Smith's *Theory of Moral Sentiments* (1759) the so-called *non-economic drives the economic* (Hirschman [1977] 1997: 109), or, as Dr Johnson framed it: 'Dangerous human proclivities can be canalized into comparatively harmless channels by the existence of opportunity for money-making and private wealth ...' (Hirschman [1977] 1997: 134). According to Hirschman, capitalism was set up to overcome what is now its 'worst feature' (Hirschman [1977] 1997: 132). From this we may presume that the seventeenth and eighteenth century vision of a moral capitalism failed as capitalism was turned into the passion of greed. However, what is significant from this brief excursion into the history of economic ideas is the 'non-economic springs of economic action' (Hirschman [1977] 1997: 110). This idea of the non-economic can be linked back to my earlier discussion of Bourdieu's idea of symbolic capital, it is another sign of the constant splintering of economics and non-economics, showing the cultural embedded nature of economics.[12] Like the separation of religion and culture, the separation of economics and culture becomes a political foregrounding of a certain type of knowledge in the social order. The separation of economics from the wider aspects of the non-economic is the moment economics becomes detached, to recall McCloskey (2002), from life itself and its underlying philosophical imagining of being human. It is the moment the ethical foundations of economic knowledge become silenced.

The non-economic economy: Robert Heilbroner and Deepak Lal

Economic historians and critical voices in the subject are always noting how the area is largely misunderstood. The domination of neo-classical economics prevents conceptual questions outside *networked mathesis*, which an historical account makes evident. The economic drive for order and measurement dominates ideas, even while the non-economic disrupts such sensibilities and the market remains unpredictable. There is here a desire to control life at its unpredictable edges in an obsession with calculation and the imagination of a science; the same dynamic that drives attitudes in psychology. In this uneasy management of knowledge, the links between economics and psychology are often accepted at the point these two domains work on empirical analysis and share the object of controlled mapping, with economic benefit, but the empirical hides philosophical and disciplinary errors. Inside these philosophical ruptures of thought, historians of economics are seen by their disciplinary regime as awkward figures because, as in most disciplines, historians reveal the artificial nature of disciplinary boundaries and the historical fragility of concepts. As Roger Backhouse's recent study of the history of economics states: '[I]t is simply not possible to draw a clear dividing line between what constitutes economic analysis and what does not, or between what constitutes "proper" or "real" economics and what does not' (2002: 6). Disciplines close down what appears to upset the rules of the discourse by employing strategies of coherence and reasserting cherished values of an operational domain. What keeps the incoherence from emerging is the institutional lock of statements supported by the economic social order. Economists and politicians give the impression of navigating the known, but in practice the storms of philosophical ambiguity constantly disorientate the disciplinary compass. The desperation felt by those economists like McCloskey (2002) is because knowledge has already been closed by power.

The central point of Backhouse's study of economics is that the field has only recently (the last 100 years or so) been the domain of economic specialists called 'economists'. As with psychology and religion, the modern specialists control knowledge only to lose it in the restriction of what constitutes the subject of knowledge. The later development of neo-classical economics is based on the assumption that you could work out a mathematical formula for wealth distribution and the management of resources. However, in the past economic ideas were, as Backhouse shows, developed by 'theologians, lawyers, philosophers, businessmen and government officials' (Backhouse 2002: 2). The important fact here, as we have already indicated, is that 'economic ideas are an integral component of culture'. This cultural shaping of economic ideas is taken up by a number of economic thinkers, usually with an historical eye (Throsby 2001). For example, the economist Deepak Lal, in his Phlin Memorial Lectures delivered at the Stockholm School of Economics in 1995 (and published in his book *Unintended Consequences*), develops an historical and cross-cultural analysis of economics to explore the development of factor endowments (land, labour and capital), culture and politics. Deepak Lal attempts to identify the 'cultural correlates of a market economy' (Lal 1998: 5). In his exploration of Western and Asian market economies Lal, not surprisngly, points towards the rise of 'individualism' in the West. He takes his analysis back to Augustine, but not in any simple way. Following Louis Dumont (1986), he argues that the history of Christian individualism is not like modern individualism, namely that in Christianity there is an 'out-worldly individualism', but in the modern world there is an 'in-worldly individualism'. As Dumont (1986: 27) states with reference to Troeltsch: 'There is no doubt about the fundamental conception of man that flowed from the teaching of Christ: as Troeltsch said, man is an *individual in-relation-to God*; for our purposes this means that man is in essence an outworldly individual'.

The key moment is when the out-worldly individualism of Christianity is transformed into in-worldly individualism. Deepak Lal identifies the roots of this, not in the industrial revolution or even like Weber in the Reformation, but in Pope Gregory I in the sixth century and his statements on the family (changes in the marriage system to prevent marriage to a close relative or kin and changes in the strategies of heirship/inheritance) and Pope Gregory VII in the eleventh century, who in 1075 set the foundation for the modern legal institutions (establishment of papal supremacy and independence of the clergy from the state, the framework of Western economy being established in the 'law of the merchants' including bills of exchange and promissory notes). These points of history were, according to Lal, to have lasting effects on the West. Historically accurate or not, the central issue here is that there is, as Lal (2002: 94) states, 'a complex interaction between ideas – the cosmological beliefs of culture as we defined them –institutions, and material interests'.

What is missing from Lal's analysis is the historical emergence of psychology for understanding the late modern economics of capitalism. It is not 'individualism' as such which results in certain economic realities, but a specific ideological framing of individualism. Psychological individualism is an in-worldly individualism, which serves particular ideological purposes. This omission is one of the central problems in the dialogue between religion and economics – as seen in Brennan and Waterman's (1994) *Economics and Religion: Are They Distinct?* In fact, in the same book, Sheila Dow rightly notes: 'The nature of the economic system, and the influence of religion, depend very much on the depiction of individual behaviour and decision-making' (Dow 1994: 200). With few exceptions, the full force of this statement has never been picked up in economics, but it is I think crucial in mapping economics and why I seek to find a sub-structure in economics for thinking about the psychology of religion. It is the 'depiction' of the 'individual' and the 'decision-making' of *mathesis* that are central ethical–political features in the making of modern economics and psychology.

One of the few writers to make the key association between economics and psychology is the economist Robert Heilbroner,[13] who in his extension of economic analysis in his 1988 book *Behind the Veil of Economics* (from which the title of this chapter is taken), recognised the importance of the ideology or vision behind economics. He attempts to identify the underlying 'premises and values' of economics. In this sense he sees economics as the 'process by which society marshalls and coordinates the activities required for its provisioning' (Heilbroner 1988: 14). Like Lal, he sees traditions as an important component in this matter. He argues that there is an underlying process or 'substratum of beliefs that causes us to structure our perceptions', which 'escapes our recognition' (Heilbroner 1988: 196, 17). He points out that:

> ... powerful aspects of the market process throw a veil over other processes – a veil that obscures understandings and recognitions that, were they present, would cause 'economics' as well as market societies to look very differently from the way they do.
>
> (Heilbroner 1988: 17)

Following the Austrian economist Karl Polanyi, Heilbroner sees economics 'embedded in non-economic institutions' (Heilbroner 1988: 17). One discourse that Heilbroner identifies in his economic examination is the value of psychology, particular psychoanalysis, for understanding these hidden processes. This emerges particularly in his earlier book *An Inquiry into the Human Prospect* (1975) and is carried into his *Behind the Veil of Economics* (1988). While Heilbroner rightly acknowledges the 'subjective element of motivation or behaviour' in the economic sphere and the way political power requires 'political obedience' (Heilbroner 1975: 102), he remains uncritical in his reading of psychology is a similar 'veil' to the veil of economics he so condemns. *Psychology veils its economic substrate as market economics veils its psychological ideology.* As Heilbroner comments, critical of the veil of economics:

> By screening out all aspects of domination and acquiescence, as well as those of affect and trust, it [economics] encourages us to understand capitalism as fundamentally 'economic' – not social or political – in nature. Indeed, as we have seen, it establishes the concept of 'economics' itself as a mode of social articulation that is separated from – not built atop – older modes of social orchestration. (192)

To read economics as requiring acknowledgement of human nature is different to assuming psychology can give you a correct map of the human being. Heilbroner is correct to point us towards the fact that economic systems can only be put in place if the building blocks for the system are established, but it is wrong to assume the models of psychology are not wrapped in the economic veil. Economic systems require a model of being human to make the system effective and this must lead us to question why the USA is the most highly saturated psychological market in the world; many forms of American individualized psychology support its economic infrastructure (see Chapter 4). Heilbroner enables us to see psychology as one of the blocks of economic thought, but he does not make the leap of interrogating psychology as a hidden ideology. It is, however, this aspect of a 'hidden ideology' that interests Heilbroner, as he pointed out:

> Blatant ideology is thus not the aspect of the veil of economics that I find interesting or important. Of far greater consequence are statements that have none of these egregious defects but that must nonetheless be revealed as 'ideological' because they can be shown to be false or contradictory, *although not wittingly so.*
>
> (Heilbroner 1988: 189–90)

Psychology and economics need to be shown as holding ideological effects behind the disciplinary veils they use to hide their incoherent statements. The greatest veil of Western knowledge is to separate disciplinary knowledge as if it is self-contained. To move back the veil of psychology is to move back the veil of economics (and, in turn, the veil of the psychology of religion). Moving back the veil of economics is to see the interconnected nature of all knowledge and it reflects non-empirical values, interests and beliefs. As Heilbroner (1988: 196) states:

> That which remains unacknowledged ... is the substratum of beliefs that causes us to structure our perceptions in terms of an 'economy' rather than a socio-political order; or to see individuals rather than individuated social beings; or two realms rather than a single unstably constituted regime.

If we reject the disciplinary regimes of knowledge then it might be possible to see just how psychological models of thinking are linked to economics according to in-worldly individualism and how the adoption of such a model of being human by psychologists of religion and pastoral theologians supports such wider social orders. Disciplinary regimes and concepts are thus ethical systems of framing the world and they require our philosophical scrutiny and moral evaluation.

The politics of introspection

The human sciences are vulnerable subjects because of their disciplinary leakage. Their statements seep through the cracks, their concepts melt in philosophical dialogue and their values ooze in the aspirations to hard science. If economics can be shown to leak into psychology, it is now important to show how the appeal to the individual in psychology leaks into the social world and how this reveals the ineffectiveness of disciplinary isolation. I will explore the specific inter-relation of psychological theories of religion to the realm of economics in the second part of the book in detail, but here I wish to continue the historical overview in order to highlight the way psychology holds a social utility in its own disciplinary emergence and how it seeks to stabilize the category of the individual for such purposes. What this history reveals is that modern forms of introspection are established through a specific social employment of individualism and the calculation of *mathesis*, particularly in the separation of psychology from theology.

In his excellent account of the historical origins of psychology, Kurt Danziger (1990) highlights the political and epistemological context for the emergence of psychology. He demonstrates how the field emerged out of the existing subjects of philosophy and physiology and the problems of establishing the need for an 'experimental' method 'for producing a social consensus about "the facts"' (Danziger 1990: 27). He argues that the production of psychological knowledge was established through the '*community* of investigators' built around the laboratory set up in Leipzig by Wilhelm Wundt in 1879 – the arbitrary date for the foundation of psychology, although William James established a similar laboratory in 1875 (Danziger 1990: 28; Taylor 2005). It was the rapid institutionalization of the methods, seen in the establishment of a more 'concrete' and 'standardized' discourse that brought about the success of psychological experimentation in both Germany and the USA. The other key factor in the successful development of psychology was its application to other institutional structures. As Danziger (1990: 101) states: 'The fact is that almost from the beginning of the twentieth century psychology ceased to be a purely academic discipline and began to market its products in the outside world'. The application of psychology to wider social needs and demands was central to its knowledge claims (Danziger 1990: 180). However, as Danziger notes, psychology had to offer methods that were socially useful to the requirements of the particular market demand, such that the professional alliance with the educational system reflected the desire for methods of measurement required by a new educational administration in the USA (Danziger 1990: 101ff). A point confirmed by the historian of psychology Graham Richards (2000: 72): 'Education and psychology provided an especially promising market, and within these Christian educators and ministers constituted a substantial proportion of psychology's potential audience'.

In a similar way to how Foucault (1975) demonstrated the evolution of the prison system, Danziger reveals how psychological knowledge in education reflected new social demands for control. The work of psychologists in the first part of the twentieth century reflected the demands for the educational system to deal with mass urban populations. Measurement and comparison were needed by the educational administrators for purposes of efficiency, which led in turn to the development of mental tests and methods of individual differentiation (Danziger 1990: 107ff). Control of the masses through the details of educational measurement and categorisation were easily transferred to the demands of industrial efficiency. The history of psychology is therefore the history of political and economic demands for a certain type of knowledge product; which continues today when psychologists are supported in developing individualistic and mathematical models of the self. The social and political demand for efficient knowledge management utilises the ideas of psychology as a form of governmentality. As Danziger (1990: 180) states, in regard the early history of the subject:

> Like all human productive activities the production of scientific knowledge is highly goal-directed. This directive component manifests itself not only in the fact that so much scientific activity is explicitly devoted to hypothesis testing, but also in the more implicit commitment to the search for a certain type of knowledge.

Following a more specifically Foucauldian line, Nikolas Rose (1996: 107–16) also identifies the ways that psychological knowledge was implanted into the cultural patterns of Western society. He lists these as 'phenomenotechnics' (the art of producing in reality what is already produced in thought), 'regimes of truth' (like Danziger's communal networks which produced the truth), 'disciplinization' (programmes for the stabilization of subject knowledge); 'psychologization' (the reading of issues in terms of the psychological) and, finally, 'institutional epistemology' (the development of an institutional location for psychological knowledge). It is the fourth of these five areas I want to focus upon, that of 'psychologization' (Rose 1996: 113). It is important to recognise that 'psychologization', for Rose, does not mean imposing a certain model of the person, particularly as psychology is not a 'coherent "paradigm"', but as Rose states, the social reality of psychology is 'a complex and heterogeneous network of agents, sites, practices, and techniques for the production, dissemination, legitimation, and utilization of psychological truth' (Rose 1996: 114). Psychological truth is not, therefore, one-dimensional, as can be seen from the diversity of theories within psychological knowledge. What grounds the psychological truth is the attempt to stabilize self-knowledge according to a new ordering of the individual in society and employing more detailed forms of calculation. The individual is structured in the neo-classical economic system by stabilizing a framework of measurability and closing those areas that escape measurability. What is missed is the 'Jevons philosophical jump', the hidden moment in each age when knowledge slides blindly into the calculative logic of making human life efficient.

Institutions stabilise knowledge about the self by providing a value-laden apparatus for thinking about the self. The human sciences thus operate by making an object appear fixed in the very fluidity of assumptions. Jerrold Seigel (2005: 652) makes this clear at the end of his extensive history of the self when reflecting on the appeal to the sciences for self-understanding:

> As interesting as such new perspectives may be, however, it is unlikely that they will ever provide definitive answers to our questions, given that science is a changing and restless enterprise. In addition, trying to say what the self truly is requires not just better understanding of its components, but *an account of how they stand in relation to one another*, and here advances in the sciences may bear considerably less promise. The reason is that the matter of how biology, society, and reflection all contribute to the self's nature is a value-laden question, answers to which cannot help but be colored by the particular concepts or categories we use to think about it. (emphasis added)

Fixing the object of self is therefore also tied to disciplinary distinction, limitation and concealment. I will explore these fault lines of thought in more detail in the next chapter, when I examine the problem of the individual and the social in disciplinary knowledge and how they operate according to what I call disciplinary amnesia, but what I want to mark out here is something of the history of different forms of introspection and the way self-knowledge is stabilized for new forms of political economy. The history of introspection, from its pre-modern theological roots to modern psychological measurement, reveals the epistemological separation of self-knowledge from out-worldly theology, in the same way as we outlined in the emergence of economics. To recall Dumont (1986: 53):

> My thesis is simple: with Calvin, the hierarchical dichotomy that characterised our field of consideration comes to an end; the antagonistic worldly element that individualism had hitherto to accommodate disappears entirely in Calvin's theocracy. The field is absolutely unified. *The individual is now in the world, and the individualist value rules without restriction or limitation.* The in-worldly individual is before us.

Once introspective knowledge is anchored according to an in-worldly individual the horizon of the self moves from pastoral 'accounting' to questions of political economic 'accounting' (Foucault 1982a, 1982b; Roberts 2002; Jacobs 2002; Jacobs and Walker 2002). The shift from theological accounting of the self to the contemporary economic accounting, or auditing, is through the technology of individualism and *mathesis* as it is dispersed through the industrial disciplinary fields of knowledge and beyond. I will first explore the calculative order of *mathesis* and then return to the problem of individualism.

Psychological knowledge can be seen as the gradual winnowing out of the theological introspection through the index of measurement. Such that the move from Christian introspection in the theology of Augustine's *The Confessions* (*c.* 397–8) to Friedrich Schleiermacher's *The Christian Faith* (1821) to the founding fathers of psychology in the work of Wilhelm Wundt and William James in the 1880s and the atomistic modelling of modern cognitive science in 1990s is established through an ever-reducing horizon for framing the individual and an increase in forms of measurement. But this historical journey is not some wonderful progression to accuracy, but rather the blurring of the value-laden conditions of introspection and the closure of a space to control and limit analysis. It requires the isolation of the individual from the context of everything else in order to isolate an empirical self for *mathesis*. For example, in the work of Wilhelm Wundt, according to Danziger (1990: 35), there was a distinction between 'actual introspection' (*Selbstbeobachtung*) and internal perception (*innere Wahrnehmung*). 'Actual introspection' was the simple perception of subjective events, while 'internal perception', was the observation in some methodical way. Psychology structured introspection through a systematic analysis.

Introspection in the history of psychology is, therefore, different from the history of theological introspection because of its methical and structured processes. There is nothing wrong with measurement as such, but the process of isolating the individual as a domain for measurement in psychology more broadly is determined by a certain politics of knowledge and something constituted by the setting up of categories to capture the human object inside the criteria of calculation. This is important because to formalise the nature of the human being according to experimental practices is to develop a utility of functions from a community of specialists. It requires isolating what is measurable and holding up the isolated feature as prior to all other forms of knowledge. Such strategies are not about revealing the truth of being human, but rather the stabilization of a certain truth of the human being for a new type of society based upon an instrumental rationality of calculation for efficiency and control.

If the calculation of introspection marked the site of the emergence of psychological knowledge, the second difference was the deployment of a new concept of the individual. The different orders of individualism can be seen by following the Foucauldian narrative of the shift from pastoral power to state-apparatus, even as we must conclude its limits in accounting for present forms of knowledge. What Foucault enables us to see is that the dynamic of 'individualism' as a form of social order works across both theological and psychological institutions. The individual is therefore a social category shaped by various forms of institutional regimes. In Augustine's classic model of the Trinitarian self in the *De Trinitate* (The Trinity [*c*. 420] 1988), with the various models of the mind (such as mind, self-love and self-knowledge, and memory, understanding and will), we see how the self is woven together by the pre-existing set of beliefs that structure the individual (Augustine [*c*. 420] 1988, Books 9–10). Augustine's inwardness relates to what Foucault called 'pastoral power', as an 'individualising' force (Foucault 1978: 123, 1979: 136). Christianity established a religious perspective that believed in the individual relation to God, in individual salvation and that the individual was cared for in specific terms. This, according to Foucault, was a new emphasis in the ancient world and one that would be carried into the heart of European history.

The key problem in the Christian tradition was when this individual knowledge of self in pastoral power encountered the state apparatus in the eighteenth century under very different political and economic conditions. At this time there was a 'new distribution, a new organisation of this kind of individualising power', or as Foucault called it, a 'new pastoral power' (Foucault 1982a: 214–15). The modern art of government, according to Foucault, arises through a combination of pastoral power, the reason of the state ('principles and methods of state government') and the theory of police ('objects of the state's rational activity' – a broader definition than we find today) (Foucault 1979: 145). This model of government replaces previous ideas of the ruler of the kingdom, as in the submission to the King or, as in Thomas Aquinas, government of the kingdom under God's Divine Law. Modern government also broke with the Machiavellian model of ruler and state (Foucault 1979: 146–7; Simons 1995: 39). This reason of the state also required the knowledge of the state's strength, which meant it co-existed with a law and order – that is the police – in the broad sense of organisation of life. As the political scientist Jon Simons indicates: 'Reason of state relies on the technology of police to make individuals useful' (Simons 1995: 39). When the reason of state and the theory of police integrate pastoral power there is an emergence of the politics of welfare and a concern with population, which became the apparatus of psychology. As Foucault (1982a: 215) argued: '[P]ower of a pastoral type, which over centuries – for more than a millennium – had been linked to a defined religious institution, suddenly spread out into the whole social body; it found support in a multitude of institutions'.

Foucault's narrative may well be contested according to some of its historical details, but the epistemological ground of his work is clear. The individual is a social category of government. This point is important to my central argument that knowledge in the industrial disciplines of the human sciences is caught in a false closure. The problem is that knowledge in economics and psychology employ strategies to hide this correlation of the individual and social, because it reveals the underlying *a priori* values of knowledge and the institutional interests. Psychology as the science of the 'individual' collapses into the political economy of governing society and economics as the science of resource allocation collapses into the modelling of the 'individual'. To put it simply, psychology and economics have a co-dependency, because self-knowledge and social-knowledge are permeable forms.

In my narrative so far I have done no more than sketch some relational problems between economics and psychology and my work depends largely on the historians of the human sciences in these respective domains. If this mapping holds sufficiently it will at least unsettle late nineteenth century disciplinary constellations around the problem of the individual and the social in Western thought. What I have wanted to show is that the formations of knowledge in the human sciences are fluid rather than fixed, that they leak rather than contain, but that they reflect the artificial organisation of knowledge for an industrial society. The situation is such that the academic disciplines under question mask the knowledge values in order to sustain the existing social institutions. However, the reordering of knowledge in the 'knowledge economy' brings about a new constellation of knowledge that transforms the disciplinary structures of the nineteenth century by taking forward individualism and *mathesis* in a more radical way. This new ordering, by default, allows us to see more clearly the ethical foundation of knowledge and how the domains of economics and psychology are fused, especially when *all* knowledge is presently determined by the rationality of economic institutions.

The ethics of the knowledge economy

The idea of the knowledge economy has slowly been dominating public discourses since the late-1980s, after the deregulation of the world markets and linked technological processes of globalization (Houghton and Sheehan 2000: 2). Statements about the knowledge economy are now a major part of international global financial and government policy and much of the rhetoric is difficult to disentangle. The World Bank and the Organisation for Economic Co-operation and Development (OECD) have been at the forefront of the discourse of knowledge economy with various reports (World Bank 1998; OECD 1996, 1999). Following Brinkley (2006: 3–12), we can identify two key aspects in the diverse set of statements surrounding the term, first, the transformation of knowledge in new technologies and, second, knowledge as a renewable economic source. In their critical exploration of the literature for educational debate Peters and Besley (2006: 66) believe the 'received view' of the knowledge economy can be related to five key areas: 'the economics of abundance, the annihilation of distance, the deterritorialization of the state, the importance of local knowledge and the investment in human capital'.[14] It would seem that the dominant epistemological category of labour that Foucault saw as dominating economics in the modern period has now been superseded by the category of knowledge itself (Drucker 1993: 38). While science and technology are the central subjects of this new economy, the wider shifts in social and cultural life increasingly displace all subjects. However, the importance of the term is its ability to capture a radical structural change in social and political life, as Dominique Foray cogently argues (2004: x):

> The term *knowledge-based economy* also enables readers to fully understand a qualitative innovation in the organization and conduct of modern economic life – namely, the factors determining the success of firms and national economies are more dependent than ever on the capacity to produce and use knowledge.

Foray (2004: 18) builds the new discipline of the 'economics of knowledge' with the aim to 'analyze and discuss institutions, technologies, and social regulations that can facilitate the efficient production and use of knowledge'. It is also important to realise that the rhetoric of the knowledge economy – the reordering of knowledge for the market – arises from the domination of economic institutions in the new global environment and the impact they have on the entire social and cultural order. All knowledge is now under the sign of economics, even if knowledge and life are more than economics. Even resistance to such a regime, as Mansfield (2003) indicated, is always caught in the process, because economics (allocation of resources and material exchanges) have always been a central and unavoidable ground of life (even if constituted by the non-economic).

There are various roots to the term 'knowledge economy', but the idea of the knowledge economy is often attributed to the now prophetic insights of economist and management guru Peter Drucker in his 1969 study *The Age of Discontinuity: Guidelines to our Changing Society*. In this book he set out to explore the possible lines of continuity and discontinuity for the future changes in economics and technology. As he argues (1969: 248): 'What matters is that knowledge has become the central "factor of production" in an advanced, developed economy'. Operating on a distinction between *knowledge* (economically applied) as an economic good and *information* (data, non-applied) the idea operates by a disguised encroachment of all knowledge for economic benefit (Drucker 1969: 252; Foray 2004: 1). Indeed, the term knowledge economy has held its own rhetorical non-usefulness according to some reports and the concept is often refined to exploit the economic specificity (Institute for New Technologies Discussion, 2003 quoted in Brinkley 2006: 3).

Drucker's analysis reflects on how different organisations seek different types of specialist knowledge for economic benefit. Reflecting on the marketization of knowledge, he writes: 'Few areas of learning are not in demand by organizations of our pluralist society. There is, I admit, little call for the consulting services of the Classics faculty. But there is more demand for the theologians than most people realize' (Drucker 1969: 250–1). The commodification of knowledge has become more sophisticated since 1969 and the market take-over now extends freely to the use of old forms of knowledge for market success (see Carrette and King 2005). However, what remains clear from Drucker's (1969: 326) work is that 'the meaning, and the structure of knowledge' is 'drastically changing'. Recognizing that knowledge structures are becoming complex, not only in the central application and utility, but also in the link to political regimes, he writes: 'We can no longer maintain the traditional line between "dirty politics" and "pure knowledge"' (Drucker 1969: 345). While Drucker recognises that the knowledge producers find it hard to accept the link of knowledge to political decisions (Drucker 1969: 349), he does have a clear sense, as we noted, of how the new knowledge system creates new forms of disciplinary association and the effects this would have on the academic subjects. 'The organization of knowledge', he argued (Drucker 1969: 331), 'and with it the organization of the university, is of necessity becoming both more complex and more controversial. A simple organization is no longer possible'.

Drucker's post-1968 statements grasped the shifts towards knowledge and politics and new subject regimes for the post-war world, but the post-1980s would be far beyond his imagination in terms of the global network of knowledge and the neo-liberal university. The decades that followed have made knowledge formulations within the university more complex by the concealed economic ideologies of codified knowledge (built on individualism and mathesis), especially in the human sciences, where fact and value are more easily blurred. What Drucker (1969: 347) makes clear from his prediction from the present is that much is at stake for the condition of knowledge:

> All one can say today is that application has become the centre of knowledge, of the knowledge effort, and of the organized search for knowledge. As a result, knowledge has become the very foundation of modern economy and modern society and the principle of social action. This is so great a change that it must have a major impact on knowledge itself and must make it a central philosophical and political issue in the knowledge society.

In his later work *Post-capitalist Society* (1993: 18), Drucker explored the changes in Western knowledge under the impact of capitalism and how in the knowledge economy 'Capitalism – with a capital C – became society'. He argues that knowledge has gone through three radical shifts in Western history from 1750. It has changed from being applied to purpose (skills and technology) and production (industry) to *'applying knowledge to knowledge'* in the management revolution (Drucker 1993: 36). While the traditional factors of production, such a land (resources), labour and capital still have a role, they are secondary to knowledge, because knowledge can 'obtain' these factors (Drucker 1993: 38). According to Drucker (1993: 40–1), it is the fact that knowledge has become '*the* resource, rather than *a* resource' which makes society 'post-capitalist'. What is particularly striking in Drucker's later reflections is the way this new form of knowledge is interested in 'results' and the way these 'results' are seen as '*outside* the person' and inside society and economy, how they 'convert *ad hoc* experience into system' (Drucker 1993: 42). Here is the end of 'man' as the foundation of modern knowledge and the rise of the knowledge economy as the space of our present predicament. We have become *exterior* to ourselves and alienated from the making of our experience. The nature of the individual and the discourse of experience are now framed by knowledge production, mediated capital, where the central register of what we are is external and separate from any sense of who we are and the 'only thing that increasingly will matter in national as well as in international economics is management's performance in making knowledge productive' (Drucker 1993: 176).

It is clear from Drucker analysis that self-knowledge is now determined by productive results, we are not simply determined by the external criteria of efficiency, we are externalised efficiency. Knowledge has been removed from the subject and the individual has become a collective enactment. Such knowledge is thus able to rethink subjects according to the logic of the knowledge economy and the only knowledge that will matter is codified (*networked mathesis*), because it rests outside the imaginative resources of the human agent as an independent mechanism. It is a knowledge that is translated into economic results, because in the renewed and more sophisticated application of the Jevons philosophical jump the non-calculable no longer matters. As a result all subjects of the old industrial human sciences become reordered according to this rationale. Economics and psychology become computer logic, programmed and measurable, in the codified cognitive science.

Drucker's adventure into the knowledge economy, while valuing specialists of knowledge – specialists of productive knowledge – at least concedes that the knowledge economy will raise questions 'of values, of vision, of beliefs, that is of all things that hold society together and give meaning to life' (Drucker 1993: 42). It is the values beneath the knowledge economy, beneath the calculated order, that we need to uncover inside thinking about the individual and the social. The management of knowledge in the knowledge economy is a vital historical juncture that enables us to address these values of knowledge. We are faced with a new opportunity to see how knowledge excludes and includes, how it protects and privileges and how it closes and opens ways of knowing and understanding. The inter-disciplinary spaces of knowledge will be the arena for this new drama, but whether we can seize this opportunity and take ethical responsibility for our knowledge is still not clear.

Inter-disciplinary thinking in the knowledge economy

In his major study of the economics of knowledge, the French management theorist Dominique Foray (2004), plays on the distinction in the French – not unlike like Foucault (1969) – between *savoir* and *connaissance*, which have no equivalent in English. He believes that this can be appreciated by the qualifier 'certified' or, in his paper with Paul David, 'reliable' (David and Foray 2003: 20). Certified knowledge ('savoir') is institutionally legitimized knowledge through scientific peer review or other forms of ritualised systems of verification. 'Connaissance' is knowledge that has not been put through such tests. Foray believes that both forms of knowledge can be employed in the knowledge economy, but such a position does not appreciate the 'savoir' of economic utility. While both forms of knowledge can be used in the knowledge economy, certain forms of knowledge can be enhanced by being tested according to the principles of economically certified criteria, such as audit and measurement. In the knowledge economy we are finding a new form of subject displacement, which is market-led and economically productive – *codified* knowledge (formed through individualism and networked mathesis). This is the basis of a new type of *inter-disciplinary* thinking. As Peter Drucker's ([1968] 1969: 326–8) early prediction of the knowledge economy illustrates:

> The most probable assumption is that every single one of the old demarcations, disciplines, and faculties is going to become obsolete and a barrier to learning as well as understanding ... Inter-disciplinary work has rapidly grown everywhere during the last twenty-years ... Increasingly such inter-disciplinary work mobilizes the energies of the university and determines its direction. This is a symptom of the shift in the meaning of knowledge from an end in itself to a resource, that is, a means to some result. What used to be knowledge is becoming information. What used to be technology is becoming knowledge. Knowledge as the central energy of a modern society exists altogether in application and when it is put to work. Work, however, cannot be defined in terms of disciplines. End results are inter-disciplinary.

The situation in 1969 has been magnified enormously, especially with increased networks and communications and new forms of economic global domination. While the old disciplines have not entirely become 'obsolete' there is certainly a reordering of priorities and values and a reconfiguration of previous disciplinary domains. There are now new forms of hegemonic inter-disciplinary knowledge overriding the old disciplines with a second order of appeal; such as cognitive science, that reads across modern subject divisions by imposing a one-dimensional reading of knowledge in terms of a privileged or certified category.[15] The overarching category of this new inter-disciplinary group and related to all other types of knowledge is the contemporary imperialism of neo-classical economic discourse; born out of the early disciplinary formations but mutated by its cultural and institutional domination in contemporary neo-liberal forms (Saad-Filho and Johnston 2005).

The new forms of hegemonic inter-disciplinary thought are based on the economic substrate of codification. Codified knowledge infiltrates old disciplinary systems by making knowledge containable, without leakage, or rather it finds ways of concealing leakage by isolating units of knowledge *as if* they did not depend on exterior forms of value-judgement. Measurement hides an epistemology of control that can be used by ideologies that wish to control. This form of thinking develops units of knowledge for production and depends on epistemic closure. It also depends on an ideological masking of its knowledge content. It is a continuation of the old individual ways of thinking but intensified in technological advancement and global economic domination. Above all, this way of thinking masks the social and political correlation of its statements by imagining a neutral place outside the self. This is the space of *networked mathesis* – the mechanistic re-evaluation of all values.

It is my argument that we are entering an age of controlled knowing marked by hyper-calculation, which conceals its hidden ethic of knowledge. The sign of empiricism marks such thinking in the human sciences, but the preliminary assumptions of such empiricism mask the philosophical values. It is the philosophical construction of the object in the human sciences (as opposed to the natural sciences) that defies the logic of the knowledge economy. The striking feature of this form of knowledge is that the placing of all knowledge under the sign of *networked mathesis* allows us to reveal the values at the points of traditional leakage. Knowledge stumbles into the shadowy world of the inter-dependence of all knowledge and at these junctures we see the life-blood of its values.

The knowledge economy enables us to rethink the relationship between the old disciplines by returning knowledge to its history of errors; it enables to rethink economics, psychology and religion in a critical context by showing the shadow economy of the psychological knowledge of religion. The knowledge economy, as Carnoy (2000) argues, 'constitutes a new kind of struggle over the meaning and value of knowledge' (quoted in Peters and Besley 2006: 50). The crisis of the old disciplines, therefore, leads to the radical questioning of other subject areas – as we see with the critical questioning of the category of religion – but these questions and concerns are caused by the very displacement of such subjects in a new order of knowledge in the knowledge economy. The return to definitions within subject areas is a return to the points of leakage, to the fluid nature of knowledge in the shifting political environments. It reveals the political intensity of concepts and the disciplinary points of closure. The epistemological ground of knowledge in economics, psychology and religion is now open to new examination in the knowledge economy; even if we reject the political structures that sustain the knowledge economy the issues it raises return us to the ethics of all knowledge.

The central underlying question in the knowledge economy is how knowledge formations operate in relation to the socio-political world or, as Joel Mokyr (2005: 2) indicates, how knowledge relates to technological and economic change; which becomes in turn a question of how knowledge becomes '*useful*-knowledge'. The utility of an idea implies that knowledge is always linked to issues of choice and selection (Mokyr 2005: 218–9); not all knowledge can be carried forward for economic benefit because they resist the rules of economic logic. The types of knowledge that persists are related to a utility value. As Mokyr argues: 'Knowledge in Ω [propositional form] will become tighter and more difficult to resist if it maps into techniques that actually can be shown to work. To put it crudely, the way we are persuaded that science is true is that its recommendations work visibly' (Mokyr 2005: 228). While Mokyr highlights the utility driving knowledge, he is still aware of the fact that economic development depends on 'the importance of institutions and politics' (Mokyr 2005: 282). Utility is defined by policy and social-individual desire. In an economic environment of utility, we need to expose the language of use-value in any system of knowledge. To whom is knowledge useful and who is benefiting from the utility?[16]

The economic utility of knowledge is increased in a system where the economic institutions dominate, because forms of knowledge are given a cost-benefit value rather than an ethical-communal value. Formations of knowledge have an increasing utility value in the economic environment and new forms of inter-disciplinary knowledge in the human sciences can be read in this way. If nineteenth-century disciplines can be seen to reflect institutional structures of an industrial socio-economic order, then the new global institutions of late capitalism can be seen to value 'useful-knowledge' within the new forms of economic growth in the knowledge economy. The old disciplines of the human sciences do not disappear, because the institutional embeddedness allows for continuation, but the leakage between subjects allows for new ideological refashioning. This is because society is always layered and holds multiple sites of knowledge; the error of Foucault's episteme is that it failed to see how forms of knowledge were carried along into later historical periods, even when they no longer dominate. The new knowledge constellations allow for new forms of inter-disciplinary thinking or reorders of the old disciplines.[17] Knowledge in the human sciences is now framing itself according to a new economic order of utility, resulting in an increase of forms of individualism and *mathesis*.

The human sciences are reshaped for economic use by reducing these forms of knowledge to the economically translatable registers of value; that is, the language of audit and measurement. The quantifiable dimensions of knowledge can be linked to economic assessments and thus have an exchange value. Other aspects of the human sciences are maintained for wider cultural enrichment (longer and more imprecise economic return) and the disciplinary isolationism of niche academic markets. However, it is important to realise that certain forms of knowledge are seen as valuable cultural wastage or excess. Such ideas are contained in an elite professional orbit and never become threatening, because they function as intellectual pressure valves of unrest and protest, and thus never touch the dominant institutional power. In the knowledge economy, threatening creative energies are burnt off in their non-utility, while 'useful-knowledge' is transmitted directly to the economic centre. Subjects that can be economically translated into the new language of 'codification' (measurement and empirical reduction) can be carried forward in the new economy. The knowledge economy therefore reconstitutes knowledge into useful forms – economically generating new subjects.

This link between the theory of knowledge and the economy is not something new, as the philosopher Nicholas Rescher makes clear in his essay developing such links in the work of Charles Sanders Peirce (1839–1914). As Rescher (1989: 4) outlines in his study of *Cognitive Economy*: 'Any theory of knowledge that ignores this economic aspect does so at the risk of its own adequacy'. While Rescher (1989: 150) is concerned to show the importance of rationality in economic reflection, akin to rational choice theory, his central proposition is that economic factors 'shape and condition cognitive proceedings in so fundamental a way'. While his model of cognition is open, the debate becomes even more complex when cognition itself is taken into a codified formation. The errors of the human sciences in embracing such codified forms under the sign of 'science' are evident at this point. Rescher (1989: 150) reinforces this point by also linking knowledge to affordability:

The limits of science are very real, but they are not inherently intellectual matters of human incapacity or deficient brain power. They are fundamentally economic limits imposed by the technological character of our access to the phenomena of nature. The over optimistic idea that we can push science ever onward to the solution of all questions that arise shatters in the awkward reality that the price of problem solving inexorably increases to a point beyond the limits of affordability.

The fact that knowledge is often reduced by efficiency-demands means that regimes of codification need to be carefully scrutinized. In a situation where the only value of knowledge is economic and where knowledge is reduced to the calculable and empirical (in the fact-value delusion), how we imagine ourselves and how we think become ever reduced. It may be that our knowledge is ever expanding to reduce what we are to that which we can control and predict, rather than what we might become outside the conditions we set up for making humans into objects of measurement and efficiency. These are the false imaginings that use the measurable as a mask for the illusion of knowing by controlling the known. This process occurs by dressing up the human sciences in the language of the physical sciences as a way to perpetuate the ideology of control and domination.[18] What is alarming is that the conditions of knowledge in the knowledge economy are limiting the conditions to think knowledge outside economy and codification. The economic, however, can never legitimately disassociate from the non-economic and in the leakages between subjects we see how economics, psychology and the study of religion are caught in hidden ethical assumptions about knowledge and the self.

In the next chapter, I want to explore one vital fault line in the human sciences to show how central concepts within the field of application leak into the political and economic orders of knowledge. By exposing the regimes and limits of these forms of knowledge we might be able to think again. As Foucault remarked: 'I think we have to refer to much more remote processes if we want to understand how we have been trapped in our own history' (Foucault 1979: 136). In the end, what is at stake is the ethical way we constitute the knowledge for thinking about who are and who we might become and identifying the institutional orders that support such discourses.

2 Binary knowledge and the protected category

> Individual and society are, both for historical understanding and for normative judgement, methodological concepts ... [A]ll human psychic events and ideal constructions are to be understood as contents and norms of individual life, and just as thoroughly as contents and norms of existence in social interaction ... But for all the indisputable indispensability of these individual forms, among which sociality stands uppermost, humanity and the individual remain the polar concepts for the observation of human life.
>
> Georg Simmel [1908a] (1971) 'The Categories of Human Experience' in *On Individuality and Social Forms*, University of Chicago, pp. 37–8

If knowledge in the human sciences is seen to have permeable boundaries across disciplinary domains, there is one central theoretical issue that moves across the subject areas and determines the ethical shape of knowledge. It is the individual-social binary, an irresolvable paradox that reveals foundational philosophical values. Georg Simmel ([1908a] 1971: 38) appeals to Spinoza's attribute of extension and thought to resolve the issue and attempts to hold the idea of two modes: 'una eadem que res, sed, duobus modis expressa' ('one and the same thing, but expressed in two modes'). However, Simmel's appreciation of 'dual categorization' would not resolve the tensions between psychology and sociology and in the same year as Simmel's essay two volumes appeared, both entitled *Social Psychology*, reflecting the philosophical strains; one by Edward Ross, an American sociologist, and the other by William McDougall, a British psychologist (Burr 2002: 12). This division demarcates the paradoxical dilemma of the disciplinary politic and it formed two markedly different areas, a field of Sociology (sociological social psychology) and Psychology (psychological social psychology). These two areas have different journals, different textbooks, and different sources of authorial sanction and validation of the transmission of knowledge (Still 1998: 19).

The social psychology of Psychology, as found in F.H. Allport's *Social Psychology* of 1924, brought about, according to Jones and Elcock, an 'individualisation of the social' (Jones and Elcock 2001: 123). In such cases the social is seen 'an additional variable' rather than something which is 'formative or constitutive' of the subject (Wetherell *et al.* 1998: 16). Similarly, in the sociological social psychology the assumption is that social context predetermines mental functioning. Roger Sapsford (1998: 65–74) has explored the tensions between these different levels of analysis in his discussion of 'domains' of knowledge: examining societal, group, inter-personal and intra-personal domains of knowledge. While such categories enable us to overcome some confusion in the field, by identifying the appropriate and inappropriate questions and clarifying the territory of knowledge, they still preserve a false dichotomy. The divisions in subject formation in the late nineteenth century and the beginning of the twentieth century have found little resolution to this problem, even though there have been many attempts to overcome the legacy of such knowledge formations within industrial disciplines. For example, the 'crisis' in social psychology of the 1970s and the subsequent development of 'new paradigm' schools of psychology, including discursive psychology and critical psychology, all attempt to overcome the tension between the individual-social (Shotter 1975; Westland 1978; Forgas 1981; Parker 1992). However, what is clear is that contextualisation of individual psychology in the social, or the reverse, becomes a philosophical statement of value rather than empirical facts. The very irresolvable and paradoxical nature of the binary problem means that it exposes the implicit values within knowledge formation. The point at which knowledge is stabilized for a particular articulation demands either a closure or opening to this issue and the ethics of the subject are determined by it. The individual-social binary is therefore at the heart of critique, because it draws the epistemological rules of political order and self-knowledge.

The binary politics of the individual-social goes to the heart of the methodological structure of inter-disciplinary thinking and internal debate within specific fields of study. Classical theory in the form of Wundt's 'Völkerpsychologie', Freud's 'group psychology', Jung's 'collective unconscious', Durkheim's understanding of sociology as 'collective psychology' and Lévy-Bruhl's 'représentations collectives' are all witness to the problems of the binary opposition between the individual and society. Studies in psychology and existentialist theory also interrogate the same enigma, wrestling with the individual caught in an alien social world (Laing [1960] 1965). More recent French post-structuralist thinkers, such as Althusser (1971) and Foucault (1975; 1982a), addressed the same problem in a different way, with the notion of 'asujetissement' (subjectivity/ subjectification), examining how the individual subject was constructed through social processes. In the specific domain of psychology and religion, Diane Jonte-Pace and William Parsons (2001: 57–126), mapping the state of religion and psychology, also highlighted these concerns in a series of essays examining perspectives in modernity and post-modernity. Recently the individual-social problematic has emerged in the debate about cultural psychology and its relation to the foundation and future of the subject of the psychology of religion (Belzen (2005a; 2005b). As Belzen (2005a: 157–8) writes, attempting to overcome the stagnation of the field:

> In the psychology of religion one recognises a preoccupation with individuals extracted from their culture, in the almost exclusive focus on (private) religiosity, and in the almost total neglect of religion as a topic for research in the psychology of religion. Indeed many, perhaps most, psychologists of religion defend the position that they can investigate only religiosity, the individual-personal correlate of a certain religion into which the individual is socialised, and not religion as such. This self-imposed limitation should be questioned, especially in light of the early debates on methodology in the psychology of religion ...

Any critical reading of the psychological knowledge of religion has therefore to examine the issue of the individual and social, not just in the domain specific concerns, but also at the point at which this issue emerges in a wider array of fields. As Shamdasani (2003: 271) makes clear in his historical account of this issue in Jung's psychology: '[T]he very attempt at disciplinary differentiation and hegemony was bound up with numerous intermeshings and mutual borrowings'. The theoretical enigma of the individual-social is pervasive throughout the human sciences and carries a certain ideological weight, because knowledge is radically altered according to how this issue is resolved. This becomes even more pertinent when we consider, as Elliott and Lemert (2005) identify, new forms of 'individualism' produced under the social conditions of globalization, which open this problem to a new set of economic determinants. Putting contemporary psychological statements about religion inside political-economy requires, therefore, a critical, self-reflexive, disciplinary analysis of the old binary paradigm of the individual-social as it operates along the boundaries of economics and psychology.

Indeed, there are few theoretical issues that have such far-reaching implications on how we imagine subjects and the social order. The problem not only constitutes the ethical order of disciplinary knowledge and the central rule of such discourses, but also the turbulent ideological struggle of the twentieth century and the fears of tyranny, oppression and dictatorship (Hayek [1944] 2001: 14). As I will show, the confusions surrounding the individual-social in psychology are the openings to political-economic thought and the embracing of either point on this binary divide is an ethical-political valuation. Central to my critical assessment of psychological knowledge is that it is intrinsically linked with the same set of debates within economic thinking, emerging from the late-nineteenth century at the same time as psychology. While Freud and Jung moved on the shifting sands of individual and collective representations, the Austrian school of economics under Carl Menger ([1883] 1996) established, as we have seen, the individual as the base of economic theory. These strands of individualism have enhanced neo-liberal thinking in economics through later economic writers such as Hayek ([1944] 2001), but, in the very real challenge to the collectivist ideologies of the twentieth century, the radical embracing of individualism is now becoming a dangerous turn to the very collectivism it sought to avoid. This shift illustrates a central problem of binary thinking about the individual-social and I will seek to open this critique inside the problem of psychological knowledge.

It is my contention in this chapter that the binary distinction between the individual and the social relates to a form of 'disciplinary amnesia' that suppresses the ethical-political dimensions of the psychological study of religion. The ethical-politic is located at the point the individual-social binary is forgotten and silently resolved. Such disciplinary amnesia allows, as we shall see in Part II of this book, forms of psychology to appeal to 'science' while hiding the ethical resolution of the individual-social binary. It is at the point of our paradoxes that our values become apparent. In order to demonstrate this point, I want to illustrate the problems within the binary construction of the individual and the social in a number of specific moments from the history of psychology and economics.

Significantly, the individual-social question returns us to the beginning point of my examination and James's ([1902] 1960: 49) intention to 'ignore the institutional branch entirely' and his decision to read religion as a private and individual experience. But while James's marking out of this central dilemma of psychological knowledge is a key feature of the history of the psychological examination of religion, it is not, by any means, the whole story. As will become clear throughout this book, the individual-social is a central pivot in the ethical ordering of knowledge, resulting in whole array of dualistic forms, such as individual units and atomised or codified individuals, but it also holds potential for creative alternatives in the group mind and embedded individualism. As I have suggested, none of the resolutions solve the binary problem, but they do reveal the ethical-political will-to-power. The end of political innocent in psychology, and its application to religion, is the end of innocent about the individual-social binary and its disciplinary leakage into economics. This chapter will plot some of the contours of this hidden ethical ground of disciplinary thinking.

Disciplinary amnesia and fractal distinction

The psychology of religion, from its formal disciplinary inception in the 1890s, is a subject at odds with itself. It is a discourse born out of Western Christian introspection, folded back upon itself in structured and measured conditions, and then extracted from its religious-philosophical foundation in the empirical illusion of scientific fact-value. The early experimental laboratories of James in the USA (1875) and Wundt in Germany (1879) provided a way for methodical and systematic examination of the subject. The aim was to isolate the introspective space within a methodical structure, but such structuring could not be carried over into the examination of religion without dislocating the social dimension.[1] The social and political threaten the individual subject and are managed through disciplinary amnesia, because a subject forgets the logic that threatens its existence. But to forget the past in the psychology of religion is also to avoid the possibility of understanding what the fractures of historical knowledge can reveal about disciplinary practices and the ethics of knowledge. This disciplinary amnesia about subject formation can be related to the way disciplines return to foundational problems in each successive period. Andrew Abbott (2001) develops the idea of 'cycles' of disciplinary generation in relation to the social sciences to address the problem and it enables us to see something of how the binary of the individual-social is dealt with by respective communities of scholars.

In his work *Chaos of Disciplines* (2001) Abbott argues that the social sciences develop according to a 'fractal distinction', where patterns repeat themselves from a common core of issues or an 'axis of cohesion' within the discipline (Abbot 2001: 9). He argues that new debates within a discipline are attempts to restate its key points of disciplinary axis. Disciplines, according to Abbot, develop through restating 'perennial debates', not in terms of an Hegelian dialectic, but in terms of a 'continuous revival ...

rediscovery or renaming', a process of 'self-similarity, self-replication, and rootlessness' (Abbott 2001: 15, 121). In this sense the subject develops by re-examining its foundational problems and replicating divisions according to the lines of argument dealing with such issues. Inter-disciplinary projects, of course, face more complex issues. As Abbott suggests: 'No discipline gains or loses authority in an area without displacing or enticing other disciplines' (Abbot 2001: 137). Abbott is not concerned with the psychology of religion, but we can see that the cycles of the subject continually return the discipline to foundational questions about the individual and the social and how this allows for the political amnesia at the point of the axis of cohesion. The question of the individual and the social is one particularly important ethical axis, which remains unresolved and which replicates itself in the field of psychology at different levels, particularly in the emergence of social psychology.

In such fields the devils of the collective and the social are constrained by neatly setting up a dichotomy between the individual and the social, which allows for a kind of disciplinary containment of the problem. If the individual can be set up against the social, or the collective, the dangers of contamination will not threaten the subject. But the binary opposition only serves to hide a more serious problem – the fact that psychology is itself a social process. *If you can maintain a division between the individual and the social you can maintain a division between a discipline of the individual and the socio-political processes.* Recognising this political dilemma Kusch (1999: 1) constructs his history of psychology on the basis that '[b]odies of psychological knowledge are social institutions'. It is this move that is inhibited in the binary constructions of knowledge.

I am not saying the concepts of the 'individual' and 'social' have no validity or important relationship in a discipline, such as the psychology of religion, but the attempts to make these categories divisible and the way they are set up is something the field can never resolve without a claim to a specific ethical ordering of knowledge. It is the operational flaws of a subject that confirm a set of ethical-political values at the heart of knowing, but the form in which this issue persists hides the bias. Abbott concedes that cultural shifts, in part, bring about the need for restatement of a discipline's priorities, although I think he fails fully to appreciate how this is politically and economically driven. Nonetheless, Abbott is able to capture the cycles of disciplinary division and the way debates engage in replicating foundational questions. If Abbott's thesis about fractual replication of disciplines is correct, it might be possible to plot some relationship between the 'axis of cohesion' in the disciplines of psychology and social psychology to show how the individual-social problem evolves and then map its relation to political-economy as a way of revealing the underlying values.

The psychology of religion is in some ways the brilliant art of the surgeon cutting the tendons that link the individual and the social, it is the separation of human observation from its socio-political assumptions. It is a methodological move that gets caught in a wider political operation. This piece of social surgery was never successful and the history of the psychology of religion is witness to this failure:

> Despite consistent attempts to delineate the nature and scope of the psychology of religion, continuing pluriformity can be partly attributed to the lack of clarity and consensus, and perhaps more recently some active resistance to defining its appropriate limits and boundaries *vis-à-vis* other systems of knowledge.
>
> (O'Connor 1997: 86)

The disciplinary amnesia about subject formation and division of disciplines pivots on the dichotomy between the individual and the social. The field of psychology sought to separate itself from sociology by bracketing out the social from the territory of the individual unit, following a discourse of 'systematic introspection' and mental operations, which reinforced a tradition of Western individualism from the Renaissance. It separated itself from anthropology by adopting the problematic notions of phylogeny (the development of the race) and ontogeny (the development of the individual), replicated in Jung's 'collective unconscious' and Freud's 'archaic heritage' (which I will return to below). It separated itself from physiology by asserting the importance of the category of experience and from philosophy by accentuating its methodological and empirical approach to the subject. The so-called 'methods of science' in the psychology of religion, asserted from its foundations by such writers as Edwin Starbuck (1899), were then not neutral criteria but, as Danziger notes, useful ways to maintain the discipline through 'ties of loyalty, power, and conflict' (Starbuck 1899: 1; Danziger 1990: 3). To go back to the sources of a field is to see all the confusions of a subject, its fault lines and paradoxes. By returning to the foundations of a subject we see all the provisionality and uncertainty of knowledge, which rather than being unhealthy, unscientific and untrue enable us to recognise the temporality of thought and problems of 'closure' (Lawson 2001). Returning to the individual-social dilemma in the history of psychology and economics takes us to the heart of the ethics of knowing the self and the world.

From crowds to embedded minds

It is not possible to present a detailed genealogy of the disciplinary struggle between the individual and the social in the entire history of psychology in the limits of one chapter; and others, such as Forgas (1981), Kusch (1999) and Shamdasani (2003), have already accomplished some aspects of this work in different historical traditions of psychology. However, it is worth highlighting one or two features of such historical ambivalence. My excursion will serve to provide some evidence that the history of the psychology of religion is the history of suppressing or bracketing out conceptual confusion around the individual-social binary. While it is the case that the division between the individual and the social was necessary in order to stabilise the enterprise of psychology and create a new site of knowledge at the end of the nineteenth century, it is my contention that this disciplinary arena perpetuates a binary division that prevents it embracing its political will. It is important to realise that early texts in the history of psychology did not so much outwardly suppress the dichotomy between the individual and the social, as *set these terms up against each other* in order to avoid the nightmare of disciplinary implosion and the exposure of the politics of knowledge at the roots of an aspiring science; a kind of displaced forgetting. It does this by setting up a dynamic between the individual and the social as two clearly demarcated or distinctive areas, which touch and inter-relate but do not fuse. Early projects, for example, in the psychology of religion thus took time to acknowledge the dichotomy between the individual and the social and then carefully dismissed the problem before continuing without concern (as we have witnessed in William James's seminal work in the area). This entailed an immediate closing down of other disciplinary areas in a rehearsal of the disciplinary dominant category.

In 1920, for example, James Pratt, a student of James, struggled in his study of religious consciousness to separate out the boundaries of the individual and society. He acknowledged a central relationship between the two, but sought to preserve the distinctive nature of the individual in terms of the locus of social interaction. Pratt maintains the distinction by noting that 'most "social" ideas are the products of co-operation between many individual minds'. Or, stating the situation slightly differently, Pratt argues that individual minds are seen as holding a pre-existing capacity to be 'molded by society' (Pratt [1920] 1924: 72–3). He seeks to demarcate 'the original psychical endowment of the individual' in a dialogue with the work of Durkheim, Mauss and Lévy-Bruhl (Pratt [1920] 1924: 75, 80–1). As Pratt argues:

Religion is the product both of society and of the individual. It also gets itself expressed both in society and in the individual. The social expression of religion, so far forth as it is a matter of externals, belongs not to the psychology of religion but to history, anthropology, and allied sciences. As psychologists we are interested primarily in the way religion manifests itself in the thoughts and feelings and activities of individuals (i.e. of individuals in society).

(Pratt [1920] 1924:.12–13)

While such an acknowledgement of the significance of the social for the individual is an important move in the battle for disciplinary territory, it hides the complicity of the subject to set up a binary world. By maintaining the division and positioning the subject alongside sociology it marks out a territory of professionalism which can only serve to isolate and preserve the subject from its own enigmatic construction. In effect, the struggle to find an authoritative voice in the academy required some denial of its intellectual field of enquiry, especially when considering the phenomena of religion.

What I am suggesting here is that the debates around the individual-social binary re-enact a unresolvable gesture of cohesion in every age, such that we find a theoretical trajectory that links late nineteenth-century crowd psychology (1890s), collective psychology (1920s/1930s), social character (1930s) at the foundation of the subject to the later positions of critical social psychology and the embedded mind of cognitive psychology (1990s/2000s). These are all part of the periodic fractal replications of the axis of cohesion in psychology and behind which lies the deeper ethic of knowledge that is the concern of this book. I will briefly sketch some of the historical foundations by taking three points of the 'axis of cohesion' related to the binary problem in Le Bon and McDougall, Freud and Erich Fromm. I will then ground these statements in a fourth axis, this time taken from the field of economics, in the work of Friedrich Hayek. These examples will hopefully illustrate the philosophical problem within the history of psychology and economics and show the vital ethical-political dynamic behind this binary order. This problem will become apparent through the book and particularly when we explore the problems of contemporary cognitive psychology (Chapter 5). The re-emergence of the individual-social binary at the heart of contemporary cognitive science of religion re-enacts the political amnesia of the discipline and equally hides its ethical order of knowledge.

Reflecting on this situation in cognitive science, Robert Wilson (2004: 188) reconsidered the idea of the group mind and embedded cognition to challenge internalist models. He concludes his study by arguing that the 'minds that individuals have are already the minds of individuals in groups' (Wilson 2004: 307). The problem, as Wilson (2004: 288) makes clear, is that biologists and social scientists are concerned about the lack of empirical evidence, but he suspects that it also 'reflects an ignorance of and an insensitivity to the conceptual work necessary to articulate what is it to have a mind'. The lack of 'conceptual work' becomes part of the disciplinary amnesia in so far as it reflects a forgetting of the artificial subject formation and the ethical-political ground of statements. The lack of conceptual work is also a lack of political will and a lack of ethical sensibility towards ways of knowing. Wilson (2004) attempts to offer different models and deeper histories to reframe debates, but while his work embraces a certain level of critical thinking he does not fully appreciate how the 'ignorance' and 'insensitivity' reflect a politic of knowledge around the individual-social binary axis of cohesion. Choices about what we theorize and how we theorize are statements of value, prior to the selective making of empirical facts. The parallel modelling of the individual-social binary in the history of economics makes this more transparent.

First axis: Le Bon's crowd and McDougall's social psychology

In 1895 Gustav Le Bon wrote his powerful analysis *La Psychologie des foules* (translated as *The Crowd*). It was, according to Robert Nye, to have a huge impact on Hitler's organization of Nazi Germany and the propaganda machine. In this work, Le Bon ([1895] 1995: 44) tried to identify the 'law of the mental unity of crowds' and identified different types of crowds. He showed that crowds operated according to a set of passions which overrode the individual and that understanding the psychology of crowds was the key to the 'statesman who wishes to govern them' ([1895] 1995: 39). As he proclaimed: 'To know the art of impressing the imagination of crowds is to know at the same time the art of governing them' (Le Bon [1895] 1995: 92). His work declared, particularly in the aftermath of the Dreyfus Affair in France in 1894, that the present age was about to enter 'the era of crowds' ([1895] 1995: 34). The central analysis of Le Bon was to show how the crowd was influenced not by reflection and reason, but by image and theatrical representation ([1895] 1995: 89). It was the dynamic of the imagination that determined the life of the crowd:

> The power of conquerors and the strength of States is based on the popular imagination. It is more particularly by working upon this

imagination that crowds are led. All great historical facts, the rise of Buddhism, of Christianity, of Islam, the Reformation, the French Revolution, and, in our time, the threatening invasion of Socialism, are the direct or indirect consequence of strong impressions produced on the imagination of the crowd.

(Le Bon [1895] 1995: 90)

The central contrast, as Wilson (2004: 272) confirms, is that in Le Bon the crowd is set in opposition to the notion of the rational individual. Shamdasani (2003: 287) elaborates this further by showing how Le Bon took over from the evolutionary anthropologists the idea of primitive and prehistoric; and thus crowds become primitive and irrational in opposition to the individual. The political implications of this situation are clear and, as Shamdasani (2003: 287) shows, there were many disputes amongst collective psychologists along these lines: 'The work of the crowd psychologists formed a predominant mode of the psychological understanding of society, and one which gave epistemological priority to individual psychology'. The work of collective psychology was dominant between 1895 and 1921 and formed part of a diverse range of theories of the group mind. There were, according to Wilson (2004: 269), a variety of positions in the group mind hypothesis, those that hold what he calls '*mutlilevel* traits' (where mind exists at the level of groups and individuals) and '*group-only* traits' (where mind is only held in the group). These traits were seen respectively in collective psychology and the super organism traditions of early ecology and work on social insects. This distinction allows Wilson (2004: 281) to make a further distinction in his reading of the work of William McDougall. He wishes to make the distinction between 'group psychological traits' (mental properties individuals have in groups but which are not reducible to individuals) and the 'social manifestation thesis' (individual psychological properties that appear in groups). Wilson's work enables us to see the shift in traits, the complexity of the issue against fears of replacing the individual locus of cognition and also how the language works in both literal and metaphorical terms, but, other than suggesting more research is required, his own disciplinary limits do not enable him to theorise what the inclusion of social and cultural dimensions into cognition would mean for psychological theory (Wilson 2004: 302). There is, however, one key moment in Wilson's (2004: 269) work where we find a social-political insight in his otherwise abstract theoretical study:

The tradition was largely motivated by and focused on two sweeping, related social changes: a heightening in the visible actions of politically disenfranchised or marginalized individuals in groups, including industrial strikes and peasant uprisings, and the increased activity of socialist and anarchist political organizations.

This link to the emergence of psychological theory is important for recognising the circularity of ideas about the mind/self and the social order. Psychological theory relating to the individual-social binary is caught in the very order of the problem in self-reflexive analysis. Discussion of the individual and the social within psychology reflect the ethical-political conditions of the theory; supporting the sense that values and theories unite in attempts to resolve this decisive binary problem. This becomes evident in Wilson's appeal to the history of psychology to overcome the dominant individualism in later cognitive theory, which we will explore in Chapter 5. What emerges here, however, is the tension of the individual-social binary and its political pivot.

When the great British psychologist William McDougall approached the topic of social psychology in 1908, and later in 1920, he attempted to respond to Le Bon and other crowd psychologists, but his work found much resistance. His first work *An Introduction to Social Psychology* in 1908 referred to the sub-area as a 'difficult branch of psychology' (McDougall [1908] 1912: v). He even declined to outline the relationship between psychology and sociology, believing that these questions would be worked out in time. The study of 'collective psychology' was not without its problems and the 'territory' question between psychology and sociology, especially in relation to Comte and Durkheim, was evident in much of this literature. McDougall claimed that the method of introspection in psychology was a 'narrow and paralysing view' (McDougall [1908] 1912: 6) and he acknowledged a 'premature annexation' of subjects in the formation of psychology.[2] He sought therefore to map some of the problems of individual psychology. As he argued at the beginning of his *Social Psychology*:

> It is, then, a remarkable fact that psychology, the science which claims to formulate the body of ascertained truths about the constitution and working of the mind, and which endeavours to refine and to add to this knowledge, has not been generally and practically recognised as the essential common foundation on which all the social sciences – ethics, economics, political science, philosophy of history, sociology, and cultural anthropology, and the more specialised social sciences, such as the sciences of religion, of law, of education, and art must be built.
>
> (McDougall [1908] 1912: 1)

What is also striking is that he recognised economics as fundamentally related to psychology, but such links shift in a variety of ways as we have seen. In a reference one assumes to Adam Smith's doctrine, McDougall argued it is inadequate merely to build economics on self-interest and noted that questions of suggestibility and advertising open the subject to other factors; pointing out, in his delightful example, that sewing machines worth £5 are sold for £12 (McDougall [1908] 1912: 11). At this stage McDougall seems to be suggesting that 'understanding the life of society' requires 'knowledge of the constitution of the human mind'. In his later work, *The Group Mind* in 1920, he also underlined the importance of economics to psychology, but he moves to a stronger position which suggests that there is a collective psychology and not just a useful relation between psychology and the social world (1920: 8). The delay in publishing this later work is revealing, because of the way his colleagues, enforcing the boundaries of psychology, resisted his ideas.

In the second section of McDougall's ([1908] 1912: 267, 333) earlier study of social psychology, he is concerned to show the how basic instincts of the mind (parental, pugnacity, gregarious, religious, acquisition and construction and imitation) operate in the social world. The blending of different levels of discourse from religion (Robertson Smith's *Religion of the Semites*) to economics (Thomas Malthus's 1798 treatise *An Essay on the Principle of Population as its affects the future improvement of society*) is witness to the problem of knowledge facing McDougall in his study. There is a fundamental leakage of knowledge across subject areas without a sufficient framework of coherence. In recognition of this situation he writes:

> The processes to be dealt with are so complex, their operations of the different factors are so intricately combined, their effects are so variously interwoven and fused in the forms of social organisations and institution, that it would be presumptuous to attempt to prove the truth of most of the views advanced.

The discursive structures did not provide McDougall with any easy way to bridge ideas across the binary divide of the individual-social, but the underlying problem is that he cannot place the category of the 'psychological' in the socio-political order. *The category is protected from being an object of economic or political study by virtue of its ability to represent other valued phenomena.* It is only post-1968 that the ethical-politics of knowledge overcomes the previous binary limits to find established constellation of the problem in such ideas as the post-structuralist notion of the 'subject'. The fractal replication of the individual-social binary preserves knowledge from its inevitable collapse into the terms of another discipline.

In *The Group Mind* the binary tensions are held together in a different way. McDougall (1920: 11) tried to show that the 'most highly organised groups display collective mental life in a way which justifies the conception of the group mind'. What McDougall wanted to show was that the 'abstract individual mind' of psychology did not help with 'concrete problems of human life' (McDougall 1920: 3). For example, McDougall tried to identify the psychology of the national character, examining nationhood as a psychological conception (McDougall 1920: 100). As he writes:

> It will be observed that we are getting away from the old-fashioned conception of psychology which limited its province to introspective description of the contents of the individual's consciousness. The wider conception of the science gives it new tasks and new branches, of which the study of the national mind is one.
>
> (McDougall 1920: 101)

McDougall is here following the German idealism of Kant and Hegel, which assumed a collective consciousness or super-individual, quasi-divine personality, but he rather identifies processes of social and historical formation, through which national sentiments, ideas and institutions are established (McDougall 1920: 16, 107). McDougall argues that we are who we are by the 'virtue of communities', that is the family, the nation, the institutions, the language and the 'relations of the social State' (McDougall 1920: 18). It is interesting in the artificial construction of the psychological subject how McDougall related this work to philosophical history; supporting the idea that psychology is a subject without a centre.[3] But what McDougall reveals at the foundations of the subject is the continuing unresolved ambivalence around the individual and collective at the heart of the subject and the problem of the ethical limits of knowledge.

Second axis: Freud and 'the riddle of the group'

Shamdasani (2003: 271) has uncovered how Jung's development of a 'collective trans-individual psychology' links to the wider historical thinking in collective psychology and the different levels of this discourse in ethnography and anthropology. While the collective dimension has received greater appreciation in relation to Jung, it is less widely developed in relation to Freud, which is dominated by his individual clinical material. Indeed, the two are often stylized according to an individual-collective division of the unconscious. However, the concern of scholars of religion and critical psychology have countered such limitations and highlighted the 'cultural texts' of Freud (which I will return to in the next chapter) and established a theoretical line of thinking to the Frankfurt school (Parker 1997a: 107ff; DiCenso 1999; Jonte-Pace 2001). As DiCenso (1999: 57) underlines in relation to Freud's study of culture and religion: '*Human existence is socially constituted and symbolically mediated*'. Much of the motivation behind such a focus is linked to a wider political hermeneutic arising from cultural theory, post-structuralism and feminist analysis and this provides a platform for appreciating Freud as a social thinker. Freud's work, in part, oscillates between the individual and social according to Ernst Haeckel's biogenetic idea that ontogeny replicates phylogeny, but despite the development of an 'archaic heritage' (a collective residue) he is trapped in the ontological priority of the individual (Freud [1916–17] 1986: 202). The binary tensions in Freud's individual-social can be seen in his response to the work of Le Bon and McDougall, in his 1921 *Group Psychology (Massenpsychologie) and the Analysis of the Ego*.

Along with Freud's later 'Civilization and its Discontents' (*Das Unbehagen in der Kultur*) ([1930] 1985),[4] *Group Psychology (Massenpsychologie) and the Analysis of the Ego* provides some of the key theoretical ground for understanding Freud's analysis of the individual and society. In appreciating Le Bon's 'brilliant' (Freud [1921] 1985: 109, 161) outline of the group mind, Freud ([1921] 1985: 95) embraces the theoretical dilemma: 'The contrast between individual psychology and social or group psychology, which at first glance may seem to be full of significance, loses a great deal of its sharpness when it is examined more closely'. Freud's discussion of the group ('*Masse*') follows Le Bon and McDougall in associating it with increased emotion, reduced intelligence, primitiveness and childhood. Freud, not surprisingly, also picks up the 'hypnotic' and 'suggestibility' aspects of the crowd; an influence on collective psychology that Barrows (1981) links back to Jean-Martin Charcot's work (Wilson 2004: 272). Freud builds the 'group' from its dyadic structure of love-relationships and the family out towards race, nation, caste, profession and institution; and sees the former as component parts of the crowd (Freud [1921] 1985: 96). This confuses the discussion as to what constitutes a group in Freud. He moves not only from personal affect in relationship, but also from unorganised to organised groups. While there are some useful distinctions of different types of groups in his mapping of the various writers under discussion (such as Le Bon's 'transient groups', McDougall's 'stable associations' and Trotter's 'generalized form of assemblage'), Freud's groups also contain the mythic group of the primal horde. The fact that the individual determines the shape of this last type of group is central to Freud's argumentation.

Freud is happy to see the individual as 'a component part of numerous groups, he is bound by ties of identification in many directions, and ... has a share in numerous group minds' (Freud [1921] 1985: 161). Nonetheless, the emphasis is always on the individual 'as a member of' and 'in a group' rather than the strict 'group mind' hypothesis identified in Wilson's work (Freud [1921] 1985: 96, 100). His dismissal of Trotter's 1916 *Instincts of the Herd in Peace and War* is significant. While acknowledging Trotter's 'valuable remark' that 'the tendency towards the formation of groups is biologically a continuation of the multicellular character of all the higher organisms' (Freud [1921] 1985: 115), he adds a footnote in 1923 warning against attributing to the group 'mental processes of the individual'. Freud seems rather to follow Wilson's (2004: 281) 'social manifestation thesis' (individual psychological properties that appear in groups). He, for example, accepts that the individual displays 'special characteristics' in a group, but persists in valuing characteristics of the individual as necessary for the group (Freud [1921] 1985: 115). The primacy of the individual in the group is seen from Freud's critique of Le Bon for neglecting the dynamic of the leader and his assertion that 'it is impossible to grasp the nature of a group if the leader is disregarded' (Freud [1921] 1985: 125, 150). This aspect enables Freud to take the group back to the primal horde of 'Totem and Taboo' ([1912–13] 1985) and it, in turn, places the ancient ground of group psychology on equal footing with individual psychology:

> Individual psychology must, on the contrary, be just as old as group psychology, for from the first there were two kinds of psychologies, that of the individual members of the group and that of the father, chief, or leader ... There must therefore be a possibility of transforming group psychology into individual psychology ...
>
> (Freud [1921] 1985: 155–6)

Freud acknowledges that an individual in a group 'is subjected through its influence to what is often a profound alteration in his mental activity', but the locus of the modern autonomous individual is always clear (Freud [1921] 1985: 116). Importantly, Freud does not regard 'a mere collection of people' as a group (Freud [1921] 1985: 129). While acknowledging that McDougall links the group through panic and fear, he believes that a different emotional intensity holds the group. The emotion that ties the group for Freud is found in the love relationship (eros), which is 'the essence of the group mind' (Freud [1921] 1985: 120). It is 'libidinal ties' that unite the group, but 'love instincts which have been diverted from their original aim' (Freud [1921] 1985: 133). Freud's reading of this dynamic takes him to explore the process of identification and the ego-ideal in his central epistemological priority of the individual (Freud [1921] 1985: 155, 168). It is the 'fascination' with the love-object that explains the 'intense emotional ties', established through the primary instincts of sex and self-preservation.

According to his myth of the father in the primal horde, Freud's group is established by the individual in the group, but Freud's lack of theoretical reflection about the different types of groups prevents him from appreciating other complexities. It appears that Freud's principal concern is with Le Bon's 'transient groups' and this narrows the range of his reflection. In what he regards as the 'riddle of the group' (Freud [1921] 1985: 148), it is perhaps the passing comments on McDougall's 'stable groups' that underline the problem in assessing the binary division of the individual-social in Freud's work, particularly when Freud discusses McDougall's conditions for raising the mental life of groups. Reflecting on the 'highly organised' group, Freud ([1921] 1985: 115) remarks: 'The problem consists in how to procure for the group precisely those features which were characteristic of the individual and which are extinguished in him by the formation of the group'. Freud here resists McDougall's value of the external 'organization' of the group by returning to the individual in the same way as he resists Trotter's organic group mind. Individuals are primary in all groups, but his resistance to Trotter's wider thesis of the 'generalized form of assemblage' is cause for greater concern, particularly in its contrast with his understanding of 'stable groups' in his later discussion of groups in 'Civilization and its Discontents' ([1930] 1985). In his earlier 1921 text, Freud rejects Trotter's idea of a natural instinct towards 'gregariousness' and the Aristotle's 'political animal', because of the notion of the leader and the ontogenesis of group in the horde, but these two are not necessarily mutually exclusive. The problem here is that Freud prioritizes the leader and primal horde over any other set of social feelings and this *excludes the chance to shift theoretical concern*. The problem is conceived differently when Freud entertains the *economic* question of maximising happiness in society (Freud [1930] 1985: 276). I will return to discuss Freud's use of the term economics later, but here I am concerned with it in terms of the Benthamite question of happiness that runs through the economic literature; as we saw in the last chapter. Importantly, Freud gives great credence to institutional life in his consideration of cultural systems in 'Civilization and its Discontents'. This allows for a different order of value. The individual-group relation, for example, is made more complex when he writes:

> Human life in common is only made possible when a majority comes together which is stronger than any separate individual and which remains united against all separate individuals. The power of this community is then set up as 'right' in opposition to the power of the individual, which is condemned as 'brute force'. This replacement of the power of the individual by the power of a community constitutes the decisive step of civilization.
>
> (Freud [1930] 1985: 284

Freud's attitude to groups appears to have been reversed. In 1921 the group was the irrational force, but in 1930 social groups are the civilising forces against the uncontrollable drives of the individual. The situation can only be resolved by appreciating the different types of groups. There are, however, important agreements to be found in the two texts, notably the required sublimation of forces required in the group and the basis of the group in the primal horde (Freud [1930] 1985: 286ff). We can perhaps understand the link between the two texts in Freud's own reference back to the theme of groups in the later discussion of civilization. Freud refers to the 'the psychological poverty of groups' and the danger of individuals identifying with each other rather than the leader. He brings America into his critical scope when discussing such matters and the 'damage to civilization' (Freud [1930] 1985: 307). The twist and turns of the individual-social binary in these texts of Freud are only resolved in the mythic appeal that anchors the individual reality, but there is enough ambiguity to show how Freud's individuals are at least caught inside groups, even if they are always at once separate individuals. Freud even turns to discussion of 'double individuals' to account for the fact that some love-relationships are able to produce libidinal satisfaction and common social bonds in civilization (Freud [1930] 1985: 298). It is, perhaps, not until Jacques Lacan ([1966] 2006) that we can find a more coherent psychoanalytical resolution to the individual-social binary when he sees the core of the individual in the other and reveals how we are formed through the other. This foundational 'psychosis' of the individual-social in Lacan begins to break down the Cartesian-atomistic self (Campbell 2004: 115ff).

Third axis: Erich Fromm and social character

It is in the traditions of the Frankfurt School that we find some of the most fascinating attempts to break the binary split between the individual and social, most notably in the work of Erich Fromm (1900–84). Fromm, in his attempt to develop a Freudo-Marxist position, developed the notion of 'social character'. The idea was developed throughout his work from *The Dogma of Christ* ([1930] 1963) to the late study *To Have or To Be?* ([1976] 1999), but also emerges in *The Sane Society* ([1955] 2002), *Beyond the Chains of Illusion* ([1962] 1989), *The Revolution of Hope* (1968) and in his *The Anatomy of Human Destructiveness* (1973). In its earliest formulation, although not designated conceptually, the idea referred to 'shared libidinous, and largely unconscious attitudes' that characterise society (Fromm [1930] 1963: 1–7; [1976] 1999: 133; Burston 1991: 102). It was the assumption that the group had a common pattern of life experience. Later, in his 1941 work *The Fear of Freedom*, Fromm conceptually developed the idea as central to his working method in a similar way to Max Weber's 'ideal types' (Weber [1904–5] 2001: 33; Fromm [1941] 2001: 254). Fromm's definition of 'social character' refused to give priority to either part of the binary divide of the individual-social. As he stated:

> To understand the dynamics of the social process we must understand the dynamics of the psychological processes operating within the individual, just as to understand the individual we must see him in the context of the culture which moulds him.
>
> (Fromm [1941] 2001: ix)

Such a position is not very different from the methods of social psychology or even that of James Pratt, but Fromm goes further to recognise that the social character was interacting with society. As he stated in his 1941 appendix to *The Fear of Freedom*:

> The social character results from the dynamic adaptation of human nature to the structure of society. Changing social conditions result in changes of the social character, that is, in new needs and anxieties.
>
> (Fromm [1941] 2001: 256)

The social character is not part of the individual character but something that shapes individual character. The social character 'internalizes external necessities and thus harnesses human energy for the task of a given economic and social system' (Fromm [1941] 2001: 244.). Fromm is here following

Marx's own assertion that consciousness is a social product rather than society being a product of consciousness (Marx 1967: 422). However, Fromm does not fall into the simplistic split of social psychological methods, because he recognises the cyclical process of social character, in so far that social character and social structure have a dynamic relationship (Fromm [1962] 1989). 'A change in either factor', he argues, 'means a change in both' (Fromm [1976] 1999: 134). Perhaps, more strikingly, he recognised, well before Foucault and the post-structuralists, the political dynamics of subjectification and the internalization of social discipline (Foucault 1982a: 221–2). As Fromm stated in 1955:

> It is the function of the social character to shape the energies of the members of society in such a way that their behaviour is not a matter of conscious decision as to whether or not to follow the social pattern, but one of *wanting to act as they have to act* and at the same time finding gratification in acting according to the requirements of the culture. In other words, it is the social character's function *to mold and channel human energy within a given society for the purpose of the continued functioning of this society.*
>
> ([1955] 2002: 77)

Fromm's work is one moment in the 'fractal' replication of the disciplinary question of the individual and the collective. His work was one way in which to overcome the problems of duality. But for all its innovation Fromm's work still insulated the discourse of psychology from political scrutiny by holding to the neutrality of a radical humanism.

While Fromm was able to recognise how religion was caught up in the processes of capitalism he could not – because of his humanist valuation of psychology – see how psychology was itself part of such an ideology. Fromm collapsed the distinction between the individual and the collective for his own political concerns, but he could not challenge the distinction between psychology and politics in the same way. Psychology, like Marxism in Fromm's work, was preserved from its own historical-political critique, not least because it was the basis for his own ideological response to a market-driven rationality and the spiritual crisis he believed was present in modern society. Deleuze and Guattari recognised some of the problems with Fromm's work in their polemical study *Anti-Oedipus*, poignantly sub-titled *Capitalism and Schizophrenia*. They protested:

> When Fromm denounces the existence of a psychoanalytical bureaucracy, he still doesn't go far enough, because he doesn't see what the stamp of

this bureaucracy is, and that an appeal to the pre-oedipal is not enough to escape this stamp: the pre-oedipal, like the post-oedipal, is still a way of bringing all of desiring-production – the anoedipal – back to Oedipus.

(Deleuze and Guattari [1972] 1984: 312)

What Fromm did not recognise is that by trying to solve the individual-collective problematic of psychology he preserved the discipline of psychology from far greater critique. Indeed, it is my assertion that the individual-collective dichotomy is a problem set up in the heart of the subject of psychology to hide the subject's political responsibility. It acts, as Foucault recognised in discursive formations, as a 'positive unconscious of knowledge' (Foucault [1966] 1991: xi, 1969: 60). Even the theoretical performances of correction only re-inscribed the authority of the discipline as holding a problematic of the individual and social, rather than acknowledging the emergence of this problem within Western epistemology and the historical location of psychology within the period of industrial capitalism.

Erich Fromm's social character was an attempt to make sense of the culture of mass persuasion in the 1940s and 1950s, which saw the rise of fascism and the rise of American mass consumerism. Fromm's ideas were taken up by David Riesman in his classical work of sociology *The Lonely Crowd* (1961), identifying the inner-directed and other-directed types of the 'new middle class' in the USA. According to Riesman (1961: 5), influenced by Erich Fromm, the link between society and the individual was 'to be found in the way in which society ensures some degree of conformity from the individuals who make it up'. The movement from crowd psychology through social character to the lonely crowd reveals the foundational problem of psychological knowledge and locates the political dynamic of the individual-social binary. The theoretical battle happens against the backdrop of totalitarian and democratic political regimes and shows the urgency of political and economic issues in the play of this theoretical rehearsal.

One vital feature of the individual-social debate is the way it closes examination of the politics of the subject. It masks the political heart of the subject in political economy. The framing of the question is therefore misguided. *The question for psychology is not how the individual relates to society, but how psychology as a discipline of the individual relates to social processes.* The disciplinary innocence of the subject operates on its own foundational problematic between the individual and the social. The binary problem implicates psychology in a political stabilization. Behind the binary question we find the positivistic illusion of a neutral scientific knowledge and the attempt to protect such a discourse from political scrutiny. The working paradox of the binary within psychological thinking allows for a discourse of individualisation that generates increased atomisation of society. It is only by challenging the nature of the binary problem in psychological methodology that we can begin to understand the political nature of such thinking. The binary cannot, of course, be resolved, but its operational resolution reveals the ethical values behind knowledge, something we can see by shifting the discussion of the binary problem to economics.

The economic mask of individualism

The individual-social binary ethic manifests itself more directly in sociological and economic thought, because its rules of discourse allow for more direct engagement with political thought and social policy. In such literature, the concept of the individual is openly a site of political contestation. For example, the sociologists Ulrich Beck and Elizabeth Beck-Gernsheim (2002: xxi) usefully make a distinction between the '*neo-liberal idea of the free market individual*' in economics and the notion of 'institutionalised individualism' in sociological analysis. I wish to argue that these notions merge in 'psychological individualism' and should not always be seen as separate, because neo-liberal individualism is now institutionalized through forms of codified discourse (see Chapter 5). However, what is important for Beck and Beck-Gernsheim (2002) is the central paradox in individualization, because modern society is constructed for the individual and not the group, but individualism destroys the social foundation. As they state: '"individualization" means disembedding without reembedding' (Beck and Beck-Gernsheim 2002: xxii). What is revealed in this study is the way individualisation is the new structure of the social. The individual is formed paradoxically to create a new form of social space and psychology feeds this social movement, because its own axis of cohesion requires a rehearsal of the individual-social binary as a way to methodologically avoid the substrate of its political identifications. As Beck and Beck-Gernsheim (2002: xxi) argue: '[T]he individual is becoming the basic unit of social reproduction for the first time in history'. It is a new form of society where individualisation is not a private experience, but an 'institutional and structural' one. This is not the model of the Enlightenment individual from the seventeenth century, but a model of the individual based on a manufactured-network of self-formation – that is a form of the individual shaped by and constructed within new economic conditions. The association of individualism and the socio-economic order enables us to bring the individual-social binary in psychology back to its ethical realm in the related field of economics. What is striking in locating the individual-social binary through the field of application in economics is that it illuminates the inescapable ethic of knowledge across the human sciences in approaching the same irresolvable dilemma. The key philosophical values of the human sciences are drawn together at this point of the individual-social binary.

The problems becomes manifest clearly in John Davis's study *The Theory of the Individual in Economics* (2003), particularly in his attempt to embed the individual in the social context against neo-classical models. As Davis (2003: 2) rightly points out: 'How economics understands individuals has extremely important social consequences'. Davis makes the important distinction between 'orthodox economics' holding to a model of atomistic individuals and 'heterodox economics' arguing for social models of individuality. The idea of collective intentionality is a valuable corrective to atomistic conceptions of the individual, but in both positions the water in still very muddied and confused inside the binary distinction between the individual and the social. This ambiguity enables us to see the importance of the binary problem in its fluid movement across disciplines, because the workings of this binary are economically and politically grounded.

Davis (2003: 134–6; 2002: 14–19) develops this idea by exploring the work of the Finnish philosopher Raimo Tuomela and his account of collective intentionality. Davis argues that while mental life occurs within individuals not all intentions are individual. To support his assumption he examines the language of 'we-intentions' when one is a member of a group. As he states: '[A] we-intention is an individual's attribution of an intention to a group that the individual believes is reciprocally held by the over individuals in the same group' (Davis 2002: 14). He maps this onto the language of 'rules' and 'norms', where rules govern institutions as we-attitudes and norms form the basis of social values as we-intentions. According to Davis, mainstream economics lacks a model of how individuals mediate between groups and individuals and for this reason he argues it is not a surprise that it holds the language of 'unintended consequences', which we saw in the last chapter. In such a socially embedded model of economic functions, individual economic behaviour has to be reassessed as reflecting 'rules and norms associated with their membership in groups' (Davis 2002: 19). What Davis establishes, in his insightful analysis, is that the 'individual' is removed as a theoretical question:

> The lack of attention given to the theory of the individual in economics
> reflects economists' widely held and generally unexamined belief that

individuals are *exogenous* to the economic process. Most economists, that is, do not believe that individuals are changed in nature by the economic process, or that individuals and the nature of individuality might be *endogenous* to the economic process. They believe these things in spite of obvious historical evidence that the economic process is a record of the continual transformation and destruction of individuals.

(Davis 2003: 11)

The binary politic of the individual-social can again be seen to hold an ethical-political dynamic and invisibility; or, to return to my earlier metaphor, the amnesia of the disciplinary formation is itself ethically determined. The theoretical questions we ask and close down reflect an ethical-political will to power and this is nowhere greater than in the perplexing space of the individual-social binary. The political tension is between what has been called 'methodological individualism' (the social explained in terms of the individual) versus 'methodological collectivism' (the individual explained in terms of the social) (see Davis 2003: 35–8; Infantino 1998: xi). Much networked activity surrounds discussion of these concepts and the academic debates are attempts to offer critical perspective to one or other position.

The ideological battle is clearly visible when we contrast the two groups along the individual-social binary within economic theory in the work of Davis and in Lorenzo Infantino's study *Individualism in Modern Thought* (1998), a work critical of 'methodological collectivism'. Davis (2003: 17) proposes the argument that orthodox economics, built on individual analysis, offers an inadequate model of the individual, but heterodox economic, not concerned with the individual, offers a more adequate model of the individual. In contrast, Infantino (1998) argues that methodological collectivism always results in political collectivism (he explores Comte and Marx to support his position). He then contends: 'There is no link of this kind in the case of methodological individualism; it does not serve political individualism' (Infantino 1998: 131). The intellectual manoeuvres are revealing, as they play out the individual-social binary ethic. They enable us to see how the ethical-political drives the theory and how they silence the political will-to-power in their own apparently neutral theoretical assertions. Davis's more affirmative position in heterodox economics is less concealed, but it nonetheless rests of the assumption of what constitutes an 'adequate' theory of the individual.

It would appear, recalling Wilson's (2004) earlier concerns, that *we under-theorize at the point that our values becomes evident*. The aspiration to a neutral logic covers the points at which the ethical drive manifests itself in thought. The leakage of the binary problem across the human sciences, from psychology to economics, reveals the intrinsic nature of the ethical ground of the individual-social. It also reveals the reasons it is concealed and disassociated from political assertion. But when the questions are explored the values become clear; as we will see from a final consideration of the axis of cohesion, but this time from the history of economics.

Fourth axis: Hayek and true individualism

Infantino's (1998: 1, 173) work is framed in terms of an appreciation of Friedrich Hayek's (1899–1992)[5] contribution to economics and the social sciences, particularly because he believes his work led 'economics to a higher level of awareness'. It is, therefore, appropriate to explore his binary schema in greater detail. Hayek, one of the neo-liberal visionaries of Margaret Thatcher and Ronald Reagan, picks up the work of Adam Smith in an essay in his *Individualism and Economic Order* ([1949] 1976)[6] and ventures to suggest that Smith's *The Wealth of Nations* teaches us more about human behaviour than 'the more pretentious modern treatises on "social psychology"' (Hayek [1949] 1976: 11). This sanction of disciplinary leakage is enough to return us to our philosophical binary problem at the intersection of disciplines. In the same essay, which formed Hayek's 1945 Finlay Lecture at the University College, Dublin, 'Individualism: *True or False*', he wanted to rescue the term 'individualism' from its negative connotations in a battle with socialism and the 'collectivist character'. Indeed, he suggests that at times he regrets being associated with some of the descriptions of individualism and seeks to rescue individualism from its negative socialist representations.

Hayek's assessment of what he calls 'true' individualism is fascinating for its construction of the individual-social relationship. He wants to see individualism as part of society rather than fall into, what he calls, 'pseudo-individualism which results in 'collectivism' (Hayek [1949] 1976: 6). He argues: 'The first thing that should be said is that it [individualism] is primarily a *theory* of society, an attempt to understand the forces which determine the social life of man, and only in the second instance a set of political maxims derived from this view of society' (Hayek [1949] 1976: 6). He continues: 'This fact should by itself be sufficient to refute the silliest of the common misunderstandings: the belief that individualism postulates (or bases its argument on the assumption of) the existence of isolated or self-contained individuals, instead of starting from men whose whole nature and character is determined by their existence in society'. Hayek's individualism is based within the social order, but separated from collective processes of individualism. What makes Hayek's theory of the individual so fascinating for our purposes is that he appreciates how the term functions differently and how this makes him directly compete for a specific – 'true' – view of individualism; it illustrates precisely what is at stake in the individual-social binary. I will take each of Hayek's strategic constructions of individualism in his 1945 essay to illustrate the politic of knowledge involved in the very setting up of the division between true and false individualism, which runs across the binary tension.[7]

Hayek (1945a: 4, n.3) follows Carl Menger's 'methodological individualism' in reading all social phenomena as individual actions. Social operations cannot 'exist independently of the individuals which compose them' (Hayek 1945a: 6). Here Hayek plays on the paradoxical notion of the individual-social binary by arguing that social organisation requires individualism, but the social organisation of the individual destroys individualism and cannot therefore be regarded as individualism. To carry out these theoretical operations Hayek makes the distinction between 'true individualism' and 'individualism' (or what we can call to establish greater clarity in his work, 'design' individualism) by identifying two traditions; one from the British tradition of John Locke through to Adam Smith and the other from the Continental tradition of Descartes and Rousseau. After setting up this distinction, Hayek's task is to isolate cleverly a specific form of individualism opposed to collectivism. The distinction is between individual-individualism and collective-individualism. The binary politic allows Hayek to set up through the text a series of strategic binary moves along this basic philosophical division: true verses false (Hayek 1945a: 4, 6); anti-rational verses rational (Hayek 1945a: 11); spontaneous verses deliberate (Hayek 1945a: 10, 27); unforeseen verses predicted (Hayek 1945a: 8); freedom verses servitude (Hayek 1945a: 12, 16); inequality verses equality (Hayek 1945a: 30); not-known verses the known (Hayek 1945: 25); unconscious verses conscious (Hayek 1945a: 25); and democratic verses totalitarian (Hayek 1945a: 29). To give even greater clarity to this binary schema, in a kind of Pythagorean table of opposites, we can represent it as in the table overleaf

Hayek's thinking becomes caught in his own binary politic, because inside this schema are a number of factors that reflect his 'assumptions and propositions about knowledge', as he states in his 1936 essay 'Economics and Knowledge' (Hayek 1936: 33). His values emerge in the *a priori* grounds of his true individualism. First, we see that 'institutions' are needed to protect the choice and freedom (Hayek 1945a: 7). Second, this requires the setting up of the basic 'rules' – not the government 'orders' of collectivism – of individualism (Hayek 1945a: 17–18, 21). Third, true individualism requires

Individual-individualism	Collective-individualism
true	false
anti-rational	rational
spontaneous	deliberate
unforeseen	predicted
freedom	servitude
inequality	equality
not-known	the known
unconscious	conscious
democratic	totalitarian

the 'rights and obligations of ownership' (Hayek 1945a: 20). Fourth, individual free society requires the respect of 'traditions and conventions', but importantly these are 'the products of a social process which nobody has designed' (Hayek 1945a: 23). Hayek is rightly attempting to find a way to overcome the horrors of totalitarian thinking, in either fascism or socialism, in a post-war context, which he seeks to establish by building a market-led society of dynamic change. The ambition is to be respected, but there is a central 'blindness' to his circular logic, because the above conditions reveal that his own 'non-designed' individualism is also a form of 'designed' individualism (albeit with different institutions). It is precisely this move than reflects how neo-liberal ideology moves into a new form of collectivism, such that Hayek's individualism is a form of 'collective-individualism' hidden by his binary schema. Note, for, example, his attempt to offer a protection against totalitarian models by preventing designed individualism: 'So long as men are not omniscient, the only way in which freedom can be given to the individual is by such general rules to delimit the sphere in which the decision is his' (Hayek 1945a: 19). The problem is that in the attempt to overcome the oppressions of total-government and shifting the control to non-government 'institutions' and 'traditions and conventions' he is only shifting the collective locus of operation *not collectivity*. Once Hayek recognises the need for social organisations, which are part of his individualism, he is then caught in the nature of such social organisations. The binary paradox unravels his own individualism inside a new collective, which, in the evolved post-1980s political structure, becomes the power of the global corporate organisations and the World Bank. The new collective-individualism is non-governmental (albeit protected by the 'rules' of law and government).

A striking feature of Hayek's individual-social binary is his critique of modernity as 'controlled' in opposition to his desired 'spontaneous' society of the market.[8] He is critical of the modern attitude that wants to have a rational understanding of social processes. As he argues, extending his position to morality and science:

> We meet the same tendency in the field of morals and conventions, in the desire to substitute an artificial for the existing languages, and in the whole modern attitude toward processes which govern the growth of knowledge. The belief that only a synthetic system of morals, an artificial language, or even an artificial society can be justified in an age of science, as well as the increasing unwillingness to bow before any moral rules whose utility is not rationally demonstrated, or to conform with conventions whose rationale is not known, are all manifestations of the same basic view which wants all social activity to be recognizably part of a single coherent plan.
>
> (Hayek 1945a: 25)

The stakes in Hayek's logic are great at this point, because his corrective against government control is blinding him against seeing an even greater non-government organisational control; he, perhaps, at this stage, could not see the full global and totalitarian forms of his viewpoint. We particularly need to watch the logic in his individual-social binary schema, because it becomes complex in the appeal to the 'not-known', 'unintelligible' and 'irrational' to cover the highly rational, controlled and financially managed operations (Hayek 1945a: 22). Hayek's post-modern play conceals his modernism. The political mask and assumed values of knowledge are evident in the deliberate attempt to hide the known in the unknown. As I will show in my conclusion, the known and not-known are ethical categories of the self and Hayek's appeal to these terms is clever but seriously misguided, because he cannot see how his counter-move against designed individualism is another designed system and the request to accept without question the forces of the market is collective-individualism. We might say, to use Hayek's rhetorical play on individualism, that Hayek's 'not-known' is a '*known*-not-knowing' and not a 'true-not-knowing', because it is based on the specific epistemic conditions of competition, which demands an ideological space of risk and uncertainty for the maintenance of the unquestioned authority of managed financial organisation. Hayek's (1945a: 22) binary play conceals his value-judgements and collective competitive design:

[T]he individual, in participating in the social processes, must be ready and willing to adjust himself to changes and to submit to conventions which are not the result of intelligent design, whose justification in the particular instance may not be recognizable, and which to him will often appear unintelligible and irrational.

Hayek's logic collapses in his binary will-to-power, because the paradox is that this language is equally applicable to the totalitarian system. The rhetoric of 'blind forces' of the uncontrolled market only works on the 'controlled' operations of organisations (as Hayek has conceded) supporting those values. What the binary ethic reveals is that the attempt to overcome the totalitarian regimes of fascist and socialist government has resulted in the non-governmental financial and corporate totalitarian system. The so-called 'spontaneous' individual formations are collective systems.

What I have wanted to demonstrate is that the individual-social binary is in part always value motivated and, consequently, politically fuelled. It cannot be resolved without an *a priori* assertion of the values one holds about being human. We might value Hayek's ideal dynamic to overcome total systems, but not his blindness to the new fascism of the market. Hayek is correct to realise that 'traditions and conventions' of smaller groupings are needed to overcome the constraints of government control, because smaller groupings in 'traditions and conventions' protect against total systems of oppression. Such groupings are the dynamic of the individual-social binary in resistance against 'individualism' and 'collectivism'.

Thinking with the unknown

Hayek's discussion of individualism enables us to see how the binary division of the individual-social rests at the base of both economic and psychological knowledge. It becomes clear in this situation that psychological knowledge cannot operate on 'methodological individualism' from the assumed innocence of scientific neutrality, because the epistemological ground is pulled away by a set of *a priori* ethical values. Economic concerns about individuality mirror the psychological subject and what is at stake is both individual and social. My argument is that the individual-social binary in psychology, and its application to religion, is hiding a more serious ethical question about the subject. To ignore it is not just to be complicit with the dominant system, but also to perpetuate actively its late modern totalitarian logic. There is a need to enter the complex world of knowledge politics, because it is the ways we think and create a problem that reveal the hidden assertions of value. As Hayek (1936: 50) rightly recognised: 'Clearly there is a problem of the *division of knowledge* which is quite analogous to, and at least as important as, the problem of the division of labour'. This is the problem of the knowledge economy, which is raised but not examined. As we have seen, it is the problems of knowledge that the human sciences do not theorize that mask the deepest values. Hayek, as an economist, openly establishes many political links with his theory of the individual, but his values go even deeper into the ethical ordering of knowledge.

Although Hayek ideologically hid behind the 'unknown', he rightly valued the force of not-knowing, because it is the dynamic of change, especially when we begin to think in the known and highly controlled knowledge economy. Hayek was blind to his own market totalitarianism and known rules, but his genuine desire to overcome such ways of thinking is important. In this respect, he rightly recognised the need for 'humility' in terms of our imaginations. As he insightfully concluded his 1945 essay: 'The great question at this moment is whether man's mind will be allowed to continue to grow as part of this process or whether human reason is to place itself in chains of its own making' (Hayek 1945a: 32). Although Hayek is making a general comment, it is also highly pertinent for specific cognitive theories of the mind in the age of the knowledge economy. Such an opening out of Hayek's 'economic' questions, in the fluid spaces of the human sciences, enables me to rethink the ambiguous practices of the psychology of religion through the ethical ground of knowledge that economic discourse reveals.

What, we may ask, is unknown and under-theorized in the psychology of religion since James? To what extent are psychologists of religion internalising wider cultural and economic processes of individualism? To what extent are the economic processes impinging upon the creation of valid knowledge in the discipline? If these questions may seem uncomfortable or even outrageous to psychologists and their 'scientific' mind, we only have to review the history of science to show how scientific fact can create errors and how this shifts with the economic reality in each period of history. The knowledge of discovery has to be constantly kept in check by the wisdom of practice. We need to ask these questions, even if in the long run they need a more modified and nuanced presentation, in order to recognise that knowledge in the human sciences is not innocent but always politically motivated at the heart of its primary conceptual organisation. We also have to ask these questions because of the politic of the individual-social binary in all our knowledge. Such a move will enable us to see that personal distress is not simply a private affair. Human beings are caught inside wider political events, which cannot be translated into private suffering alone. As the clinical psychologist David Smail argues: 'Psychological distress occurs for reasons which make it incurable by therapy, but which are certainly not beyond the powers of human beings to influence' (Smail 1987: 1). It is for this reason that the psychology of religion, if it is to be a morally responsible subject, has to overcome its 'disciplinary amnesia' about the question of the individual and the social and its denial of the ethics of subjectivity. We need to reveal the pre-existing conceptual values prior to the possibility of a human science.

To return psychology to political economy is to return our visions back to our will-to-power, it is to bring theory back to an ethical value of knowledge and to bring those half-baked human 'sciences' back to their primary philosophical categories. The discourses of economics-psychology-religion (forms of the human sciences) are united in a value-system of how we imagine ourselves as human beings. The ethic of knowledge behind such values is the basis of my critique.

In the next part of the book, I will take this critique into three different traditions of the psychology of religion and show how the link to political-economy can reveal the ethical ground of such knowledge. I will also show how we now inevitably rewrite such engagements between economics-psychology-religion inside the ethical framework of the knowledge economy. My aim overall is to use the object of 'economy' to draw out the ethics of knowledge in the psychology of religion. This ethics of knowledge will be revealed in the binary tensions, the protected categories and the moments of closure in each successive wave of thinking.

Part II

Economic formations of psychology and religion

3   Religion, politics and
psychoanalysis

What people think and feel is rooted in their character and their character
is moulded by the total configuration of their practice of life – more
precisely, by the socioeconomic and political structure of their society.

Erich Fromm [1950] (1978) *Psychoanalysis and Religion*,
Yale University, p. 52

While the important correlation between subjectivity and the political order
has marked the border of psychoanalysis and produced a fascinating lineage
of revolutionary psycho-social thinkers, there has been a disturbing absence of
sustained political and economic discourse within psychoanalytical theories
of religion. The engagement between psychoanalysis and religion – as with
the psychology of religion as a whole – silences the political-economic object
through its particular disciplinary logic. The naïve viewpoint has been that
the psychoanalysis of religion returns the cultural object of religion to the
private world of inner experience and unconscious process and reorders the
political in the logic that phylogeny replicates ontogeny. While the individual-
social binary positions the locus of its statements of truth it further deflects
the object of politic economy through a selective ordering of its knowledge.
Indeed, the quasi-scientific interventions of a psychological discourse are
seen to produce a neutral political assessment of religious practices and a
stable object of religion.

The disciplinary strategy of the psychoanalysis of religion also involves
a hegemonic hermeneutics to silence politics and economics in its own
dominant double-talk, which removes the politic-economic by, for example,
superimposing categories of repression, shadow and projection and
reinstating the unity of the imagined unconscious-religious object or, even
more cleverly, reducing the object by producing a mock political-economy
that it can read in terms of its own insufficient and inadequate language. Such
that the economic object is reduced in value for some deeper unconscious

religious-truth, reducing its political effect by disguising its domain of influence within the self. The disciplinary amnesia is effective at this point, because the signifying magic of the discursive regime constantly separates – some might even say 'splits' – the order of truth into the *psychological* and *religious* as uncontaminated areas of the material and political world. The early psychoanalysis of religion in Freud and Jung and their exponents produce, in effect, a largely depoliticised and non-economic object. Even as *Jewish* psychoanalysts were forced to leave the political world of *fascist* Germany and relocate themselves in the 'new economic world' of *American* prosperity and power, talk of psychoanalysis and religion remained at the level of *science* against *religion* and the political-economic marker dutifully silenced.

With a few notable exceptions, to be explored later, it was not until the emergence of feminist and post-structuralist theory[1] in the post-war world that some of the basic categories of the psychology of religion started to be questioned and the personal became more political; but even then the psychoanalysis of religion remained restricted in its discursive straitjacket. Feminist theory[2] at least started to recognise the political organisation of the self and in critique of the isolated monad of patriarchal religion started to explore 'relational' and 'maternal' models to re-imagine the religious space (see, for example, Jonte-Pace 1997). The re-imagining of the *cultural* in post-structuralism, social theory and creative hermeneutical readings also advanced a more nuanced rendering of the religious-cultural aspects of depth psychology. In a creative attempt to read the socio-political world, there have also been some applications of psychoanalytic theory to the problem of 'religious' violence (see Jones 2002). But despite these extremely important moves into the cultural 'other' of psychoanalysis, which I will return to later, the psychoanalysis of religion was reluctant to embrace its own discourse as a political-economic reality. The tools of application are removed from scrutiny in the privilege of the interpretative act. Indeed, the category of 'religion', as an object of study, appears to increase the displacement of critique towards the method, because of its specific status in the modern economy of knowledge (something I will explore more closely in the next chapter).

In this chapter, I want to explore what can and cannot be said in the area of the psychoanalytical study of religion. In exploring the nature of the discourse, I want to reveal something of the hidden limits of the subject and explore some rules of the discourse with regard to the political-economic order. In line with the wider argument of this book, my aim is examine why the historical conditions of the discourse did not allow the political-economic to become an integrated order of analysis and here I wish to make a kind of test case of psychoanalysis and religion. The psychoanalysis of religion is a useful case example to examine these issues, not only because it is one of the bedrocks of the psychology of religion as an area of study, but because it allows us to see something of the strategy of silence found within modern affluent regimes of thought. What is also striking is that the economic unconscious of psychoanalytical discourse did emerge at various points in its history, but the interventions were limited and detracted from what are seen as the key problems of knowledge in the study of 'religion'. The conditions of reception were not right for developing these complex socio-economic readings of methodology. Even the innovative inter-disciplinary space of the study of religion with its implicit cultural dimension did not permit a more integrated analysis of the economic subject. The problem rests on the question of what a discipline is permitted to say and how its imagined object operates for the institutional apparatus, whether it is the medical authority, the religious pastoral or the academy (see Foucault [1970] 1972).

My approach to this problem will take a number of stages of argumentation. First, I will briefly sketch my opening polemic that psychoanalytic engagements with religion are established from cultures of satisfaction that mask wider socio-economic problems. Second, I will then show how the psychoanalytic study of religion imagines its own unique religious object in terms of the science-religion dialectic, which insulates itself from wider inter-disciplinary engagement with political and economic orders. Third, I will briefly plot something of the history of the 'economic' in psychoanalysis and the Freudian Left, not least across its European and American location. I will look in particular at Reich, Fromm and Lacan as they hold a particular European-American tension.[3] This exploration will enable me to explore why the psychoanalytical study of religion, as with psychoanalysis as a whole, is not receptive to the political-economic order. This will then lead me, fourth, to examine the more recent *cultural* examinations of Freud and religion, bridging formative thought in the work of Peter Homans and recent studies in feminism, particularly by Diane Jonte-Pace, and innovative hermeneutical readings by James DiCenso. My outline and selected examples are by no means meant to be exhaustive, but they will at least identify the ground of my position for the psychoanalytic context and its relation to my wider argument that the politics of knowledge in the human sciences limits the scope of intellectual inquiry.

In the process of this examination, I wish to construct two political orders of the psychoanalytical study of religion; first, the order of the *same* (that which increases disciplinary specialism, reduces the political value of the study, sustains traditional categories of thought and thus supports late-capitalist orders) and an order of the *other* (that which collapses the disciplinary regime, increases political engagement, challenges thought and questions late capitalist orders of truth). It will also follow that the theoretical order of the *same* is ego-driven and individualistic and that the order of the *other* is focused on unconscious-drives and social identity. The positions reflect the politics of the individual-social binary in so far as the former separates self and society and the latter unites such categories. The economic and political readings in psychoanalysis can be mapped on to this division, but they also reflect a political attitude to knowledge between closure and openness, and control and change.

A little more provocatively, I would like to assert that the order of the *same* is largely a reflection of certain dominant American readings of psychoanalysis and that the order of the *other* reflects a European edge and the voice of the oppressed within American culture. I wish to push this argument, because I want to show how the conditions of thought are linked to social location and wealth production. As I have shown, securing subject boundaries is also securing social orders. My argument also rests on the fact that transformative theory (as opposed to theory that colludes with and propagates the dominant ideology) emerges at points of social tension and struggle; and even persecution. Indeed, the 'revolution' of psychoanalysis and its model of sexuality informed and emerged at a point of cultural transition and change, which was subsequently pacified and 'put to work in the market economy, and in the process it has lost much of its ideological bite' (Robinson [1969] 1990: xv). The social tensions that created psychoanalysis shifted to a new set of social realities and a new abstract object. The fact that sexuality is now located within the market underlines my argument that in the new economy of knowledge all thought is shaped by a regime of economics and that new problems arise from this situation. Psychoanalysis was born out of European social change and struggle, but it was absorbed into the market society of America. In turn, these contexts change the order of the object of study in religion and culture.

In the post-war society of affluence, the new economy of thought sustained what I will call 'discourses of satisfaction', through which forms of disciplinary knowledge insulate themselves from the messy world of politics by separating the self from social order. It is a gesture of collusion or even appreciation of certain freedoms and wealth (which in turn hides those without freedom or wealth). The psychoanalytical study of religion is caught within this political economy of knowledge and thus I wish to mark out a certain economy of privilege surrounding American 'psychology of religion' that ethically informs its categories of knowledge. But while it is important to identify the specific political-economy of the psychoanalytical study of religion in America, it is also important to recognise those *other* political voices and the oppressed within American culture who have utilised the discourse.

Along with the Freudian Left, the cultural other of psychoanalysis holds potential to be used by the oppressed within and outside America and has played a significant part in feminist and race theory. The question is how the psychoanalysis of religion can become a discourse of the *other* and why the dominant institutions refuse this *other* in the making of the subject. I am therefore concerned to explore why one area excludes the *other* and builds the empire of the *same*. In such a disciplinary space, thought only produces clones to reproduce *introductions* and *course readers* – valid as such exercises are to those who wish to build the empire of the *same* and those who make a living teaching the subject – it is however time we were dissatisfied with this way of thinking and started to liberate thought to its *other* disciplinary revolution. As Naomi Goldenberg (1979: 71) rightly argues, in her own critical psychology of religion: 'Our constructions need to be various and flexible in order to let human nature attempt to define itself in new terms'. It is through highlighting the excluded categories and the protected categories that we can identify the ethical-political foundation of knowledge and facilitate a renewal of critical thinking for each success age.

Politics of satisfaction

Philip Rieff, in his excellent assessment of faith after Freud, argued that the religious person 'was born to be saved' and that 'psychological man is born to be pleased' (Rieff [1966] 1987: 24–5). Those studying the psychoanalysis of religion were in this sense rightly capturing the shift of symbolic registers, but they were also inadvertently servicing the new political therapeutics that Rieff so usefully uncovered. The psychoanalysis of religion was therefore a social mirror of the pleasures of a therapeutic culture. Such work indulges in the skill and imaginative invention of the psychoanalytical-religious object by returning all reality back to the ever-expanding 'unconscious' object of the *same*. In the hermeneutical excesses of the psychoanalytical religious readings one could take pleasure in the creation or destruction of the 'religious' object, according to which reading one desired, by reading it in terms of the new signification. Psychoanalysis was 'rich' enough to offer flexibility and even revision, without concern for the 'poverty' of economic knowledge. This process obviously, as Rieff's work indicated, was part of a

longer social and cultural history.[4] The discourse shifted in both time and space and although the material conditions played a part in these changes it was always masked by a different order of representation. It is the rhetoric of science and metaphysics that provides the great mask of economic truth.

The discourse of satisfaction within the psychoanalytical study of religion is established under the sign of the *objective* truth of the human subject, where truth is a metaphysical imaginary in the unity of science and religion. This discourse, in effect, marginalises the material reality and political conditions of knowledge in a bizarre alliance that diverts notions of 'truth' from the conditions of truth-production. However, in a theory of the new economy of knowledge (explored in the preliminary chapters) both science and religion can no longer be innocent, because thought is already within the totality of economics – it is already part of the institutional apparatus of knowledge production and exchange. The rules of psychoanalytic discourse about religion can be seen then to operate according to a 'partial' truth presented as 'the' truth; an assumption that one discourse can offer the authority to dismiss the other. We have already seen how the discipline forms useful amnesia about its own production in order to preserve its 'sacred' object, but these processes of articulation are always within the conditions of their time. What then are the conditions that bring this refusal of the political-economic in the psychoanalytic study of religion?

The psychoanalytic study of religion is by far the most successful dialogue in the field of religion and psychology. Furthermore, according to Eric Sharpe (1986), psychoanalysis was a defining foundational field of 'religious studies' and all the more remarkable for its institutional assimilation. Despite obvious concerns about reductionism, psychoanalytical work provided the supreme apparatus for the re-imagining of religious discourse for the new world of the twentieth century political subject, particularly in a post-war industrial context. The social influence of psychoanalytical theory is captured in W.H. Auden's (1940) poem on the death of Freud, when he recognised that he was 'now but a whole climate of opinion'. The psychoanalytical discourse was embraced into an ever-increasing privatized world of the individual and as church power shifted in the post-war nation-state a different order of truth started to blossom. This 'psychical' truth allowed a reading of religion as 'inner' truth, unadulterated by the trauma of war and promising salvation as unconscious character-formation. 'Religion' was usefully accommodated as ritual, image and transformation within the various church-state organisations within European and North American culture. The 'psy' disciplines (Rose 1998) reordered the Western world and, within the new economic prosperity of the bourgeoisie individual, a new re-imagining of the religious self emerged, alongside the mass psychology of the pastoral system.

However, behind the dynamic reordering of religion as psychic practice, there was some rearguard resistance to reducing the transcendent God to the modern self. This now forgotten debate was a useful distraction, a delightful piece of intellectual theatre for later debates in the science of religion to proclaim the neutrality of science, but what it masked was not the shift from church to modern post-war state, but rather the birth of the new transcendent of late-capitalism. While theologians and scientists debated the finer academic details – as if they constituted some terrible change in their self-important worlds – and the American dollars supported institutions of psychology, the 'invisible hand' of the economy silently waved goodbye to the old world and greeted the consumer-religion. The army of psychologists and, in turn, the scholars of religion established their dazzling journals and textbooks to provide a professional witness to their ignorance of political change. However, outside the literature of psychology – that most unaware political discourse – there were concerns, particularly in France, that maybe the new American psychoanalysis was but another demonstration of the booming American economy and that perhaps psychoanalysis had been imported from the old Europe only to be adapted to the economic-self of American consumerist society. America provided the economic conditions for turning knowledge of the self and 'psychoanalysis' into an entirely different political entity than its roots in Europe.

The scientific mask of economics

In order to grasp something of what I am trying to provoke in the imagination, it is worth recalling some of the rhetorical masks in the engagement between psychoanalysis and religion in the early literature and its mock resistance. My aim here is not to explore the traditional science and religion debate in psychology (which has been adequately done elsewhere, see Watts 2002), but rather to show how negotiating the territory of the relationship covers the political-economic object. The striking aspect of the early engagements is the theoretical dance – not battle – along the science-religion frontier and the way this safely delimits the domain of concern away from the modern economy. Given the institutional location of the founders of this new 'analysis' of religion, it is no surprise that the power struggles would be acted out at the level of the metaphysics of 'truth', involving the dialectical of thesis and antithesis and exploiting all the appropriate territorial rhetoric of atheistic-reductionism, objective-subjective division and cultural evolutions.

The medical-religious model contains the debate in the neat categories of knowledge, while the gods of the economy were in full production. For example, the rise of psychoanalysis in the Germanic world is seen to reflect the shift from the old European institutions of religion – Freud's Judaism and Jung's Swiss Protestantism – to the ever-increasing domain of power established within medical science, but the new apparatus of social control supported by the two prongs of the nation-state politics and industrialization is never sufficiently brought into the private analysis. Let me characterise the mask of the religion-science model in some early, and somewhat forgotten texts, as a way of highlighting the camouflage of the economic interventions that I will go on to discuss in detail.

In his historical assessment of the early relation between psychology and the churches in the first part of the twentieth century Graham Richards (2000) notes that, unlike debates in the natural science and religion, where there was conflict, the relationship with psychology has been (with the exception of some psychoanalytical literature) a congenial one. Indeed, Barry, writing in 1923, argues that psychology was an 'ally of supreme importance' and even goes on to argue that psychology supplies the 'data and vocabulary for a true theology of the Holy Spirit (Barry 1923: 188):

> We are all psychologists to-day. Psychology has become 'popular' more rapidly than any science previously, and a positive spate of books pours forth from publishers on psycho-analysis and the New Psychology. The general public as well as professional thinkers are coming more and more under its spell. History and the social sciences, industrial organisations, generalship, over and above the technique of medicine, are being re-thought in psychological terms. And the tide is advancing up the religious beaches.
>
> (Barry 1923: 188)

This positive alliance between psychology and the churches is, Richards argues, the reason why a conflict model fails to characterise the history of the early twentieth century encounter between these subjects. According to the literature from 1920s and 1930s, Richards identifies the 'clear benefits for both parties' and finds few 'anti-psychology mainstream Christian texts for most of the inter-war period' (Richards 2000: 69, 74); although there are key exceptions, such as the Rev. J.C.M. Conn (1939) in his informed work *The Menace of the New Psychology*.[5] The pastoral demand during the war years certainly created a therapeutic alliance to deal with the horrors and devastation. This is not to say that the transition was without any tension and, as Richards points out, psychoanalysis did engender certain amounts of concern from those with pre-modern convictions. In Barry's 1923 lectures it is important to recognise that he carefully qualifies the positive relationship with psychology. He states that 'psychology is certainly an ally', but as he goes onto argue, 'a dangerous ally, to the Christian thinker' (Barry 1923: vi). The churches embraced psychology, but the early texts did not approach the New Psychology and psychoanalysis without some critical sensitivity.

Alfred Garvie, for example, in his 1930 work *The Christian Ideal for Human Society* notes that psychology was 'at its beginnings' and that 'it has made, and is making mistakes' (Garvie 1930: 36). With shrewd insight into the nature of psychological knowledge, Barry also stated that there were problems in assuming that psychology could provide 'rigid conclusions'. He argued: 'Personality is always a not wholly calculable factor; and any science of man (sic) which for simplification ignores this factor cannot give an adequate account of its subject' (Barry 1923: 37). Garvie also makes some other important social qualifications, even if he did not have the political-economic dimension in mind. He recognises that it is 'a false and vain abstraction' to separate 'the human personality from the human society' (Garvie 1930: 36). There was also the concern, often addressed to Carl Jung, that psychology was in danger of making metaphysical assumptions and over-stepping its boundaries. As Garvie rightly observed: 'There is a danger of psychology becoming metaphysics, of the science forgetting its own limitations, and attempting to solve the problem of philosophy' (Garvie 1930: 215)

Textbooks on the psychology of religion rehearse these metaphysical debates between science and religion. The 'critical appraisal' sections, to take Michael Palmer's nomenclature, offer discussion – along with other concerns about historical fact and accuracy – about the nature of readings about religious truth. For example, the Swiss Pastor Oskar Pfister is used to qualify Freud's atheism and Catholic theologian Victor White and Jewish philosopher Martin Buber are brought to offer critical reflections on Jung's theological excursions (Palmer 1997: 76–7, 167–8, 185–7; Wulff 1997: 33–4, 315, 464–5, 467–8). These territorial anxieties are a battle for discursive authority and psychology wins the struggle by enabling psychological reality to become the guardian of spiritual development in the twentieth century, as the pastoral theologian Don Browning notes, even in his broad approval of the subject in 1987:

> The religious leaders of our culture – our ministers, priests, and rabbis – all receive large doses of psychotherapeutic psychology, personality

theory, and developmental psychology in their professional education, often without much careful reflection on how this knowledge squares with what they have learned about humans from a religious and theological perspective.

(Browning 1987: 2)

The embracing of the psychological by religious practitioners and scholars of religion – which was in the first instance at least the embracing of psychoanalytical interpretation – was a fairly amicable struggle. There were a range of positions entertaining either models of reductive integration, equality in dialogue and pastoral application (see Watts 2002: 3–15). These various power relations have subsequently been exposed in the very framing of the subject area through the different transformations of practice from 'psychology *of* religion' and 'religious psychology' to 'religion and psychological studies' and 'psychology *as* religion' (see Jonte-Pace and Parsons 2001: 3–6). The language of psychoanalysis did not, however, make the various power relations transparent. For example, those, like Fromm, saw the threat to religion not in Freud's ethically informed, and thus religiously grounded, atheism, but in Jung's more subtle psychologism; a position supported by later commentators such as Palmer (Fromm [1950] 1978: 20; Palmer 1997: 168). Shifting the analysis in a different way, David Bakan's opinion was 'that the degree of strain between religion and science is the direct function of the degree of idolatry', reading idolatry as the 'over quick fixing upon any method or device or concept' (Bakan 1967: 154, 158). The play on idolatry is fascinating for in its double-edged critique, Bakan recognises the 'searching' quality of science and religion as open-ended systems for examining life and the way both attempt to possess truth in a positivist assertion. However, the binary of science and religion does not adequately portray the ideological issues related to the study of psychoanalysis and religion, because they both inherit the concepts and frames from the history of Western thought that cross Greco-Roman philosophy, the Judaic-Christian tradition as well physiological discourses. By locating such fields of thought in the history of ideas there are as many continuities and discontinuities and, significantly, psychological discourse can easily be seen to carry older models of theological introspection, particularly in the *a priori* assumptions of the self (see Carrette 1993/4; 2005c).

It is my contention that the debates between psychoanalysis and religion were positioned according to a set of *veiled* points of engagement, not in terms of some great conspiracy, because the institutional exponents *only had the vantage point of their own discipline and associated disciplines.* The disciplinary frame of truth restricted the rhetoric and meant that the dialogue took place in terms of what could be articulated in terms of the associated institutions. This is not to say that disciplinary transgression did not occur, but when it did it often had a limited trajectory, because the discipline suitably policed the impostor; such are the methods of silencing those who unsettle the politic of knowledge. Added to this complexity is the fact that the so-called 'science of religion' ideologically wanted to find alliances across discourses to create a stable object for the study of religion. The cross-fertilization of psychoanalysis and religion became an ideal candidate for 'manufacturing consent' in the apparatus of modern knowledge (Herman and Chomsky 1995; cf. McCutcheon 2003). It is precisely in the blind desire for sites of 'science' that the late nineteenth-century scholars of religion repeatedly failed to examine the ground of inter-disciplinary objects and only after the rise of behavioural theory in psychology did psychoanalysis become questionable for those wanting a new hyper-rational scientific method. Psychoanalysis would be policed according to the logic of science that masked its own economy.

Repressed economy: the psychoanalytical Left and religion

It is well known, but rarely contemplated in depth, that in Freud's meta-psychology he used, alongside the dynamic and topographical, an economic model for the unconscious. As Freud explained:

> We see how we have gradually been led into adopting a third point of view in our account of psychical phenomena. Besides the dynamic and the topographical points of view, we have adopted the *economic* one. This endeavours to follow out the vicissitudes of amounts of excitation and to arrive at least at some *relative* estimate of their magnitude.
>
> (Freud [1915] 1984: 184)

The borrowing of metaphors across disciplines is a revealing discursive act and important for the politic of deferring the meaning along the disciplinary chain (Derrida 1978). It is not just words, but groups of discourse that differ meaning in the endless search for the mystique of authority. Laplanche and Pontalis believe this language of the economic emerges from the 'scientific spirit' of Freud's thought and that it is the 'most hypothetical aspect of Freud's metapsychology' (Laplanche and Pontalis [1973] 1988: 128). They argue that it cannot be read in its own terms unless one thinks of an exchange of values and such values are seen as finite (Laplanche and Pontalis [1973]

1988: 127–9). However, Freud is a man of his time and, as we noted earlier, in a revealing set of works within the history of economics, Mirowski (1989, 2002) has shown how the natural science metaphors permeate the field of economics. The cross-fertilization of metaphors within specialist discourses reveal the dynamic of knowledge as strategic metaphorical truth, rather than empirical-truth, and it is worth contemplating the metaphorical shifts within such systems of knowledge for its account of truth.

Lawrence Birken in rare examination of Freud's use of the term 'economic' believes that the idea, originally taken from Freud's work in neurophysiology, is 'no mere metaphor, but a fundamental set of axioms about the function of individuals and the world in which they lived' (Birken 1999: 312). Birken, while appreciating Freud's knowledge of economics was 'sketchy', finds agreement with Austrian economist Carl Menger in recognising 'needs' as based on individual drives (Birken 1999: 317–18). Birken's conclusion is that Freud's libido theory was a kind of 'unified field theory' and that *homo oeconomicus* gave way to *homo sexualis*, but we might add that when sexuality was taken into the neo-liberal market *homo sexualis* return to *homo oeconomicus* once again (Birken 1999: 327).

Another writer who has explored the rhetoric of economics outside its own field is the Dutch economist Peter-Wim Zuidhof (2002). According to Zuidhof, Freud, no doubt aware of the Austrian School of Economics in taking this central metaphor, develops and expands a variety of different ideas of economics that eventually 'dissolve' in meaning. Zuidhof's returns Freud to Bataille and Derrida and a reading of 'general economy' as forms of excess, but in doing so he opens important questions about, what he conjectures, might be a form of 'economic imperialism' in our culture. My own reading of the economic proliferation of economic terms follows a different path. The contemporary saturation of economics across different social and institutional contexts can be seen as part of the neo-liberal takeover of all aspects of cultural life (Carrette and King 2005). However, Freud's use of the term 'economic' cannot be framed according to developments of post-war capitalism, or neo-liberal society, and we therefore need to explore why economics is not only a metaphorical language of the unconscious, but something that remains marginal to the psychoanalytical tradition.

In Stephen Frosh's important survey of the political dynamic of psychoanalysis he recognises the 'complex contradictions' in establishing a politics of subjectivity within psychoanalysis (Frosh 1999: 15). However, while he is aware of the bourgeois nature of the discipline, the individualistic analysis and the retrogressive nature of some of its theory, not least on gender, he recognises that the field holds a certain political complexity, because 'many psychoanalytical approaches have both progressive and reactionary components' (Frosh 1999: 313). Surveying the diverse political aspects of psychoanalysis – through Freud, Neo-Freudians and Post-Freudians – he sees that there is 'no neat synthesis' to be made of the political visions found within the literature and rightly qualifies that it is not a 'social theory nor a programme for revolutionary activity' (Frosh 1999: 315, 317). Nonetheless, he is aware, along with many later theorists, such as Žižek, that psychoanalysis 'is always politically relevant' and, as he goes on to point out, 'the politics of psychoanalysis always has a critical and subversive tinge to it' (Frosh 1999: 312; Žižek 1991). This edge is established from the fact that the idea of the unconscious, notions of social repression and concepts of fantasy – not least established from the work of Melanie Klein – offer a rich vocabulary for a political hermeneutic of society in its configuration of the individual-social order.

While Frosh's analysis rightly establishes the potential value of psychoanalytical theory for political thought, he makes it clear that his approach to the question identifies two strands of the 'politics of psychoanalysis'; first, a politics of the theory, or the implications of the theory, and, second, the application of psychoanalysis in forms of psychoanalytical social theory (Frosh 1999: 12–13). What is striking about this arrangement is that in a footnote he recognises a third strand of the politics 'within' the psychoanalytic movement, which he is sees as the 'province of sociology or journalism'; something he believes can be seem in works such as Sherry Turkle's ([1978] 1992) account of the Lacan and Lacanian politics (which I will briefly explore later). This division is revealing, because it prevents him from framing the political question in terms of the sociology of knowledge and from seeing the implications of the knowledge economy on the very discursive formation of psychoanalysis. Frosh does appreciate, particularly in his other works, the volatile nature of late modernity and identity politics within this, but he does not follow through the political analysis of discourse that I am suggesting in this work (see Frosh 1999: 190–5; 1991). Despite this theoretical orientation there is enough evidence in Frosh's survey to make one wonder again why scholars of the psychoanalysis of religion have not taken up the subversive political quality of the inter-disciplinary engagement, not least from those figures of the Freudian Left. I will briefly think through this question by examining the reception and reading of two revolutionary figures, Wilhelm Reich and Erich Fromm, before turning to Lacan.

Reich and Fromm: religious prophets of political psychology

If the scientific and metaphysical focus of the psychoanalytical study of religion eradicated the political nature of the discourse then how did it deal with some of the explicit features of the Freudian Left? The answer is twofold, avoidance and neutralisation. In what is clearly the best overview textbook to date in the field of the psychology of religion by David Wulff (1997), Reich and Lacan are never mentioned and Fromm is neutralized in a discussion of 'humanism' – his own limiting essentialism – that dilutes the political force of his work; eliding his politics with philosophy in the passing location of his 'humanist-socialist view' (Wulff 1997: 595). Strikingly, Wulff makes only a passing comment on Marx's influence on Fromm (rightly qualifying the introduction of such a thinker as distinct from the 'vulgar Soviet misinterpretations'). He makes no reference to Fromm's radical critique of capitalism, submerging this in a brief reference to the 'market character' to be replaced by the humanistic-religious one (Wulff 1997: 595–604). The disciplinary policing is effective, but the problem is not Wulff's as such, it is rather the conditions of thought that make the field possible. Wulff, it should be noted, is not politically unaware in his own readings of psychology and makes important changes to his second edition to note recent 'postmodern' critiques of the field and even ends his marathon work by talking about a 'situation of crisis' in relation to environmentalist concerns (Wulff 1997: 641). Nonetheless, his textbook is not 'critical' in its introduction of the canon of the field and certainly not engaging with the Freudian Left in the work of Reich, Lacan and Fromm.[6]

Wulff, to be fair, is discipline-making rather than critically challenging. His viewpoint is thus by its nature reflecting the rules of the discourse to marginalise the outwardly political (other than his final comments and mapping of existing critical voices). Wulff's psychology of religion is represented according to the mask of science and not open to political economy or the institutional politic of the field. For example, he notes that there is 'little empirical research' that can be linked with Fromm's humanistic models of thought (Wulff 1997: 603). Clearly the politics of textbooks are another matter and by definition one cannot displace the object they seek to create, but according to what political discourse of satisfaction does this situation remain unexamined? Why do those thinkers that bring Freud into dialogue with Marx become marginalised in the examination of religion? Is it because atheism shrouds their religiosity or because those working within the knowledge parameters of the psychology of religion want to eradicate the political? Or perhaps the inter-disciplinary web they demand of thought is just too overwhelming for comfort? Disciplinary spaces thus adequately police what can and cannot be said. It is precisely in this situation that we need to unearth the values that exclude and protect categories of knowledge about the self and the world.

Listen, little theory! Reich's radical psychology of religion

Wilhelm Reich (1897–1957) does not offer any comfort for the reader both in his disruptive style and his politically inspired disciplinary transgressions. Indeed, as Robinson's discussion of the Freudian Left makes clear, Reich is 'a difficult intellectual' (Robinson [1969] 1990: 9). Even sympathetic biographies open by admitting he 'manifest forms of hypomania with an attendant psychic inflation' (Corrington 2003: x). Nevertheless, the psychoanalytical movement carries forward equally unsettled voices without effectively silencing their work. Unfortunately, the bits of critical insight littered in the complex writings of Reich's political psychoanalysis are dismissed before they even reach thinking within the psychology of religion.

The Freudian Left works effectively to bring together Marx's sense of alienation and Freud's social repression to at least demand that the subject take seriously the question of political-economy. Reich offers valuable material for understanding the individual-social relationship, not least in his work on *Character-Analysis* ([1945] 1980) that identified the process of social armouring, which in turn inhibited full expression. He also weaves the economic into the psychological. As he states:

> The ideology of every social formation has the function not only of reflecting the economic process of this society, but also and more significantly of embedding this economic process in the *psychic structures of the people who make up the society.*
>
> (Reich [1933] 1970: 18)

Reich's appreciation of the economic order, developed from his reading of Marx, is striking for its attempt to bridge different fields of knowledge. Reich moves easily from the biological to the political and establishes his own social-psychological approach of *sex-economy* – the mapping of ideology onto the body politic of orgasmic pleasure.

While writers such as Mitchell ([1974] 1990) and Frosh (1999) are rightly aware of the problems, both in terms of Reich's focus on genitality and his biological essentialism, his links between politics, religion and psychology are important for building a theoretical framework for a critical psychoanalysis of religion, not least, in his 1933 work *The Mass Psychology of Fascism*. Here he makes the inter-disciplinary connections when he asserts: 'The psychology of the unconscious added a *psychological* interpretation to the sociological interpretation of religion. The dependency of religious cults upon socio-economic factors was understood' (Reich [1933] 1970: 145). Although one has to struggle through the excesses of his work and the polemical and somewhat dated Marxist readings, this study makes intriguing use of categories of religion and economics, which allows us to break disciplinary locations.

In the tradition of crowd psychology from Gustav Le Bon's 1895 *The Crowd* and echoing anthropological works on 'mystical' participation in the group, *The Mass Psychology of Fascism* examines the religiosity of fascism (cf. Poewe 2006). The work develops a notion of 'mysticism', which can at times mean simply 'religion' and a rather dry Leftist critique, to show the collective control of pleasure. More importantly, he recognises that 'religious forms' and 'contents' are dependant on 'socio-economic conditions' (Reich [1933] 1970: 144). By bridging psychological and sociological readings of religion and the economic, Reich is able to show how ideas are not 'imposed' upon individuals but rather embedded within them, not unlike post-structuralist forms of subject-formation where the sense of self is both externally and internally produced (Reich [1933] 1970: 146). Culture becomes 'imperialistic mysticism' and patriarchal religion the 'negation of sexual need' (Reich [1933] 1970: 146). There are, however, gestures in the work to a more positive appreciation of religion. In discussion of a Protestant Pastor, he notes that it was 'capitalism's abuse of religion that was at fault' (Reich [1933] 1970: 127) and later he seems to suggest that it was the separation of sexual and religious feelings that created the negative appreciation of sex within religion (Reich [1933] 1970: 148). Religious ecstasy was for Reich 'sexual excitation' (Reich [1933] 1970: 149), but it was the added dimension of economic thought that takes Reich beyond previous psychoanalytical models. The theoretical ground is not very well-established, but he has signalled the possibility that religion, politics and psychology were somehow intimately connected. Unfortunately, the wider trajectory of Reich's life, his Nietzschean like outbursts, in *Listen, Little Man!* ([1948] 1975), and his imprisonment, following accusations of fraud by the Federal Food and Drug Administration in 1954, led to a tragic and comic end that prevents his more searching and largely fragmented insights from being heard.

There is, however, one notable exception to the voices of dismissal. Philip Rieff gives equal weight to Jung's language of faith as he does to what he calls 'Reich's Religion of Energy' (Rieff [1966] 1987: 141–88). Rieff is able to hold the tension of the 'brilliance' and 'absurdities' of Reich's work and paints a compassionate picture of a suffering life that returns to the 'religious' (Rieff [1966] 1987: 173). According to Rieff, Reich develops an 'oceanic feeling' of cosmic unity in his later work, forgetting both Freud and Marx, in what becomes for Rieff a life that represents the 'private self-transformation' in a world that misunderstands (Rieff [1966] 1987: 178). In Reich's return to God, Rieff sees the important recognition of love as the 'supreme energy' at the centre of his world (Rieff [1966] 1987: 187). These lines of thinking can be seen in Reich's extraordinary work, *The Murder of Christ* ([1953] 1971), which is an attempt to read Christianity through a new hermeneutic of cosmic energy. Not unlike Freud's imaginative reconstruction of Jewish history in terms of his own vision of life in *Moses and Monotheism*, Reich's meditation on the life of Christ and forms of Christology articulates his own private theory of Cosmic orgone forces (natural life forces that held orgastic qualities and which could be measured). As Corrington (2003: 223) perceives, there is in Reich's identification an 'ecstatic naturalism' through which he blends Christian thought to his notion of life energy. Christ becomes the life energy, but his murder is maintained by oppressive systems:

> Christ's problem is much more comprehensive. *It concerns the conflict of motion again frozen structures.* Motion alone is infinite. Structure is finite and tight ... The Murder of Christ could happen and does happen today as it happened then. The economic and social conflicts are even exact duplicates today of what they were then: Emperors and foreign governors and an enslaved nation, and tax burdens and national hatred and religious zeal and collaboration of the subjugated people's leaders with the conquerors, and tactics and diplomacy and all the rest of the show. In order to comprehend Christ's story, you must start thinking in cosmic dimensions.
>
> (Reich [1953] 1971: 58)

Reich's late visionary text holds the quality of many theological voices of liberation, combined with a touch of body and liberation theology. The turn to religion in the later work is remarkable not only for its shift from his earlier Marxist and Leninist critique, but also for the fact that, as Robinson notes, 'religion represented a positive good, since it alone had preserved man's awareness of the forces of life' (Robinson [1969] 1990: 69). However, as Robinson continues, in his assessment of Reich's religiosity:

> The Science of Orgonomy was as fantastic and elaborate as any theological system, and its content was identical with that of the great religions of salvation: it promised both a total interpretation of reality and a total therapy for man's individual and social ills.
>
> (Robinson [1969] 1990: 70)

This radical move towards a theological metaphysics has been taken up in Corrington's biography where he develops the 'unsaid' aspects of Reich's 'ecstatic naturalist metaphysics' and hopes that a new appreciation of Reich's philosophy can be found (Corrington 2003: 247). This positioning of the late works of Reich in the metaphysical, rather than promoting the political Reich of the 1930s, demonstrates the constant splitting of economy from the psychological and religious. Reich is appreciated in the different phases of his work according to their thematic anchoring in the disciplinary codes and the complexity of inter-disciplinary politics becomes an expression of the exaggerated and the mad. The mixing of discourses is difficult and adds to the mechanism of dismissal. For example, the play of economics, religion and psychology becomes part of the tragic and comic in Reich's life; which Robinson concedes ends in perhaps an 'appropriate … farce' (Robinson [1969] 1990: 73). Again like Nietzsche, there is a narrative of madness which conveniently enables the important insights on political-economy to be merged into the crazy departure from science, coupled as it is today with an outdated Marxism.

Rieff's sensitive reading of therapeutic faith and Corrington's sympathy for his metaphysics, while demonstrating the persistence of the so-called religious, do little to avoid the disciplinary separations and the marginalisation of *homo oeconomicus* inside the psychological and the religious. Reich is left in the 'wasteland', dismissed by the Left for embracing religious ideology, condemned by religion for his politics, rejected by psychoanalysis for his dissent from orthodox Freudian theory and silenced by science for his excessive and undisciplined creativity or madness. He becomes in the end a cult figure of avant-garde films – the 1974 Yugoslavian film *W.R.: Mysteries of the Organism*[7] – delighting in his bizarre sexual and political revolution of the 1960s, which remains his economic time (see Chasseguet-Smirgel and Grunberger 1986).

There is something in all of these rejections that needs to be brought into a critical appreciation of Reich, but what is left in the ruins of the unconscious are the unsettling links between political-economy and knowledge. Reich's insights are often overplayed, but the fact that his work constantly brings us back to an ideological narrative pushes us towards a much-needed inter-disciplinary critique of society and the body. His original links between psychoanalysis and economics would however return like a phoenix from the flames, they would be a marker of the conditions of thought and the repression of the economic. The return of these links to the economic would not be a return to Marx, but in a post-Cold War world of neo-liberalism the uncomfortable recognition that psychology, religion and economics are caught in a new knowledge economy. It is yet to be seen if the time is right for revisiting the past to make sense of our present.

It is not surprising that in a later edition of Reich's *The Mass Psychology of Fascism* he made reference to Erich Fromm's *Fear of Freedom* ([1941] 2001), because, as Robinson points out, there are striking parallels (Robinson [1969] 1990: 46). Fromm and Reich also interconnect in bringing together religion, economics and Freudian psychology. Despite this confluence, Reich was critical of Fromm's neglect of the sexual problem and in related ways Fromm suffered badly from internal political debates in the psychoanalytical tradition about loyalty to Freud, not least from his friend at the Frankfurt School, Herbert Marcuse (Reich [1933] 1970: 219; Marcuse [1950] 1966; see also Frosh 1999: 163–75).[8] I am not primarily concerned with the neo-Freudian politic in the psychoanalytical tradition, which has been well-document elsewhere (see Frosh 1999; Jacoby 1975). What is important for my concern is to show how Fromm's inter-disciplinarity of religion, psychology and economics is contained and repressed. I am concerned with how Fromm's politic becomes silenced in the humanistic and how his radical attempt at a critical psychology of religion goes underground.

Counter-knowledge: Fromm's political-economy

Erich Fromm (1900–80), as we have already noted in Chapter 2, attempted to break the individual-social divide in his own thinking, even though his work never adequately placed psychological discourse under detailed economic scrutiny.[9] The problem of weaving discourses together is precisely why the political force of his analysis of economic life has been insufficiently carried forward in the study of religion. The object of study is always fragmented and the unexamined rules of a discourse effectively manage the said and unsaid by refracting the light into the institutional and discursive alliance of the material order of silence. The work of Fromm is itself a demonstration of his own struggle to hold together the realms of religion, psychology and economics, such that while his early work *The Dogma of Christ* ([1930] 1963) overcame the central theoretical problems, his work on *Psychoanalysis and Religion* ([1950] 1978) struggles to maintain a coherent focus on these questions, due largely to the lack of an inter-disciplinary rationale. The categories of economics, psychology and religion are only briefly locked together, because, as he admits in the later work, '[s]uch a sociopsychological analysis goes far beyond the context of these chapters' (Fromm [1950] 1978: 52). As Fromm confirms: 'The history of religion gives ample evidence of this correlation between social structure and kinds of religious experience' (Fromm [1950] 1978: 52). If this is the case then it also implies that psychological discourse of religion is a reflection of a certain social structure, but Fromm never fully embraces this implication of his position.

Nonetheless, all the strands of a critical psychoanalytical theory of religion are present and Fromm's view – even if not developed in consistent terms – recognises the socio-economic base of religion and psychology. If Reich offered some initial fragments for a political-economy of the psychological discourse of religion, Fromm was the first architect of such critical thinking. Even though his thought was never sufficiently developed, he drew the necessary lines between political-economy, religion and psychology that few could even see in the pages of his books. The conditions of thought were not ready for his radical insights; clouded as they were by internal psychoanalytical politics, traditional concepts of religion and an inability to represent the economic structure of psychology and religious discourse outside the Left–Right politics of the Cold War. Fromm's theoretical insights on the politics of knowledge are also easily silenced because of the power of the American political Right, the subsequent collapse of Communism and the fear of ideological rhetoric. The irony is that in the politics of the knowledge economy, established in a world of neo-liberalism, we are able to appreciate Fromm's inter-disciplinary structure of thought for a new critique and a new political age. Perhaps, the fact it is neo-liberalism, rather than Marxist ideology, that returns us to Fromm will enable some to appreciate his theory; but do not be surprised if they find other ways to rebury his thought, because his prophetic voice highlights the profound injustice of the market. For this reason it is necessary to explore his specific model of knowledge in more detail.

Fromm's work integrates psychological, religious and economic knowledge through the figure of 'man' in the social world. These categories thus interact at the point of Fromm's humanistic essentialism, a base of the human condition shaped by the social structure and alienated by the market driven world. Only on a very few occasions does the harmony of this inter-disciplinary politic emerge; but nevertheless each specific step in the discussion is given clear articulation. I will take the three steps of this model in turn: religion embedded in the economic, psychology embedded in the economic and, finally, religion embedded in the psychological. The first two are linked through a Marxist ideological superstructure and the last step through a 'soul-orientation' of the human search for meaning. The end result of these theoretical linkages is – at least – the beginning of an inter-disciplinary critical psychology of religion.

The first locking of categories is apparent in one of the most under-explored, but, in my view, one of the most important texts in the history of the psychology of religion, Fromm's Frankfurt School inspired work *The Dogma of Christ*, written in 1930 (see Carrette 2004b). Here we find the development of an economic theology, where religious dogmas, rather then appearing to be simply grand metaphysical reflections of a disembodied Christian faith, reflect the material and social conditions of an evolving community of people (Fromm [1963] 2004: 56). In plotting the shift of Christianity in the first three centuries, Fromm explores the way Christianity moved from being a 'religion of the oppressed to the religion of the rulers' (Fromm [1963] 2004: 54). The individual psyche, religious expression and the 'existing social situation' are entwined in this historical development (Fromm [1963] 2004: 11). As Fromm explained: 'The change in the economic situation and in the social composition of the Christian community altered the psychical attitude of the believers' (Fromm [1963] 2004: 81). What Fromm is articulating is the complex evolution of utterances about Christian belief and how they interact with the economic (material) and social forces, which in turn create new orders of power. Religion becomes for Fromm a human affair and in many ways he is putting forward a model of the 'social function of Christianity' (Fromm [1963] 2004: 58). If we follow the assumption of the social and material conditions shaping religion then it becomes imperative for later theorists to explore the material and social conditions of psychological models of faith. Fromm does not pose this question, but he does establish, like Reich, the capitalist distortion of religious concepts later in his work:

> We use symbols belonging to a genuinely religious tradition and transform them into formulas serving the purpose of alienated man. Religion has become an empty shell; it has been transformed into a self-help device for increasing one's own powers for success. God becomes a partner in business.
>
> (Fromm [1963] 2004: 87)

The embedding of religion in the economic is conceptually a clear development of Marx, but a Marx always cushioned with a Freudian humanity. The location of Freudian psychology within the ideological apparatus was a more challenging move and it was not until his exposure to American capitalism that the full force of this critique was visible, not least in relation to American ego-psychology. In his sharply critical essay 'The Crisis of Psychoanalysis' in 1970 we see Fromm challenge the state of psychoanalysis in America – not least tinged with his own alienation from the International Psychoanalytic Association – by noting the shift from 'a radical to a conformist theory' (Fromm 1970: 14). The early radical elements found within the bourgeois liberalism of psychoanalysis changed under 'new economic and political forces' and subsequently created increased 'bureaucratization and the alienation of thought' (Fromm 1970: 24–5). These changes were mirrored in the history of political, philosophical and religious movements, but it is the 'crisis of psychoanalysis' that is Fromm's central concern and the political edge is clear:

> In contrast to this majority there was a small minority of radical psychoanalysts – the psychoanalytical 'left' – who tried to continue and develop the system of the radical Freud, and to create a harmony between the psychoanalytical views of Freud and the sociological and psychological views of Marx.
>
> (Fromm 1970: 25)

Fromm goes on to outline the conformist nature of psychoanalytical thinking. In this critique, Marcuse's work and the ego-psychologists are the principal focus of his intervention (see Frosh 1999 for a more detailed account). Fromm's critique of Marcuse rests on setting up a distinction between philosophical abstractions and the clinical base in outlining the misuse of Freud's ideas of repression and the reality principle. Fromm allows for a greater potential for change in the social world and accuses Marcuse of misreading Freud and creating a vision of non-repressive society, which he regards as 'infantile regression' rather a mature development (Fromm 1970: 31–5). The critique of ego-psychology is more sustained. Fromm argued that Freud remained an id psychologist and by putting emphasis on rational adaptation Fromm believed the work of ego-psychology reflected a conformist mentality:

> The ego psychological revision did not only start by studying the psychology of adaptation, it *is* in itself a psychology of the adaptation of

psychoanalysis to twentieth-century social science and to the dominant spirit in Western society.

(Fromm 1970: 43)

We shall see later how Lacan critiqued the same trend in American psychology, but what Fromm reveals is the way psychological thought is conditioned by the American social context. Unfortunately, the power game of who is 'conforming' and 'true' to Freud extinguished the political weight of Fromm's insights. Marcuse ([1950] 1966) believed the neo-Freudians (including Fromm) moved from the unconscious biological base to preconceived notions of social structure by turning to cultural facts. Russell Jacoby, in taking up defence of Marcuse, played on the idea of amnesia in forgetting Freud and accused Fromm, along with the ego-psychologists, of conformity. This conformity was established by moving from a 'biological and instinctual psychology toward a humanist, existential, and personal one' (Jacoby 1975: 47). The debate as to what constitutes a 'critical psychology' loyal to Freud marks out Jacoby's text, but perhaps in the end his most important insight – made in passing – is that '[s]ocial analysis decays into group loyalty' (Jacoby 1975: 117).

There were, as Frosh so clearly shows, genuine problems in formulating a Freudo-Marxist position with 'conformism and insipid humanism' on one side and 'a monstrous vision of libidinal self-gratification which offers little but individualistic hedonism' on the other (Frosh 1999: 179). However, despite its failures there is a central theoretical agreement that psychological theory interfaces with society. Fromm sets down the central political question when he sees how psychology is used by capitalism: 'Psychological knowledge ("*Menschenkenntniss*") has assumed as a particular function in capitalist society, a function and a meaning quite different from the meanings implied in "Know Thyself"' (Fromm [1963] 2004: 157). It is this recognition of the influence of American capitalism on psychological ideas that needs to be taken to the heart of a critical psychology of religion. It was in this sense that Fromm called for forms of 'negative psychology' to stand alongside 'negative theology' to preserve human life from the market forces (Fromm [1994] 2005: 162). From this point onwards we can no longer be innocent in the way psychology is brought into engagement with cultural-religious practice, a fact important for those wishing to rely on psychology for a 'science of religion' and those wanting to implant psychology into the pastoral world of faith communities. Critique becomes the only way to be suspicious of the dominant regime of psychology, particularly in American society.

The final link between psychology and religion in Fromm's mapping of a critical psychology of religion is established through his critique of forms of academic psychology 'trying to imitate the natural sciences and laboratory methods' (Fromm [1950] 1978: 6). According to Fromm's therapeutic outlook, psychoanalysis is concerned 'with the same problems as philosophy and theology' (Fromm [1950] 1978: 7). This attitude is the same as Jung's in *Modern Man in Search of a Soul* (1933) and it is by using the idea of 'soul' that Fromm attempts to interlock the questions of these different domains concerned with the human exploration of love, reason, conscience and values (Fromm [1950] 1978: 6). The move to merge these areas of enquiry is part of Fromm's wider questioning of the idea of 'religion' in terms of economics and psychology and it is worth pursuing this a little to show how the different strands of Fromm's thinking are held together in the assertion of an underlying human essence.

Fromm is aware of the problem of the term 'religious' and its Western construction. Anticipating contemporary post-colonial assessments of the category religion, he declared, in a posthumously published work discussing Marx and religion: 'Europeans were arrogant enough through the centuries to proclaim the white man's symbol to be constitutive for any religion' ([1994] 2005: 133) Fromm's appreciation came from both his interest in Eastern traditions and his attempt to establish an existential reading of all systems of meaning. In 1950 he confirms the 'terminological difficulty' of examining religion and, unlike James who set up for the purposes of his 1902 lecture an individual model, Fromm firmly holds to his social psychological formation of the subject. As he wrote in 1950:

> We simply have no word to denote religion as a general human phenomenon in such a way that some association with a specific type of religion does not creep in and colour the concept … I understand by religion *any system of thought and action shared by a group which gives the individual a frame of orientation and an object of devotion.*
>
> (Fromm [1950] 1978: 21)

While Fromm does not fully appreciate the Western construction of the category, he is at least suspicious of the term 'religion' and its function. His use of the idea of 'orientation' anticipates contemporary work on 'religion as orientation' (Long 1986; see also Carrette and Keller 1999). At one point Fromm also appears to read the religious attitude as a 'way of life', which appeals to his general atheistic humanism and attempts to get around the 'concept of God' in thinking about religion ([1994] 2005: 138).

Fromm's appreciation of Marx's attitude to religion is the key to his critical reading, because he sees the dialogue between these two areas as holding 'insurmountable obstacles' caused by the unfortunate preconceptions of Western history and political misunderstandings of Marx ([1994] 2005: 133). Fromm took a lot of time, not least because of the Cold War politic of American society, to represent Marx's idea of 'man' and of religion ([1961/6] 2004, [1994] 2005: 132–70). Fromm attempts to take Marx out of the political prejudice of Communism – which Fromm rejects along with capitalism – in order to valorise his humanity and social concern. He even wishes to correct misreadings of his view of religion by going beyond the infamous 'opium' idea to the later passages of appreciating religion as 'the heart of a heartless world' ([1994] 2005: 166–7). Fromm's final rescue of Marx comes in his linking of the German medieval mystic Meister Eckhart with Marx through a 'negative theological' appreciation of religion without religion, not unlike Bonhoeffer's 'Godless Christianity', which Fromm makes reference to in the 1967 foreword of *Psychoanalysis and Religion* ([1950] 1978: viii, [1976] 1999, [1994] 2005: 113ff):

> There is little difference, except in terminology, between Eckhart's atheistic mysticism and Marx's concept of man as the highest being for himself. Both are atheistic, both speak against the idolization of man, for both the fulfilment of man lies in the unfolding of his essential power as a purpose in itself. If Eckhart was an atheistic mystic speaking the language of theology, Marx was an atheistic mystic speaking the language of post-Hegelian philosophy.
>
> (Fromm [1994] 2005: 169)

The uniting of such diverse thinkers around the question of a central 'humanism' and Fromm's appeals to this discourse are cause for concern from a politic of difference, but the ground of his essentialism reveals much about the interweaving of the discourse of psychoanalysis and religion. It becomes clear, in Fromm's later work, that his imagined object of the 'human' has profound roots in a Judaic-Christian model of social justice. According to Rainer Funk (2000: 12), Fromm had wanted to make a life work studying the Talmud and his Orthodox Jewish background achieves some harmony within his later work when he reflects on the prophetic 'messianic' vision. In many ways his work establishes a line of thinking from the eighth century Jewish prophets of Isaiah, Jeremiah, Amos and Hosea to Marx and his own work (Fromm [1961/6] 2004: 166–74). This confluence of religion and political vision is the ground of his psychoanalytical work, but as Frosh (1999: 175) recognises, along with the wider political Left in psychoanalysis, such statements were more effective for 'morale' rather than 'strategy'. Fromm's inter-disciplinary challenge to psychology, religion and economics was difficult to develop in social structures that were invested in the disconnection of specialist isolation/illusion. In this sense, Fromm remains uncomfortable for disciplinary thinkers who wish to imagine they are important in their own terms.

Reich and Fromm remain voices of unrealised potential, but they are also witness to the repression of the unconscious economy of the subject. Elizabeth Ann Danto's study of social liberalism in the psychoanalytic tradition between 1918 and 1938 recognises this lack of analysis of the political history of psychoanalysis. 'That the history of political activism in psychoanalysis', Danto (2005: 8) comments, 'has been consistently withheld from public view is puzzling'. In her work examining psychoanalysis and social justice between 1918 and 1938, she discovers an important social consciousness to the psychoanalytic movement and the setting up of clinics for the poor. She believed that psychoanalysis had 'cared' until 1938 and engaged with important political and economic realities. It would be wrong to romanticise social activism in psychoanalysis before 1938 and the edge of social concern in Freud's writing about the individual and the collective, but equally it is wrong not to be aware of the shift in focus when psychoanalysis begins to be dominated by American cultural politics. The theoretical priorities of psychoanalysis according to some critical thinkers certainly did change when psychoanalytical thought shifted its geo-political location, but the question remains as to whether some of the theoretical concerns can be brought into the very different political conditions of today or whether these documents remain historical ventures of their time.

Commenting on the collapse of the Freudian Left and his later change of opinion – including a shift to the Right – Robinson rightly notes, in the second edition of his work on the subject, that 'important intellectual and political developments during the past two decades have effectively undermined the conceptual pillars on which the tradition rested' (Robinson [1969] 1990: xii). Robinson believes the second edition of his work on the Freudian Left has only historical value, but then surprisingly argues that 'the social and psychological reality they [the Freudian Left] set out to criticize is ... as bad as ever' (Robinson [1969] 1990: xviii). As my own work seeks to show, in a neo-liberal world, inter-disciplinary questions are now framed by late capitalism not the Left. The social questions of justice, following the collapse of the Left, emerge today in a different set of conceptual sites, not least those explored by new academic interest in cultural studies and identity politics.

However, the political domination of American corporate and military power also means that knowledge from within that economy requires a particular critical consciousness. In the remaining sections of this chapter, I will go on to explore psychoanalytical politics through the Franco-American tension drawn out in the work of Jacques Lacan and then, to conclude, I will show how political economy remains hidden in American academic study of religion and psychology, not least behind the signification of the cultural.

Lacan and American psychology

In the course of Fromm's critical inter-disciplinary thinking he drew attention to the nature of American market-driven culture and its impact on psychological discourse. The critique of ego-psychology and its adaptation to American culture also finds support in a different fashion in the work of the French psychoanalyst Jacques Lacan (1901–81).[10] His work is important for my argument for two reasons. He, first, shows the political significance of subjectivity, written as it is through language and the social order, and, second, he provides a different cultural context for the development of psychoanalytic theory to ground my argument that socio-economic factors shape psychological theory; which in turn requires our critical suspicion. The position I am developing has been carefully explored in Sherry Turkle's excellent work on *Psychoanalytical Politics* ([1978] 1992), which examines the sociology of the Lacanian psychoanalytical movement in France. This work highlights the differences between the reception of psychoanalysis in France and the USA and provides a base for understanding the conditions of any psychological project. Turkle's argument is that there is a 'cultural plasticity' (Turkle [1978] 1992: xxiii) of psychoanalytical ideas and in the process shows the difference between its European and North American emergence. This cultural variation of ideas is true of all forms of thinking and, in this respect, she notes that just as there are national forms of Calvinism there are different forms of psychoanalysis (Turkle [1978] 1992: 49). Following Lacan's critical charge against American psychoanalysis, which in places becomes outwardly political in tone, she highlights the difference between American optimism and its conservative theory, in the work of such writers as Erikson, and the situation in France. 'In France', she argues, '... there is a strong political and intellectual Left, psychoanalysis became deeply involved in radical social criticism, and French social criticism became deeply involved in psychoanalysis' (Turkle [1978] 1992: xxiii–iv).

The cultural differences between France and the USA can also be seen in the different national patterns of development in the psychology of religion.

Beyond the early work of Pierre Janet and Theodule Ribot (and excluding French speaking Switzerland) the field did not develop. As Wulff (1997: 46–7) notes, in contrast to Germany and America, there was no 'sustained development' in France and today it has the smallest representation in the European network of the psychology of religion.[11] However, no political reading of this situation is offered. The secular structure of Republican French society, with its division of church and state and its order of laïcité, is a key factor, and, as Turkle illustrates, the late arrival of psychoanalysis to France and its link to the political Left are obviously additional elements. The nature of Leftist atheism causes a kind of blind spot to the academic study of religion – there are no departments of 'Religious Studies' – in France; although the 'study of religion' occurs in other disciplinary spaces. Few have explored how Lacan's Catholic background regularly manifests itself in his work, that his idea of the Big Other ('le grand Autre') resembles theological categories, how his reading of *jouissance* evokes a mystical theology, how his practice and thinking corresponds to Zen Buddhism, and the fact that his 'search for the absolute' led to him to examine a range of enigmatic cultural forms (Roudinesco 1997: 12, 205–6, 351ff).[12] The conditions of theorizing in France have not produced the necessary object of analysis, but this also highlights the fact that the distinctive nature of the religio-socio-economic conditions of American psychoanalytic thinking about religion cannot be ignored. Lacan's critique of American ego-psychology brings this into greater perspective.

According to Lacan, the individualism and cultural adaptation of American psychoanalysis separated it from Freud's more radical reading of the unconscious. Lacan's critical view is set out in his famous Rome discourse of 1953:

> [I]t seems indisputable that the conception of psychoanalysis in the United States has been inflected toward the adaptation of the individual to the social environment, the search for the behaviour patterns, and all the objectification implied in the notion of 'human relations'. And the indigenous term, 'human engineering', strongly implies a privileged position of exclusion with respect to the human object.
>
> (Lacan [1966] 2006: 204)

Lacan was concerned that the ego had replaced the unconscious and this reduced psychoanalysis to the *'well-beaten paths of general psychology'* (Lacan [1978] 1991: 11). The order of the same had replaced the order of the other. The radical European Freud has been replaced by a conservative

American dream. In critique of Heinz Hartmann and the 'autonomous ego', Lacan rejected the assumptions of a stable ego and attempted to return the discussion to the central conflict of its formation between the id and the superego. According to Lacan, the ego is an illusory unity formed at the 'mirror stage', between 6 and 18 months, when there is recognition of the infant's own image in a mirror and, importantly, it is another person – the parent – who confirms the identification at this moment. The key part of this transformation of the subject is that it is formed through an external identification and it is thus an imaginary construction through the other:

> These notions are opposed by the whole of analytic experience, insofar as it teaches us not to regard the ego as centred on the *perception-consciousness system* or as organized by the 'reality principle' – the expression of a scientific bias most hostile to the dialectic of knowledge – but, rather, to take as our point of departure the *function of misrecognition* that characterizes the ego in all the defensive structures so forcefully articulated by Anna Freud.
>
> (Lacan [1966] 2006: 80)

The entry of the child into the Symbolic order of language is another process through which the subject is formed by otherness. Speech, as Lacan argues, 'is founded in the existence of the Other, the true one, language is so made as to return us to the objectified other ...' (Lacan [1978] 1991: 244). This linking together of structural linguistics and psychological formation is Lacan's historically determined inspiration and it is also the point at which his work opens out to the political climate of 1960s France.[13] It is precisely this aspect that Turkle develops in her own sociological evaluation of May 1968 and the embracing of the Lacanian 'notions that man is constituted by his language, that our discourse embodies the society beyond, and that there is no autonomous ego' (Turkle [1978] 1992: 242). The Lacanian subject is social in its very formation and divided through this very sociality. The decentred subject in Lacan bridges the psychoanalytical and the political. As Frosh notes in his more detailed summary: 'The politics implicit in Lacan's theory are provocative' (Frosh 1999: 150). While Frosh notes the dangers of such an anti-humanist position, he recognises the value of the theory of subjectivity that 'focuses on its structuring in accordance with cultural forces, and which provides an account of the way these forces operate at the deepest levels of the individual's experience' (Frosh 1999: 151). Lacan's linking of the subject and politics has been a central part of the emergence of critical psychology, not least in the jointly authored work *Changing the*

Subject (Henriques *et al.* [1984] 1998), incorporating ideas from other post-structuralists, such as Althusser (1971) and Foucault (1975), in the new challenge to psychology. The question remains why this political subject was not carried into the Anglo-American discourse of the psychology of religion and its disciplinary statements.

Other cultures and the forgotten economy

The silencing of the political economy in the psychoanalytic study of religion becomes even more striking when we observe how the examination of Freud's cultural texts constantly omit this dimension; even as such studies open the space for 'otherness' and the culturally repressed. It would appear that the politics of identity, within studies of psychoanalysis and religion since the 1980s cultural turn, is still unable to see how material exchange and political order cushion the privilege accounts of the culturally shaped religious psyche. The neutrality myth of science is not as dominant in the examination of psychoanalysis, religion and culture and thus cannot explain the continued avoidance. It is my view that the mask of the economic shifts in these later works to a different late modern form of economic obfuscation in the category of 'culture' itself.

I want to take briefly three texts that have a 'cultural' focus within the psychology of religion to map some of the common points of silence. The texts I will examine explore the cultural texts of Freud in relation to religion and emerge at the borders of three distinct areas where economic thought could appear: sociology, feminism and post-Lacan hermeneutics. The critique here is as much about a disciplinary apparatus that limits discursive exploration as an individual blindness to the political economy of a subject. I should add that I take these texts out of admiration for their engagement with the cultural and their attempt to remove Freud's work and the psychology of religion from a restricted individualism. It is the very act of critical adventure beyond the private to the cultural that makes them valuable and necessary parts of a critical psychology, but their position at the threshold of culture makes the absence of serious engagement with political economy even more striking.

In a complex text, that is yet to be fully appreciated for its creative disjunction of disciplines, Peter Homans in his work *The Ability to Mourn* (1989) attempts to show how psychoanalysis emerges out of distinctive social and historical processes, not least the shift in the social order of religious traditions. He argues that psychoanalysis is a 'creative response' to the loss of symbols in the process of secularization and rationalization. While not wishing to construct a 'general theory of culture' (Homans 1989: 5–6) his concern is nonetheless with Western culture and with the traditions of Christianity and Judaism. His argument is that in what he calls the 'cultural texts' of Freud there is 'a profound and mournful sense that the past of Western culture – the common cultures of the West – has been lost' (Homans 1989: 8). Homans's study is striking for its inter-disciplinary courage to think both within and outside sociology and psychology and also for his attempt to locate Freud in the 'social, political and cultural forces' (Homans 1989: 17). Indeed, Homans goes on to argue that psychoanalysis is a social and physical science, pointing out that it 'is unthinkable apart from a social ethos in which science has been institutionalized' (Homans 1989: 211).

Within such a theoretical understanding, it might be assumed that the economic order would be crucially engaged. Homans even tentatively breaks the disciplinary categories by reading Max Weber's thought and life through the psychological apparatus to establish connections with the life of Freud and an echo of economy is heard, but sadly not sustained. While Homans's work constantly brushes up against the economic question, it remains like some forbidden fruit never to be grasped. He entertains Weber's *The Protestant Ethic and the Spirit of Capitalism* as a text reflecting 'comparative cultural studies', but the connection between economy and psychology is never drawn in any detail (Homans 1989: 233). In outlining the tensions in Freud's theory of culture he sees how the psychodynamic understanding is 'welded to the contemporary liberal-democratic ethos' that has created the 'society of psychological man', but there is no rooting of this insight in political economy (Homans 1989: 265). Homans also rightly sees psychological society as holding a 'technologizing of fantasy' in industrialization, but it is never clear why technology is highlighted and the order of finance that sustains it is silenced (Homans 1989: 268, 310). The fantasy of advertising and the screen of television and cinema mask the deeper fantasies of money (see Goodchild 2002).

When Homans, following Lacan, wishes to remove psychoanalysis from the strictures of 'exact science' he makes the important point that 'it is also simply unthinkable apart from a culture in which science and industrialization are the principal elements and that it is completely structured by these elements' (Homans 1989: 295). The 'unthinkable' separation of psychoanalysis from culture takes on a different edge when we realise that today culture is inseparable from the economic forces in the social world, but what is disturbing is why this is 'unthinkable' for those working in the cultural domains of psychological and religious discourse. Homans brings psychology into the social, but the politics of fantasy he articulates are contained by the fantasy of what is impossible to think.

Before concluding this section, it is worth noting two other studies that have highlighted Freud's cultural texts in the psychoanalytic study of religion. First, in James DiCenso's refreshing re-examination of Freud's cultural texts on religion we find a linking of subjectivity and culture, using insights from Lacan, Derrida and Kristeva, what he calls the '*postmodern* theorists' (DiCenso 1999: 13). There is here a distinct shift from Homans's modernity within sociology to the new late modern – some might say late capitalist – discipline of cultural studies (see Jameson 1992). His aim is to reveal an '*other* Freud, concerned with issues of psycho-cultural formation and transformation' (DiCenso 1999: 3).

DiCenso's new hermeneutical reading of Freud certainly brings a richness to the field, but the cultural arena remains limited in its scope. He rightly recognises that Lacan and Kristeva help us to appreciate that the relationship between the cultural, religious and psychoanalytical studies are 'more complex' than has previously been assumed, but the space of the 'cultural' requires greater differentiation. Despite extending the cultural to the religious and the ethical, the generality of the cultural hides its political polemic. For example, he rightly creates new opportunity for cultural critique by recognising the 'constitutive function of symbolic forms' (DiCenso 1999: 144). As he goes on to state in his conclusion: 'We are indeed dependent on cultural forms to provide ideational tools and resources to actualize our human potentialities, and this certainly makes us vulnerable to cultural conditioning' (DiCenso 1999: 146). DiCenso points us in the right direction and adds theoretical weight to the ethical subject in Freud, but the 'cultural' remains seriously under-theorized and its lack of specificity hides important questions. Indeed, we can even go as far to say that the signification of the *cultural* masks the specificity of the material relations. As Terry Eagleton (2003) has shown in relation to cultural studies, there is always a danger that models of the cultural become the short-hand endorsements of the political reality behind them, even if this is never intended. This is not a personal critique of DiCenso, it is rather a critique of the cultural politics of the disciplinary space which controls the individual utterance.

The question of the 'unspeakable' is explored in another illuminating examination of Freud's cultural texts by Diane Jonte-Pace. In her work *Speaking the Unspeakable* (2001), she carries out a detailed textual reading of Freud's work and uncovers a 'counter thesis' to the central Oedipal thesis. The counter thesis is a 'set of sites' or 'complex of ideas' around the themes of mothers, death, Jewishness, the (un)canny and immortality, which are touched upon but never fully articulated in Freud's writing (Jonte-Pace 2001: 74, 107, 120). The central drive of Jonte-Pace's work is to link psyche to society, which in turn reveals the underlying misogyny. Jonte-Pace's brilliant excavation of Freud's texts follows closely Peter Homans's cultural process of mourning in psychoanalysis and she brings this reading of Freud into a cultural dialogue with her own concern with feminism and, in particular, Kristeva. The themes of secularization and rationalization are brought forward and a non-economic Weber echoes the cultural shifts (Jonte-Pace 2001: 129). Unfortunately, like Homans, Jonte-Pace's analysis of society and culture lacks material and economic substance and, while she rightly draws our awareness to the powerful unspoken aspects of our cultural order, she in turn marks out culture without an economy. When Jonte-Pace refers to the 'broader cultural pattern' behind Freud's work there is little sense of how the cultural is constituted (Jonte-Pace 2001: 133, 139).

To be fair to Jonte-Pace, the value of her work is directed to a creative and important reading of Freud that exposes the misogyny within our cultural fantasies, but what is apparent is that Jonte-Pace continues a psychoanalytical closure of the cultural by remaining in the logic of modern disciplinary thinking. In moving beyond the intra-psychic and interpersonal, as Jonte-Pace so rightly does in her discussion, the 'intersections of body, psyche, and society' are never developed at the site of political economy (Jonte-Pace 2001: 3). I am not, as such, asking a question of whether a feminist analysis of cultural misogyny and xenophobia should include an economic question. Valid as such a question may be, we cannot examine everything in every study, but what I am trying to show is that contemporary advances into the examination of 'culture', particularly within texts broadly exploring psychoanalytical readings of religion, do not sufficiently articulate the material conditions and exchanges of economy in the shaping of cultural realities. What I am seeking to entertain is the implication of articulating the economics of cultural life and why this is silenced in the most progressive texts in the study of religion and psychology. This is not a problem of individual interventions it is a problem of the ethics of knowledge and the values that include and exclude categories.

The work of Homans, DiCenso and Jonte-Pace all reflect major advances in thinking about religion, culture and psychoanalysis. Indeed, I would argue they represent one of the most important developments in psychological studies of religion in the last 20 years – the cultural location of the psychology of religion. But for all their incisive analysis and overcoming of simple individualism they do not see how the 'cultural' is now being transformed by the overriding power of economic forces. As Throsby wrestling with the relation between economics and culture has argued: 'Cultural relationships and processes can also be seen to exist within an economic environment and can themselves be interpreted in economic terms' (Throsby 2001: 10). Throsby is, of course, aware that this is a two-way relationship, but this returns us to the murky water of what constitutes the 'culture' and how this term operates along the lines of its own ambiguity in the social world (see Throsby 2001: 3; cf. Williams 1976). I do not wish to reduce culture to economics or turn economics into another protected category, some old-fashioned Marxist misreading, rather I want to see how the power of the knowledge economy has brought us to a point in human history where we are now caught inescapably in a world driven by financial directives, which ethically reshape our ways of knowing. What seems important in this contemporary situation is that the 'plasticity' of our psychoanalytical thinking about religion is also reinforcing such a world by its disciplinary structures. The limits of what a discipline can and cannot say silence the truth of transgressive thinking. What is more alarming is the fact that even in a 'cultural logic' driven by a market society the economic dimension is obfuscated (Jameson 1992).

The psychoanalytic study of religion is able to silence political economy through both its detached discourse of science and its over-embedded discourse of culture. More importantly, the rules of the discourse also manage to silence those voices that connected psychological and religious thought to the economic realm. However, these voices are returning from the past under a new political regime and a different economy of knowledge. In the knowledge economy thought is saturated by the category of economy and there is no exteriority for the subject. The act of avoiding the economic is act of avoiding an acute ethical aspect of contemporary forms of knowledge, because knowledge is now driven by an economic fantasy. The problem now is imagining the possibility of a subject outside the economic. To think economy inside the psychoanalytical theory of religion is to move towards the limits of what can be said inside those discourses of the *same* and to stumble into the unknown of the *other*. It takes us to the heart of the ethics of knowledge and the categories by which we think. It may be that we have to change the discourse, particularly as many scholars of the psychoanalytical study of religion claim not to think politically. Such scholars, in their disciplinary innocence and purity, are leaving those who are not privileged enough to think with such detachment with a far greater wound, drawn from the hidden claws of their scientific and cultural beasts.

In the knowledge economy it is time to articulate the unconscious economy and overcome the excess wastage of thought found in our discourses of satisfaction, sustained as it is by the limits of the disciplinary imagination. Before we can accomplish such an exercise, inside such a critical project, we must first establish in greater detail the hidden ideology behind psychological discourse and its related category of religion. In the next two chapters I will examine the protected and privileged categories in humanistic and cognitive psychology. I will show how they carry forward the ethical-political values of Western political economy in their modes of representation and how the inter-disciplinary object of 'religion' can facilitate and mask this order of power.

4 Maslow's economy of religious experience

People know what they do; they frequently know why they do what they do; but what they don't know is what what they do does.

Michel Foucault (1982) 'Personal Communication' in Dreyfus, H.L. and Rabinow, P., *Michel Foucault: Beyond Structuralism and Hermeneutics*, Harvester Wheatsheaf, p. 187

It is also a challenge to all intellectuals, or at least those who express a commitment to democracy, to take a long, hard look in the mirror and to ask themselves in whose interests, and for what values, do they do their work.

Robert McChesney (1999) in Chomsky, N., *Profit Over People*, Seven Stories Press, p. 14

The link between economy and psychology shows the correlation between models of the self and the material values of a culture. It shows that if psychological theory operates without an awareness of its embedded economic foundation (the non-economic factors of economy, to recall my earlier discussion) it can easily carry forward the values of its host economy without critique. The development of psychological theory in post-war American capitalism is a good example of this fusion of psychology and economy, not least because it also shows how the categories of 'religion' and 'spirituality' contribute to this process. If psychology changes its nature within American culture then its application to older forms of introspection (found within, for example, the traditions of Buddhism, Judaism and Christianity) will reveal the contrasting models of the self and the shift in authority to make statements about being human. It will reveal the shift from a metaphysical order to a material order, from the pre-modern to the modern ideology of human definition and subjectivity. In this chapter I want to explore how the 'psychology of religion' in humanistic psychology acts as a hidden cultural reordering of introspection (thinking about the self and experience) for a capitalistic culture. I want to show how psychology adapts the language of older forms of introspection and how it shifts the ethical-political values in its theorizing for a new economy of knowledge. In addition, I want to show how the ideas of 'religion' and 'spirituality' facilitate and constitute the psychologization of experience.

In each success age, the knowledge of what it is to be human is a central site of contestation, because to claim authority on the nature of being human is the technology of government.[1] To know what we are is to know what we should be doing or, more precisely, to construct and politically imagine a discourse of what we are is to convince people voluntarily to become 'subject' to such knowledge; even if this is by the sheer force of institutional practice. General psychology, for instance, provides the anthropological sub-structure for capitalism, because it provides a utility and measurement of human functioning and performance for modes of production and consumption. This is, to recall Dumont's (1986: 26–7) conceptual distinction, the logic of an 'in-worldly', as opposed to an 'out-worldly' individualism. The unity of psychology and capitalism, established through the politics of 'in-worldly individualism', was not simply an economic alliance, but an operation of the nation state to order populations.

If populations were to be ordered it was also necessary to pacify potential revolutionary discourses, which may disrupt the economic order. It was therefore necessary, as Nikolas Rose (1996: 113–14) has shown, to 'psychologize' society through a network of institutions and practices. The rise of the nation state is, therefore, also the assimilation of all aspects of life – the policing of life – through technologies of the psychologized self. This policing of life required a knowledge of self which would undermine the rationality of existing discourses of being human, or at least pacify such categories of knowledge for the service of the state. It is my contention in this chapter that the gradual psychologization of experience and the embedding of the category of 'religion' inside such a process in the twentieth century, is the rejection of an 'out-worldly individualism' found in Christianity and Judaism; it was part of the disarming of a theological knowledge of the self and related forms of introspective discourse. The psychologized subject of capitalism provided the technology for rethinking the ontology of ourselves through the acts of measurement and analysis, which closed down the liminality of self found in the 'sacrifice of the self', which Foucault ([1980] 1999: 180) identified in Christian history.

I am not suggesting a return to a theological self as such, or that 'out-worldly individualism' is not without its own order of control and oppression, but rather setting up a contrast with types of subjectivity as a way to show the rise of a capitalist self and the economic reframing of the discourse of self in the 'psychology of religion'; or rather the psychological *creation* of a 'religious' subject. The reordering of introspection is part of an economic adaptation that brings about institutional shifts within the cultural logic of the self, which operates upon the creation of the inter-dependent objects 'psychology' and 'religion'. These objects appear to reflect different institutional orders of power, but the strategic setting up of the categories allows a shift in the order of self and economy. This is carried out in a double movement in the 'psychology of religion'. The category of 'religion' stabilizes the disparate traditions of introspective experience found in the institutional networks of Christianity, Judaism and Buddhism (the amorphous traditions that are the focus of the texts I will study) and then reorganises them by superimposing the institutional categories of psychological discourse embedded in American capitalism.

In the ideological shifts of the twentieth century, this double movement shows how the critique of the category of 'religion' can never innocently protect the methodological discourse, which is also implicated in the economic reordering of introspection. Reading the introspective traditions of, for example, Christianity inside psychology is made easier by locating them in the modern category of 'religion'. It enables knowledge to be abstractly refashioned according to the new economy of self and, importantly, brings about an institutional blending with, rather than threat to, the culturally dominant order.[2] Psychology and 'religion' were, therefore, deceptive friends to pre-modern forms of introspection. The Christian institutions, particularly in their pastoral formations, did not recognise that such an alliance had wider political ramifications for the construction of a 'religious subject'.

The appropriation of the discourse of 'spirituality'[3] by psychology in the twentieth century is one instance of the psychologization of human beings for the services of capitalism and the undermining of pre-modern traditions of introspection (see Carrette and King 2005). This is not to presume that psychologists or theologians were always aware of what they were doing, but to recognise that the psychologization of life provided a new currency for thinking about being human. The ideas of 'religion' and 'spirituality' assume a particular importance in the history of Western capitalism because they allow American psychology to invade the territory of older forms of introspection more efficiently and ease the epistemological takeover of experience. In this process, the 'out-worldly' individualism of pre-modern introspection is converted into the capitalistic utility of psychological knowledge through the category of 'religion'. In the twentieth century, the trajectory of such psychologization of introspective discourse can be traced through the work of William James, Gordon Allport and Abraham Maslow in the USA. Even though they would not necessarily sanction the political ideologies that supported their work, they were nonetheless, due to their popularity, key players in the shift of introspection towards a private, individual construction. In order to understand how this shift occurred, I will examine one of the key figures in the cultural transformation of such a discourse, one historical vignette of a complex historical transformation of introspection and its dependency on the category of 'religion'.

Abraham Maslow

I want to demonstrate the psychological shift in the representation of subjectivity, in the ideological space of individualism, by focusing on the work of Abraham Maslow (1908–70) – often regarded as the most significant psychologist in the mid-twentieth century. I want to concentrate on his work, not because he initiated the move towards the psychologization of introspection, but because his work in the USA reflects a very poignant ideological transformation inside American capitalism. Indeed, I would want to go further and suggest that Maslow's psychology was caught in a wider post-war market demand for a rethinking of traditional values in order to make them compatible with capitalistic ideology and the material culture. In this sense, Maslow's alignment with the values of American capitalism is not some personal ideological crusade, but rather an institutional-cultural reordering of knowledge. Indeed, Maslow's gradual awareness, as a culturally sensitive and compassionate man, of the dangers of his own psychologization of introspection is witness to the hidden ethical-political currents shaping his discourse. Unfortunately, he failed sufficiently to pinpoint the problems in the market because of his inability to see psychology as embedded in economy.

I will begin by giving a brief context to Maslow's psychological accounts of 'religion' and then show how he categorised the 'religious' as 'psychological' in a discursive political battle for authority over experience. This psychological categorisation is the attempt to shift the register of experience out of a pre-modern realm into the modern 'psychological-capitalistic realm' – that is a realm of representing experience through models of self which ideologically restrict the subject to measurement, management and mass-consumption, instead of opening or losing the self in ideas of liminality, sacrifice and illusion, terms which signify the paradox, construction, or non-essentialism of self found in more ancient forms of introspection.

In conclusion, what I am suggesting is that psychology, and Maslow's psychology in particular, is an ideological reconfiguration of certain forms of pre-modern introspection, which prepares the ground for creating the psychological object of 'religion' as a product of individual consumption; something that allows for the emergence of the discourse of 'spirituality' (Carrette and King 2005). What this means is that Maslow is taking the 'out-worldly individualism' of 'self-in-relation' to a non-empirical metaphysical ordering (self in relation to God, sacrifice, illusion) as self-referential statements of fixed, measurable, essences (self as object and unit of consumption). This reorders introspection as a private, separate and distinct mode of operation, which can be identified, measured and sold as attitudes (products), rather than seeing the self as built in relation to some order or 'truth' outside the self (that which is not fully known or understood by the self).

The central philosophical problem of the self imagining itself or testing itself is that it is caught in the self-reflexive ideology of its own imagination and categories of knowledge. Theological institutions, for example, can limit the horizon of self as much as psychological institutions, according to different orders of governmentality, but there is a strategic value of holding an open model that overcomes the self-illusion, whether this is found in a metaphysical, or existential, order of 'truth'. I am, thus, not upholding pre-modern modelling of self over modernist psychology, but rather showing strategically how pre-modern forms of introspection hold a corrective against capitalistic forms of self, even as they may hold different problems of limitation and restriction.

The other problem we witness in the psychology of *religion* is the extrapolation of concepts from different historical traditions, without the context and processes of formation, and (falsely) assuming that they describe the same experience. This shift would eventually provide the platform for the so-called 'New Age' market of 'spirituality' and the post-Thatcherite management use of 'spirituality' for marketing and personal/commercial growth.[4] By focusing on Maslow we can unravel the intricate relationship between psychology, capitalism and the psychological making of 'religion' and 'spirituality'.

Hidden relations: capitalism, psychology and religion

In his 1987 work *Religious Thought and Modern Psychologies*, Don Browning attempts to examine the ethical dimensions of modern psychology through an analysis of the metaphors embedded in the conceptual system of psychologies. He believes traditional 'religion' and modern psychology have a special relationship because 'both of them provide concepts and technologies for the ordering of the interior life' (Browning 1987: 2). He goes on to state that psychologies are 'instances of religio-ethical thinking', 'mixed disciplines' containing religious, ethical and scientific discourses (Browning 1987: 8). While recognising the value of the dialogue between theology and psychology, Browning believes it is necessary to develop a critical perspective. However, he does not follow traditions in the sociology of knowledge from the Frankfurt School, which suggest that psychologies are epiphenomena of social processes, such as capitalism. Rather, partly following Weber, he argues that modern psychologies were 'responding and coping with the forces of advanced capitalism but indeed not shaped by these forces in all aspects' (Browning 1987: 9). They are, as he states later, '*responses* to the forces and trends of capitalistic societies' and thus 'are in the background of these psychologies' (Browning 1987: 241). As Browning continues:

> Capitalistic societies form an agenda with which the psychologies are implicitly or explicitly dealing. Capitalistic societies do not necessarily dictate the responses of these psychologies, but they do present a pressure with which, in their varying images of human fulfilment, these psychologies attempt to cope.

While Browning identifies the correlation between the 'values of individualism' and capitalism in psychology, he seriously underestimates the critical project required to interrogate such a relationship. His work fails to draw out the ethical implications of the 'agenda' or the sense in which psychology is a 'response' to capitalism and the way the category of 'religion' becomes part of the psychological reordering of introspection. In many ways, capitalism is still a background context for psychology in Browning's assessment. He, for example, argues that humanistic psychology is 'partially explained by its continuity with significant strands of individualism that have characterised American history' (Browning 1987: 64). Even if this picture is 'partial' it still needs to be taken seriously in ways which Browning does not explore. The inability to foreground the ideology of humanistic psychology, for example, is the continuing desire to preserve the texts of psychology from political scrutiny.

Interestingly, Browning's work appears at the beginnings of the emergence of 'critical psychology' and he cannot therefore appreciate the technicalities of later writings in critical psychology.[5] If Browning wished to develop some ethical evaluation of psychology in dialogue with theology then he cannot simply dismiss the links with capitalism so easily. In fact, Browning's failure to carry through his analysis only poses the problem more sharply and fails to register how the 'conditions of emergence' of psychology reflected strongly the social processes of capitalism. He does, nonetheless, acknowledge that critical psychology sees the models of previous psychologies as 'unreflective, naïve, and philosophically and ethically immature if not downright dangerous (Browning 1987: 244). Nonetheless, his conclusion that critical psychology and descriptive and normative value-free psychology need to work together only waters down the ethical commitment, allowing psychologies to flourish even in their abuses. He is, however, rightly sensitive about the fact that writers in the arena of critical psychology 'seem to find no place for the role of religion' (Browning 1987: 245); although this avoidance can now be read in a more nuanced way when we consider how the category of 'religion' sustains the economic order of psychological introspection.

While there is now evidence of the need to take theological history seriously in the formation of psychological discourse and of the need to overcome the hubris of theological models of the self to challenge psychology, Browning reveals an extraordinary anxiety about the loss of the 'deep metaphors' of pre-modern introspection in a capitalistic psychology. Such a concern emphasizes the importance of taking a closer examination of the relationship between capitalism, psychology and the category of 'religion'. Maslow's so-called 'third-force', or humanistic psychology, of the 1950s and 1960s serves this purpose. It not only seeks a kind of translation of introspection into psychological discourse, but it is also firmly grounded in the context of American capitalism and the making of a 'psychology of religion', having impacts on business and other organisational structures. It is possible to suggest that Maslow provides a new 'currency' for reading 'religion' and 'spirituality' in the psychological market place, a kind of 'motivational' model for market forces and a hierarchy for capitalistic need. If critical thinking is to be effective in its analysis of self and economy it can no longer hide how the categories of 'psychology' and 'religion' anchor the reordering of introspection in capitalist society. The category of 'religion', which often simply means 'the churches' in Maslow's (1971: 362) work, is part of the cultural ideology of psychology, it becomes part of the double movement of psychological institutions in the mutation of pre-modern introspection.

Maslow's psychology

According to Ruth Cox (1987: 264), Maslow 'captured the spirit of his age' and his psychology was 'woven into the very fabric of American life'. While

Cox offered this as a positive afterword to the third edition of Maslow's 1954 *Motivation and Personality*, the very fusion of Maslow's psychology with American life is also its critical downfall. Maslow's psychology, for instance, is not born in the two-thirds world (as the developing countries of the world can be more adequately represented) or even in the land of his parents in Eastern Europe. Maslow's psychology is reflective of the optimistic post-war American political and economic climate and cannot be separated from such a context. It captures a period of economic optimism, increased production and individual consumer power. Maslow rejects the angst of European culture in Freud and the mechanistic models of Watson as negative evaluations of the human being and sets about a political reconfiguration of 'motivation' as human potential.

This focus on 'motivation' is, therefore, not simply a reflection of the biological foundations of his work and a development of Kurt Goldstein's organismic theory, which recognised a drive towards wholeness in brain injured soldiers from the First World War, it is a social statement of capitalistic desire hidden in the fabric of the so-called 'science' of his psychology. Maslow's theory of motivation shifts, in a post-war consumer society, from biology to social manifesto, particularly in its mirroring of the models of economic production. The ideas of 'deficiency' and 'growth' motivation in individuals, the distinction between 'becoming' and 'being' reflect this underlying 'efficiency' model of self. The subsequent establishment of a hierarchy of needs, which has 'self-actualisation' as its highest achievement, is a clear adoption of the values of individualism and the American dream. The capitalistic sub-structure of Maslow's psychology reflects the ideological weight of knowledge behind the self in Western culture, but what is more significant for our concerns is how such notions of 'self-actualisation', 'peak-experience' and 'B-cognition' have all played a key part in the creation of late capitalistic spiritualities. Maslow is not alone in his contribution to the commodification of introspection through the 'psychology of religion', but his concepts and framing of 'religion' and experience through the instrumental operations of psychological knowledge captures the wider representational shift of 'religion' into the psychological machine of capitalism.

Modelling psychological-religious experience

According to Maslow's biographer Edward Hoffman, after the 1954 publication of *Motivation and Personality* – the work which established Maslow's hierarchy of needs – Maslow started to gather material on so-called ecstatic and mystical experience, reading works from Eastern traditions, Krishnamurti, Watts and Jung, or, as Maslow phrased it, 'the immense literatures of mysticism, religion, art, creativeness, love, etc' (Hoffman [1988] 1999: 205–6; Maslow 1962: 67). Such reading was also accompanied by personal interviews with 80 people, 50 'unsolicited letters' and written responses by 190 college students to a set of instructions, something which reflects a distorted sample analysis involved in Maslow's work (Maslow 1962: 67). Hoffman believed no one had gathered more material on this area of 'religious' experience since William James (Hoffman [1988] 1999: 206). He listed 'transcendent' experience under the heading of '(Inner) timelessness' and identified 20 features in his 1956 paper 'Cognition of Being in the Peak-Experiences', later appearing as Chapter 6 in his 1962 *Toward a Psychology of Being*.

Maslow's overall aim was to extract from pre-modern introspective history aspects of experience for a different historical ideology and reposition them in the discursive structures of psychology. Rejecting the move by nineteenth century atheism to eradicate everything of 'religion', he states in his short work *Religions, Values and Peak-Experiences* in 1964: 'One could say that the nineteenth-century atheist had burnt down the house instead of remodelling it' (Maslow [1964] 1976: 18). The specificity of Maslow's 'remodelling' of experience is an extraordinary – and in some senses blatantly honest – adaptation of ideas of the self for the purposes of psychology. He was trying to reconfigure experience once framed by pre-modern modes of introspective discourse into a new category of 'religious' discourse inside the (pseudo) scientific analysis of psychological facts. His analysis of experience is in many ways a territorial takeover of older forms of introspection through the 'psychology of religion'. It involves the positioning of introspective experiences within Christianity, Judaism and Buddhism under the sign of 'religion', then reading these in terms of the category of 'religion' and then finally eradicating the artificial sign of 'religion' to allow psychology a dominant space in the cultural order of introspective representation.

Before taking a closer look at his use of the category 'religion' in his *Religions, Values and Peak-Experiences*, it is interesting to note *how* he framed his written instructions for data gathering for his earlier exploration of peak experiences. The instruction stated:

> I would like you to think of the most *wonderful* experience or experiences of your life; *happiest* moments, *ecstatic* moments, moments of *rapture*, perhaps from being in love, or from listening to music or suddenly 'being-hit' by a book or a painting, or from some great creative moment. First list these. And then try to tell me how you feel in such *acute* moments,

how you feel differently from the way you feel at other times, how you are at the moment a *different* person in some ways.

(Maslow 1962: 67, emphasis added)

From this instruction we can easily see how the experience is remodelled in terms of private, intense experience. Maslow has already rewritten his concepts in terms of the psychological self. The peak experience is wonderful, happy, ecstatic, rapturous, acute and leaves you different. The extraordinary element of this analysis is that, in reaction to Freud and behaviourism, Maslow has turned and fetishised the positive dimensions of experience – 'high level of maturation, health and self-fulfilment' as opposed to Freud's 'deficiency' model of neurosis, anxiety, pathology – but in the very process he has eliminated the historical fabric of experience. To highlight the 'feel good' dimensions of experience reflects an economic possibility that the conditions of expression and experience carry the value of the positive experience. It also creates the idea of 'religion' according to euphoric dimensions, rather than the complex patterns of formation found in many cultural traditions, which develop from the integration and meditation on suffering. The agonies of Job, the emptiness of the desert, the dark night of the soul and a theology of crucifixion, to recall the Judaic-Christian tradition, have all been eliminated. Maslow fails to see how 'peak' experiences could co-exist with more painful and testing events. The most rapturous experience may also be the most painful and frightening, as in some near-death experiences or the witnessing of a dying relative. Maslow's 'remodelling' is therefore creating a 'religious' experience for the purposes of a particular politic of optimism and euphoria found in an affluent culture – the hopeful dynamics of consumption without responsibility for suffering.

It is also significant that Maslow notes that no one responding to his survey reported his full 'syndrome'. This is problematic not only because of the issues of correspondence to his 'impressionistic, ideal, "composite photograph"', but because experience has been rewritten in terms of 'syndrome' (Maslow 1962: 67). The remodelling of experience in terms of 'syndrome' is an example of Rose's (1996; 1998) 'psychologization' of experience, the reading of all human experiences in terms of psychological discourse. The extent to which 'syndrome' can be grafted on pre-modern introspective discourses shows the powerful dimensions of Maslow's use of the category of 'religion' to do this work. As Frager notes, Maslow saw the revolution he and others led in psychology as 'solidly established' in 1968. 'Furthermore', as Maslow argues, 'it is beginning to be *used*, especially in education, industry, religion, organisation and management therapy and self-improvement ...' (Frager 1987: xxxv). Here we see the application of psychological knowledge becoming parasitic on existing discourses and 'remodelling' them to the concerns of a different knowledge sustainable for a new society, a society determined by instrumental rationality, efficiency regimes and market forces.

The remodelling of pre-modern introspective experience (an out-worldly event) in terms of peak-experiences (an in-worldly event) makes it a consumer product (an attitude to be sold), because it separates the 'experience' from the 'tradition' and its practices, which form the experience. There is a false assumption that 'experience' in one realm of discourse is translatable into another, as if the 'experience' is free-floating and easily definable as a distinct consumable unit, which can be siphoned off from different cultures and traditions and repackaged. This representation of experience, as we saw in the introduction, is a rhetorical and institutional reorientation. The illusion of psychology is the assumption that it is offering a neutral (scientific) judgement, when it is involved in a politics of experience – the power struggle to develop an authoritative discourse on experience by locating it within a different institutional/conceptual structure. Maslow's work reflects some of the worst aspects of this 'remodelling' in humanistic psychology, unconsciously blending his psychology with the cultural atmosphere of American capitalistic values in a distinctive and accessible manner. To appreciate this in more detail we must look more closely at his commentary on 'religious' experience from 1964.

Remodelling the transcendent

The key strategy of Maslow's appropriation of older forms of introspective language for psychology can be seen in his use and setting up of the category 'religion' to frame and hold a specific kind of psychological experience. This is a process of retaining the language and concepts of interiority and introspection from Christian, Jewish and Buddhist traditions and removing the out-worldly signification, so that it operates according to psychological regimes of knowledge. It is the creation of an epistemological rupture of experience through the orders of psychology and its correlated concept 'religion'. The move towards a psychological representation of 'religion' and spirituality in Maslow's work was initiated by his concern that those who wished to establish a legal ban on prayers in schools were somehow seen as not interested in 'spiritual values'. Maslow, in the attempt to claim institutional power for psychological organisations, sought to take 'spiritual values' away from the church by rejecting what he saw as 'the erroneous definition and concept of spiritual values' (Maslow [1964] 1976: 3). Maslow thus starts a battle to take over introspective discourse from organised 'Religion' (with, as he declares, a capital R to distinguish it from it practices) for the victory of psychology – that is to take over the power of older forms of introspective discourse and bring a new authority to the psychological institutions and practices. He rejects, in propagandist terms, the domination by organised 'Religion' of '*the* path' to a life of righteousness, justice and the good. As he states, in a revealing footnote:

> As a matter of fact, this identity is so profoundly built into the English language that it is almost impossible to speak of the 'spiritual life' (a distasteful phrase to a scientist, and especially to a psychologist) without using the vocabulary of traditional religion. There just isn't any other satisfactory language yet.
>
> (Maslow [1964] 1976: 4, n.1)

The 'yet' here is very important, because Maslow and others create a hybrid language fitting together notions of 'religious' with psychological concepts – a takeover strategy in the battle for authority. What is remarkable about this takeover is that it created a subsequent ambivalence in Maslow when the clergy and rabbis within America started to dominate his audiences. As Hoffman points out:

> Not surprisingly, Maslow's long-standing disdain for religion initially made him uneasy in the company of clergy and religionists who flocked to his lectures on peak-experiences and the B-values. It was strange to him to speak in churches, but the admiration he felt from his audiences – mostly liberal Protestants, including Unitarians, and some ecumenical Catholics – was very real.
>
> (Hoffman [1988] 1999: 245)

The brilliance of Maslow's takeover of introspective language for psychology was that it gave the impression it was in the service of the church, but paradoxically it undermined the authority of the church from the inside. Once the churches started to use psychological registers within and alongside its own institutionalized theological categories it gave away its authority to speak the 'truth' about human experience and became the host for the parasite of psychological discourse. Maslow's battle, of course, was part of a wider war going on between the pre-modern language of the churches and the ideology of the modern state apparatus, coupled as it is with a regime of science and technology. While modern physics challenged Christian cosmology, psychology reordered Christian anthropology and ontology. Unlike William James – whose work *The Will to Believe* Maslow regarded as 'the last despairing rationalisation of a previous believer in God' – Maslow eradicated the mystery of experience and read it back into human potentiality (Hoffman [1988] 1999: 38–9). As Maslow ([1964] 1976: 4) remarked: 'I want to demonstrate that spiritual values have a naturalistic meaning, that they are not the exclusive possession of organised churches, that they do not need supernatural concepts to validate them'.

A less critical reading of Maslow might suggest his work was a gallant effort to rescue 'spiritual' values for a society rejecting them, something the so-called 'New Age' movement claims as its own moral authority, but these movements are hiding the more sinister monopoly of psychologized 'truth', the operation of the category of 'religion' in such reordering and the allegiance to forms of capitalism. The new patterns of introspection are playing with a consumer mentality which Maslow – somewhat innocently – initiates in his work, a consumer mentality that creates notions of 'religion' and the 'spiritual' inside the psychological for redistribution. This redistribution occurs by bringing experience into the 'realm of human knowledge', that is to make it 'objective', 'public' and 'shared' (Maslow [1964] 1976: 6). The very act of making introspection amenable to an 'objective' and 'public' analysis of science relocates the experience according to a utility of purpose for modern institutions. Maslow's psychology attempts to establish an efficiency and refinement of experience through the psychological idea of 'religion', which makes it useful for business and the processes of capitalistic production and consumption.

'Motivational' factors are rewritten in terms of commerce and competition and there is a subtle elision of ideas, especially when an increase in human potential is indistinguishable from an increase in capital. It is always the utilization of motivation and potential towards capital not any other social task. I will return to this later, but what we see in Maslow is an efficient relocation of experience according to a set of tactical manoeuvres in the process of psychologization. We can organise these tactical manoeuvres into four areas: the rejection of those institutions that support pre-modern (non-psychological) forms of introspection, the extrapolation of ideas from traditions of introspection that are useful for psychological individualism, the territorial claim to the 'transcendent' – one of the most powerful conceptual terms of Western metaphysics – and, finally, the repositioning of experience inside psychological discourse – the final embracing of capitalistic determinism. It is worth looking at these hidden strategies in more detail, especially as the category of psychology is often over-protected in the related critique of the category 'religion'.

Tradition, science and religion

Maslow's first move in the process of psychologization, through the twin ideas of 'religion' and 'spirituality', is to reject tradition and the institutions that preserve pre-modern introspection. However, when Maslow says society can 'no longer rely on tradition', 'cultural habit' and the 'unanimity of belief', he is unaware of how traditions operate and how he sets up the very dichotomization of 'science' and 'religion' he tries to overcome. In this sense, Maslow's arguments are constructed on a manipulation of knowledge and language for advancing the ideology and authority of psychology. Maslow's argument is that the split between 'science' and 'religion' misguides 'science' and 'religion', but this false distinction is part of his own double movement of creating and collapsing terms in order to valorize the psychological. In line with Nietzsche and James before him, Maslow rejected institutional 'Religion', as dogmatic sheep-following, it was seen as 'arbitrary and authoritarian' (Maslow [1964] 1976: 14). The separation of the dogmatic and oppressive 'Religion', and the siphoning off of a set of valued 'religious' experiences from the same imaginary zone, allows a political reordering of the institutional locus for the authority of experience.

Once Maslow has marked out the territory of what constitutes 'Religion' and 'religious experiences', he then carries out his second move of psychologization by isolating those aspects of 'religion' most amenable to reinforcing a psychological self, what he identifies as the 'core' aspect in terms of 'naturalised' states of the psychological condition. According to Maslow, the 'core' of 'religion' – significantly – is read as 'private' and 'individual', which enables Maslow to isolate the institutional authority and the traditions of communities to an atomistic unit of the psychological self (Maslow [1964] 1976: 27–8). Such a model, to some extent echoes William James's analysis of individual 'religious' experience in his *The Varieties of Religious Experience* (1902), but where James consciously offers an 'arbitrary' working definition and respects the limits of his project Maslow offers no such qualifications inside his own psychologization.[6] Maslow is emphatic about the 'essential' and 'intrinsic' aspects of 'religious' experience. He argues that the 'nucleus of every known high religion ... has been the private, lonely, personal illumination, revelation, or ecstasy of some acutely sensitive prophet or seer', which it 'subsumes' under revelation, the mystical and the ecstatic or transcendent experience – what Maslow ([1964] 1976: 19) coined 'peak-experience'. The force in which he rejects institutional 'Religion' is even stronger than James. As Maslow ([1964] 1976: 28) powerfully argues: 'As a consequence, all the paraphernalia of organized religion – buildings and specialized personnel, rituals, dogmas, ceremonials, and the like – are to the "peaker" secondary, peripheral, and of doubtful value in relation to the intrinsic and essential religious or transcendent experience'.

The erosion of institutional 'Religion' and the assertion of the psychological state above community, tradition and social rituals is a central move in the psychological privatisation of experience. As Maslow ([1964] 1976: 28) goes onto acknowledge, 'each "peaker" discovers, develops, and retains his *own religion*'. The creation of a *private* 'religion' is the key category move of the psychological experience for a new economy of self. It brings Maslow's psychological evangelism into a direct relationship with the wider trends of American capitalism. What is even more interesting is the way he builds his argument openly to appeal to the American political climate of the 1960s Cold War in his attempt to eradicate those communities he constitutes under the sign of the 'religious':

> I may go so far as to say that characteristically (and I mean not only the religious organisations but also parallel organisations like the Communist Party or like revolutionary groups) these organisations can be seen as a kind of punch card or IBM version of an original revelation or mystical experience or peak-experience to make it suitable for group use and for administrative convenience.
>
> (Maslow [1964] 1976: 22)

'Religious' organisations are linked with Communism and analogies made to IBM. This rhetoric is a powerful force in engendering the regime of psychological knowledge. The irony, of course, is that Maslow's psychological structure is more of an IBM version, a distilled and abstracted template of complex traditions held within the signification of 'religion'. It shows how grouping experiences under the category of 'religion' allows for an easier political reordering of experience under the authority of psychological institutions. Maslow wants to appropriate and reformulate older categories, such as the 'mystical', inside the psychological to create a new economy of self and experience.[7] By separating experience and language, Maslow is able to essentialize the categories of introspection, assuming the existence of experience in some kind of Platonic realm. He obviously forgets the historical conditions of experience and the way concepts are fashioned by communities in each historical period. The key fact is the stabilizing of concepts *as* psychological. The concept of an original revelation or peak experience detached from the cultural environment raises the question of whether one can have such a 'raw unmediated experience' (Katz 1978: 22–74), but the psychological hermeneutic is the register of Maslow's values, even as he is unaware of how it reveals his own embedded location in the socio-economic making of the self in American culture.

History and culture create and shape experience. Experience is, as I discussed in the introduction, the conscious register of events in time and space, which by definition cannot be extrapolated from their conditions of emergence. To argue that experience is inwardly driven according to psychological events and not social ones is not only a binary valuation, it also creates the market conditions for the 'supermarket of spiritualities', the 'pick and mix' mentality of 'private' religious ideas and practices. Such a model means that everyone has their own 'private religion' created from their own 'private experience' as potential units of consumption. However much Maslow might suggest self-actualisation brings about compassion and social concern, his psychologization is a serious misunderstanding of social values, shared rituals and symbolic practices. To argue that something called 'religious' experience can be extrapolated from, for example, the Christian community is a failure to realise that psychology is itself a communal practice with its own rituals of performance, institutions and 'high priests'.[8] What Maslow is doing is using a certain ideological rhetoric to bring about a different order of power-knowledge, the psycho-politics of a post-war capitalist culture, against the weight of the reified cultural traditions of Judaism and Christianity.

My own counter-discourse, in this examination of Maslow, uses a different ideological rhetoric to bring 'psychology' under critical examination in the same way others have already rightly raised suspicion over the category of 'religion', which as we have seen always dovetails with other conceptual orders. Rather than protect the category of 'psychology' as the privileged category, to recall my reading of Proudfoot (1985), we can see how it reveals a different ethical-politic of experience in Western thought. By showing the complexity of introspection, the ideology of psychology can be questioned and ways of undermining capitalistic constructions of the self can be established. By using the history of introspective ideas we can find a political resource for rethinking the nature of psychological knowledge; it enables us to see the emperor's new clothes in the interaction of economy and self-knowledge. In this sense, history provides ethical resources for critically re-imagining psychology and capitalism; it also enables us to question those who isolate the category of 'religion' without awareness of their own valuation of self and economy inside the order of the psychological.[9] It underlines, with Foucault, how 'the self is nothing else than the historical correlation of the technology built in our history' (Foucault [1980] 1999: 181).

In order to remove the power from pre-modern models of introspection, Maslow found an affective way to undermine the value of such traditions through the discursive category of 'religion', but the language games extended to other conceptual shifts. This he does by making a third move in the psychologization process, the territorial claim to the 'transcendent'. This psychological reductive move occurs when he states that so-called 'supernatural revelation' can be seen as 'perfectly natural, human peak-experiences' (Maslow [1964] 1976: 20). The 'truth' of experience is taken outside theological authority and positioned within human (psychological) experience. The categories of psychological experience become essentalized psychological events. Echoing Huxley's perennial philosophy, Maslow makes the imperialistic move in stating that 'all religions are the same in their essence and always have been the same' (Maslow [1964] 1976: 20). Maslow has now universalised psychological knowledge and taken the imperialistic Western move in assuming that all human experience and all senses of the self are the same, irrespective of culture and history.

If such a move was not sufficient, Maslow then sets up a division between 'non-theistic religious people' and 'conventionally religious people' and makes the claim that the former have '*more* religious experiences' than the latter (Maslow [1964] 1976: 30). This is an extraordinary move that uses the imagined *quantity* of the abstract idea 'religious' experience as a register of value. The logic is deeply flawed, not only in assuming 'religiousness' is a separate and distinct process from everyday life, but also that there is something called 'religion' which can be identified as such and can be separated from culture.[10] It would in effect be like the Catholic church claiming that you could have more psychological experiences in non-psychological people, which is an absurd statement.

Maslow continues this line of argument by claiming that the individual who struggles to create 'a system of faith' has a more 'serious' relationship to values, ethics and life-philosophy, but as that 'system' – and note the irony of this word, in so far as a 'system' implies a worked out tradition of theological reflection – could be anything from personal fascism to hedonism. The individualism of creating a 'faith' can only support a system which promotes the self-creating faiths as valuable to its efficiency, notably a regime that promotes a diversity of products for strengthening the market. Maslow, therefore, uses frequency and depth as ways of rejecting organised 'Religion' and then makes the claim that '"orthodox religion" de-sacralizes much of life' (Maslow [1964] 1976: 33). Maslow is now in an all-out attack on institutional 'Religion'. He argues that 'religion' separates the 'transcendent and the secular-profane'. He then appeals to Eastern traditions to show that the 'religious' and the 'secular', the sacred and the profane, are not separate, but Maslow's entire argument is built on the assumption that these groups called 'religions' are claiming something different to naturalise psychological events. The contradictions abound, to reveal the polemical nature of Maslow's 'scientific' project.

Maslow's work reaches even more confused levels when – the exciting – peak experience is contrasted with habitual 'religious' practices, the latter dulled through 'familiarization and repetition' (Maslow [1964] 1976: 34). He argues that the 'transcendent' or 'religious' experience occurs more regularly *outside* traditional 'Religion' because of the repetition in institutional rituals. The splits and dichotomization he criticises are brought into full view. It is a rhetorical set of gestures to locate experience in a different institutional order of power. He even makes the claim, in a footnote which undermines his entire essentialized position, that 'it is easier to be "pure" outside an organisation, whether religious, political, economic, or for that matter, scientific. And yet we cannot do without organisations' (Maslow [1964] 1976: 33). His recognition that we cannot do without 'organisations' undermines this attempt to extrapolate a 'raw' experience from the fabric of institutions. The constant reference to the 'transcendent' is also a reflection of the way Maslow is dependent on the creation of a notion of 'religious' tradition in the very act of rejecting it. His entire argument is nothing more than a psychological polemic for privatising experience for an American market, not least for a generation of college students disillusioned with the past.

The fourth and final move towards psychologization comes when he repositions experience in the psychological space. He sets up a distinction between the 'naturalistic' and 'supernatural', without giving any sense of what these terms mean in practice, and argues that all the dimensions of the latter category are reflections of the capacity of human beings. He wants, for example, to find a scientific view of the 'transcendent', but the language is under great strain at this point (Maslow [1964] 1976: 44). Even Maslow thinks the 'semantic confusion' is difficult to work out. He believes, appealing to Paul Tillich's theology of Being, that 'all the concepts which have been traditionally "religious" are redefined and then used in a very different way' (Maslow [1964] 1976: 45). Tillich, of course, did provide a different ontology for theology and was sympathetic to psychoanalysis, but the move to the singular psychological referent did not occur in his work. In

Tillich ([1952] 1980), the psychoanalytic insights are partly cushioned and extended by his allegiance to existentialism.

Maslow believes that that 'religious concepts', such as the sacred, the eternal, heaven and hell, the good death 'will be explained by naturalistic investigators', which in itself is to misunderstand completely the nature of theological language, a bit like saying poetry will be scientifically calculated (Maslow [1964] 1976: 44). Perhaps, what is even more alarming is Maslow's attempt to eradicate any sense of the 'unknown', by arguing that 'mystery, ambiguity, illogic, contradiction, mystic and transcendent experiences' will be explained in the human realm. Even the human realm needs the sense of mystery and the limits of human knowledge need to be marked out, something James understood in a way Maslow did not.[11] Maslow's move is to mark out a realm of 'religion' for psychology and, in turn, to create a new (institutional) discourse (Maslow [1964] 1976: 46). He seeks an ultimate separation of 'religion' from the 'church' by arguing 'that spiritual, ethical, and moral values need have nothing to do with any church' (Maslow [1964] 1976: 57). Maslow's argument is overstated, as historically the categories of the spiritual, ethical and moral emerge from a wide set of cultural traditions, even in their Enlightenment formation. The binary construction of the secular and sacred is therefore a false separation, as so-called 'religious' ideas are formed inside the so-called 'secular' institutions. Maslow's move is, nonetheless, a tactical disassociation, as can be seen in the shifts from 'spiritual values' to 'higher values', from 'transcendent experiences' to 'peak-experience' (Maslow [1964] 1976: 52); examples of what Proudfoot (1985) would call his philosophical 'placeholders'. There is constant moving back and forth to displace historical terms and replace them within the economy of psychological language.

Maslow's ([1964] 1976: 48ff) concern is to challenge and separate 'spiritual' values from institutional 'Religion' and relocate 'spirituality' in education through psychology. He is concerned that education has become 'technological training for the acquisition of skills' without morality (Maslow [1964] 1976: 48). This is made even more bizarre by the way he makes 'religion' into a utility product and tries to eliminate the mysterious in human life. Maslow performs the task of putting 'psychological man' at the centre of the universe and forgets that 'psychological man' is no greater a creation than any other previous form of introspective discourse. His modernist assumptions about empirical 'truth' and the claims of psychology as a science prevent any critical analysis of the language and the history of ideas. As Foucault ([1969] 1991: 211) insightfully remarked: '[Y]ou may have killed God beneath the weight of all you have said; but don't imagine that, with all that you are saying, you will make a man that will live longer than he'.

Psychology, politics and economics

The ethical-political nature of Maslow's project becomes even more apparent when he attempts to pacify the role of the churches. He states:

> Even the social act of belonging to a church must be a private act, with no great social or political consequence, once religious pluralism has been accepted, once any religion is seen as a local structure, in local terms, of species-wide, core-religious transcendent experience.
>
> (Maslow [1964] 1976: 55)

This privatisation of experience performed by Maslow's psycho-politics reflects the way the self is positioned within American society. Experience and the self are brought into the private sphere, enforced by the discourse of 'religion' and 'spirituality, and, in consequence, the links between the individual and social are undermined. This becomes evident in the specific way Maslow aligns the 'philosophy of man' with social structures. While he is aware of the interconnected nature of psychology and society, he neglects to make some crucial associations within such thinking. For example, in his *Toward a Psychology of Being* he recognises the relation between psychology and economics:

> When the philosophy of man (his nature, his goals, his potentialities, his fulfilment) changes, then everything changes, not only the philosophy of politics, of *economics*, of ethics and values, of interpersonal relations and of history itself, but also the philosophy of education, the theory of how to help men become what they can and deeply need to become.
>
> (Maslow 1962: 177, emphasis added)

If we take Maslow's words seriously then the inter-relationship between his own philosophy of being human has its economic correlation. Maslow never identifies this position explicitly in his psychology, but Hoffman's biographical work does provide some insights into the political location of Maslow's thinking. His personal engagements with the business world also provide some immediate evidence of the commercial applicability of his psychology. We can, of course, never rely on these assessments alone, but they do contribute to the wider picture of Maslow's psychology and the positioning of his work. This is not to say Maslow was not concerned with justice and social values, or even that he supported capitalism as such, but that he fails to realise the economic and political implications of his psychological model.

The most revealing correspondence of Maslow's developing psychology with capitalism can be seen from the fact that in the summer of 1962 he become a visiting fellow at the Non-Linear Systems, Inc. plant in Del Mar, California, invited by its President, Andrew Kay. Impressed by their working models he formulated a response to the structures of the industry. Deborah Stephens, who reissued his work on business management, with the support of the Maslow family, has more recently promoted this alignment between Maslow and business. The original 1965 work, *Eupsychian Management*, was republished under the new title *Maslow on Management* (Maslow *et al.* 1998), which included many extracts and interviews from the leading captains of the business world. This republication of Maslow's work was also supported by a collection of pieces by Maslow called *The Maslow Business Reader* (Maslow 2000). In the preface to *The Reader*, Stephens points out that Maslow is even more important to practices of American business today. Referring to Douglas McGregor's *The Professional Manager* and Maslow's own studies, Stephens states 'both men developed theories that are now imperative to the success of business in a global economy' (Maslow 2000). The words are telling and support the general contribution Maslow's work makes towards enhancing the sub-structure of business, particularly in places like Silicon Valley. Maslow's work offered a model for 'motivating' the work force – so they could flourish in their skills – but what is never considered is how this creative flourishing in the work place is always linked to profit margins and capitalistic investment (see Carrette and King 2005: 123–68). Building models of human flourishing on the efficiency of production neglects how human flourishing requires a critical awareness of social justice and some ethical account of the knowledge we silently use to include and exclude each other. Maslow's model is human flourishing for the privileged of capitalism. It would obviously be unfair to assume that Maslow intended his work to be read in this way, because he could not see any link between the theorizing in 'science' and the socio-economic environment.

Maslow believed that his work on management was a way of reaching the wider public, beyond the restricted institutional base of education and psychology. His management model was based on the idea of a 'eupsychian' culture, that is a culture generated by self-actualising people, which moved towards 'psychological health'. The assumption was that this would create 'synergy', a 'resolution of the dichotomy between selfishness and unselfishness, or between selfishness and altruism' (Maslow 1998: 22). But this 'synergy' disguised visions of global capitalism behind a rhetoric of 'health' and 'human potential'. As Maslow indicated: 'Enlightenment economics must assume as a prerequisite synergetic institutions set up in such a way that what benefits one *benefits all*. What is good for General Motors is then good for the U.S., what is good for the U.S. is then *good for the world*, what is good for me is then good for everyone else, etc.' (Maslow 1998: 23–5, emphasis added). Such a claim reveals how the imperialism of American capitalism is naively carried forward into Maslow's own psychology.

The self-actualising of Maslow's management, despite gestures towards a sense of belonging to the group, is the self-actualising of capitalism. The criteria of actualisation are read in terms of a very limited political and social landscape, where individual selves are understood in terms of the contribution to the company and business values. The flourishing of any human being is only understood in terms of efficiency and the contribution to the product, not the spontaneous creation that offers no profit margin. As Stephens (in Maslow 1998: 1) points out: 'We can learn from self-actualising people what the ideal attitude toward work might be under the most favourable circumstances'. Work-directed flourishing, or even psychological flourishing, is a limited cultural creation of humanistic capitalistic values and only offers one option of how human beings may invent themselves. The eradication of alternative introspective traditions is not some neutral empirical endeavour, which discovers the 'truth' of being human, it is an ideological construction, which eventually leads to the sanction of capitalistic lifestyle through a new psychological language of 'religion and 'spirituality'.

Plateau and peak experience: rescuing the tradition

To Maslow's credit, he eventually saw how his and other such humanistic psychologies were being used in, or rather were mirroring, the prevailing culture. This can be seen in his later critique of the Easlen Institute and his disillusionment with how his own work was being developed (Hoffman [1998] 1999: 309; Maslow 1996: 129–31). After critiquing the values of 'religious' traditions Maslow (1996: 130) is forced to acknowledge that:

> There needs to be a better balance at the Esalen between the Dionysian and the Apollonian. There needs to be more dignity, politeness, courtesy, reserve, privacy, responsibility, and loyalty. There should be much less talk about 'instant intimacy' and 'instant love' and much more about the necessity for Apollonian controls of such a space and style.

He goes on to ask the question about whether the Esalen Institute could 'make for a better society' (Maslow 1996: 131). These revealing questions continued to concern Maslow in his later life, as seen in his 1970 presentation at the transpersonal psychology conference at Council Grove in Iowa, which led to the revised 1970 preface of his *Religions, Values and Peak Experiences* (Hoffman [1998] 1999: 310). As Hoffman ([1998] 1999: 310) shows in his biography, Maslow conceded he was 'originally naïve' about 'the dangers of an overzealous interest in mysticism and the purely experiential aspects of religion'. He was concerned about the 'over-extreme, dangerous, and one-sided' use of his work and believed he had been 'too imbalanced toward the individualistic and too hard on groups, organizations, and communities' (Maslow [1964] 1976: vii, xiii).[12] In response to this situation, Maslow revised his 'peak-experience' concept with the idea of 'plateau experiences', which were 'less intense' and required 'long hard work', as found in the traditions of formation in Christianity, Judaism and Buddhism (Maslow [1964] 1976: xv–vi). Maslow is here recognising the dangerous results of extrapolating the 'experience' from the 'tradition' which creates the experience, recognising perhaps that the marketing and psychologization of the 'religious' and 'spiritual' created an isolated experience.

In the new 1970 preface, he was critical of the American counterculture misuse of 'spiritual disciplines', believing the drug culture and consciousness expanding groups had misconstrued the insights of the 'religious' traditions; not seeing how the category itself contributed to such a process. As Hoffman recalls Maslow, there was an attempt to correct this misunderstanding:

> The great lesson from the true mystics ... [is that] the sacred is *in* the ordinary, that it is to be found in one's daily life, in one's neighbour, friends, and family, in one's backyard, and that travel may be a *flight* from confronting the sacred ... To be looking elsewhere for miracles is a sure sign of ignorance that *everything* is miraculous.
>
> (Maslow quoted in Hoffman [1988] 1999: 312)

Maslow may have realised the error of isolating specific experiences in his psychology too late, for the very marketing of intense, short-lived experiences was a joy for the capitalistic world. 'Religion' and 'spirituality' were psychological products and in the world of late-capitalism, following the deregulation of the markets by Reagan and Thatcher in the late 1980s and 1990s, the spirituality market would burgeon even more than before (see Carrette and King 2005). Maslow's efforts to reposition his psychology also faced calamity when he saw how his work inspired the privileged culture of capitalism. In an attempt to save his psychological creation from its own potential injustice Maslow had argued:

> Unfortunately, physical and economic wealth do not inevitably get used for higher need gratification. Higher needs can be gratified under poverty, it's harder, but possible if we remember what we're dealing with – respect, love, self-actualisation, *not* autos, money, bathtubs.
> (Maslow [1954] (1987): 373–4 quoted in Cox 1987: 262)

What Maslow had failed to realise is that his hierarchy of needs was a hierarchy of capitalistic values and the idea of 'self-actualisation', however much it appealed to 'synergy', was locked into a fundamental individualism and motivation of capital. Maslow could not see how his psychology was formed and shaped by capitalism, because he could not problematise the ideology of psychology and its framing of 'religious' experience. Maslow questioned traditional forms of introspection under the sign of 'religion', but he could see how this category and his reading of experience as psychological was part of a deeper historical change in self and economy.

Religion of the self

In Paul Vitz's timely little volume in 1977, *Psychology as Religion: The Cult of Self-Worship*, we see the central problems of Maslow's psychologization of 'religious' experience.[13] Maslow and humanistic psychology were putting forward a new kind of private 'religion' of the self – an 'in-worldly individualism' of utility and measurement. As Vitz argued: 'Psychology has become a religion, in particular, a form of secular humanism based on worship of the self' (Vitz [1977] 1994: 7). However, what Vitz's, somewhat limited, study did not appreciate was how this 'religion of self' was fundamentally tied to a capitalistic sub-structure within psychology, or at least he did not theorise the full economic implications of his position. This new so-called 'religion' of the self was part of the psychologised rendering of experience for capitalist cultures; and its appropriation of the discourse of 'spirituality' was it central hallmark. The attempt now to integrate 'spirituality' into health treatment and education is a complex formulation of 'religious' values, which desperately masks the social and economic vacuum of capitalistic ideology (Carrette and King 2005: 44–53). In an attempt to meet the needs of uncertainty, mystery and liminality in human life, the product of 'spirituality' – with its undifferentiated meaning – can easily be used to silence the non-psychological worlds of the human imagination in order to continue the perpetuation of a regime of knowledge which seeks nothing else but accumulation of wealth.

As long as experience and the self remain a 'psychological' construction, divorced from longer traditions of philosophical introspection, it will continue to suffocate the alternative resources for making experience – the cultural implications of which are still unclear. This does not entail an uncritical or nostalgic return to past traditions, but a critical appreciation of the new ethical-political values within the order of 'psychology' and 'religion'. Psychology is not liberation from an oppressive dogmatic introspection in the Christian church; it is the creation of a different ideological and dogmatic structure for Christian introspection and the modern atheistic world. Under the regime of psychology, the closed-self has become the new opium for a capitalistic ideology tortured by its own angst and consumer vacuum.

Paradoxically, in Maslow's revaluing and re-imagining of the categories of pre-modern introspection we can see the critical strategies for making and unmaking psychological experience. There is even the possibility of contextualising the capitalistic self found in psychologized categories of 'religion' and 'spirituality. As Foucault (1982a: 216) points out: 'May be the target nowadays is not to discover what we are, but to refuse what we are'. While humanistic psychology holds the potential to offer critique of capitalism its efforts are often betrayed by its theoretical foundations of the self inside American capitalism, which undermine its external ambitions for liberation. Critique of the 'psychology of religion' must, therefore, question both sides of this equation of knowledge.

If we are to establish greater critical awareness of the values within knowledge, we must critique the concealed foundations of knowledge and the economically embedded statements about the self. Maslow's modern capitalistic self went against some of his best intentions and was even reconstituted for a new age of global business, but much of it is now superseded by a new regime of psychological values that flourishes inside the knowledge economy. It is the codified science of cognition that now dominates psychology and economics, showing how models of the self constantly evolve according to the dominant political economy. But the politic of knowledge becomes even more complex when the very construction of knowledge is taken into the economy and when that economy is based on a redefining technology. In such a world, we lose the transparency of Maslow's post-war revisions, his naïve semantic games and innocent inventions of 'religion' and enter a strange entangled set of mind games in the imagining of self. It is to these unsettling questions of our time that I now turn.

5 Cognitive capital and the codification of religion

Mental facts cannot be properly studied apart from the physical environment of which they take cognizance.

William James [1892] (1985) *Psychology: Briefer Course,*
Harvard University Press, p. xxvii

Cognitive processes ain't all in the head ... once the hegemony of skin and skull is usurped, we may be able to see ourselves more truly as creatures of the world.

Clark, A. and Chalmers, D. (1998) 'The Extended Mind' in
Analysis, 58(1), p. 8

Scholars of religion are always inescapably dependent on other fields of study in the making and unmaking of their object of study. One of the problems that this entails is an uncritical celebration of the hybrid discourses, which are put to the service of the object to form either a 'science of religion' (the art of measuring a taxonomy) or a 'contemporary theology of the age' (the art of updating belief). What is remarkable about these inter-disciplinary engagements is the suspension of a critical politic to evaluate the inter-disciplinary discourse. One of the reasons for this blindness is the false assumption that the preliminary concepts of 'science' exclude a wider socio-economic dimension, something that maintains the ideological isolation of the religious object and the valued method. There is in effect an inter-disciplinary collusion, as the method becomes part of the process of making the object, something we have seen in relation to William James, and which continues in contemporary projects. As Harvey Whitehouse (2005A: 2, emphasis added) rightly indicates, even if he does not fully sustain the ambition: 'A scientific theory of religion must tell us what, *for the purposes of that theory,* constitutes religion'. This alliance of method and the making of the object often conceal the values of the method in the making of the object.

For those working in the *science* of religion, any critique of the supporting discourse would entail exposing the object and the approach as value-laden – killing both host and parasite. In such an intellectual space, the rules of the modernist discourse of religion have often developed strategic ways to protect the method of science from excessive scrutiny. There is a suspension of the historical, philosophical and ideological problems of the 'science' in order to exonerate the analytic power that services the religious object through either regulation or celebration. This disciplinary practice has nowhere been more (in)visible than in the cognitive and neuro-scientific making of religion. Indeed, the mind plays many tricks on itself and in the area of cognitive science there is always a delightful play of cognitive dissonance about its own object. The will-to-truth of the contemporary cognitive science of religion is so socially pervasive that the rituals of persuasion it evokes hold, in some quarters at least, as much uncritical devotion and blind allegiance as the *religion* they construct as an object of enquiry. Scholars of religion are strangely unaware of the politics of their inter-disciplinary thinking and the alliances they seek to make. By raising the ethical-political question of cognitive science, I am radicalising the work of cognitive theorists Clark and Chalmers (1998) and an important question in their watershed article 'The Extended Mind'. They pertinently ask: 'Where does the mind stop and the rest of the world begin?'. Or to 'extend' the question for my purposes: how does political-economy inform the constructions of cognitive theory?

In this chapter, I want to put the processes of cognitive science in their 'extended environment' and make *them* the object of analysis by asking what are the conditions that make the cognitive science of religion possible – cognitive or otherwise. I want to explore how the environment of the knowledge-economy shapes the cognizance of cognition. I am, in effect, making reality more complex and breaking some discursive and mental boundaries. I am seeking to show how cognitive theory can be both open and closed to this theoretical extension in a disciplinary self-reflexive move. In some ways, I am developing – and making more *complex* by *multi-disciplinary* extension – what Dan Sperber and others (Sperber 2000) have, usefully and insightfully, explored under the term 'meta-representation' ('mental representation of mental representation'). It is precisely at this point of 'meta-representation' that we can find openings to the wider environment of the brain and cognition. As Robert Wilson concurs:

> Far from being the province of an inwardly withdrawn mind, metarepresentation and the levels of cognitive performance that it

facilitates belong to the mind as it is located in the social and physical world.

(Wilson 2004: 188)

I am therefore bringing meta-representation into a higher order of analysis by examining the rules of how we represent representation of the mind; I am bringing mental representation into a political-economic space according to the wider argument of my book. In effect, I am putting brains back into their bodies and their interacting environment after they were conceptually removed by human over-identification with technological objects and systems. The problem with writings within the cognitive science of religion to date is that they remain to a large extent locked inside simple – early – models of cognition. While there are some signs of extending the discourse to the wider environment, much remains closed, isolated and individualistic in a codified theory of cognition. It is precisely this codified formation of cognition that demands an extension to the wider political variables informing cognition *about* cognition.

It is my argument in this chapter that models within cognitive science of religion are received and embedded in a wider cultural environment of the knowledge economy. The conceptual apparatus of the knowledge economy produces and sustains certain forms of cognitive modelling for new forms of capital investment in the network society. The cognitive science of religion is thus not some innocent abstract modelling (of 'truth'), but rather part of a dominant Western social and institutional reconfiguration of knowledge. This is not, as the cognitive theorists rightly remind us, a problem of 'essentialized institutions', but a question of the 'context dependency' of cognitive meta-representations within the knowledge economy (Whitehouse 2005a: 22–4, 173).[1] Indeed, there is an ideological transmission of – and receptivity towards – the abstract modelling of calculated cognition because the dominant political-economic order sustains systems that mirror technological processes and financially supports this new ordering of human knowledge for new forms of exchange. Codified cognitive science is the new capital of human resource management and those who uncritically model older forms of knowledge in such a way are remaking subjects for this new social order.

However, at the frontiers of cognitive theory there are more dynamic models of the mind, which hold the potential to disrupt certain codified forms of cognition by opening the mind to its extension in the social environment. The domination of what, I am calling here, 'codified', rather than 'dynamic' models, is linked to the rationale of the knowledge economy and its networked *mathesis*. Unfortunately, cognitive approaches to religion remain largely[2] isolated in codified cognition, because of a desire to limit the intellectual scope of cognition and provide models for control and calculation. The more dynamic models of the mind are more difficult to predict and control in the network of the knowledge economy and thus are perceived as economically inefficient and scientifically too complex to map.

At this point we need to qualify carefully the argument against misreading and misinterpretation and against the *emotive*-rationality of abstract thinkers: the tired old responses by those who do not want to think and by those who genuinely wish to make links across knowledge without realising how their projects fall into a wider politic. Even the good intentions of empirical science do not extend the context or even think how ideas are rooted in the economic context. So, at the beginning of my argument, I will carefully qualify my position. It is *not* because the signifier cognition does not correspond to something that exists. It is *not* because we do not display discernable patterns of thought located within physical environments. It is *not* because of soft-cultural relativist thinking and a denial of some universally given biological functions. It is *not* because of an old state conspiracy theory. It is *not* a Marxist reading of reality. *The reason for the social reception of contemporary cognitive thinking is because of the complexity of ideas and their social field of use (irrespective of their truth or falsity) in the knowledge economy (which is coterminous with the rise of cognitive science). It is because the knowledge economy supports codified knowledge and limits the inefficiency of 'extension' of the mind to its political environment. It is because codified forms of cognitive theory have a certain political receptivity in the present technologically driven economic environment.* However, the development of cognitive science can be wider and richer and can include, rather than exclude, other ways of thinking. Cognitive science can hold greater complexity, as has been shown in recent theories of the 'extended mind', but that complexity requires some account of both the nature of language and the nature of the political environment. By highlighting dynamic modelling of the mind we might break some of the ideological links between codified cognition and the knowledge economy and extend the cognitive theory of religion to include awareness of its own political environment.

Establishing a philosophical critique of cognitive neuroscience, Bennett and Hacker (2003) enable us to reposition cognitive theory into a political landscape by returning concepts to philosophical debates about language. As they indicate: 'Conceptual questions antecede matters of truth and falsehood' (Bennett and Hacker 2003: 2). Concepts are neither true nor false, but rather adequately represent or not, according to the established criteria of philosophical reasonableness or scientific analysis, but concepts – because they are not scientific fact – are also received, or not, in an existing social environment. This means, in terms of meta-representation, that the cognitive patterns of cognitive science have a social transmission and receptivity, which thus locate them in the social environment of the knowledge economy (whether intended or not). We could, therefore, argue that concepts are formed from multiple points of interacting forces and *not* from a single point (the illusory appeal to the brain and its correlate in simple encoded representation).

We are far more complex than some cognitive scientists would have us believe and breaking the 'scientific' mask of 'concepts' will be an important step in exposing the political order behind the academic endeavour. We have *both* innate predispositions and interacting environments and concepts are formed in the interactive space *between*, not in one order or another.[3] Those who wish to give priority of one over the other thus 'abandon scholarship for dogmatics', as Alles (2004: 271) so rightly indicates. Indeed, the most remarkable feature of the majority of writings in the cognitive science of religion is that their appeal to a mono-causal reality holds extraordinary parallels to the monotheistic dogmatism of its imagined object religion. Let us bring cognitive concepts to even greater philosophical analysis and wake up those who dream of science to the daylight of the preliminary formation of concepts in the socio-economic environment. The cognitive science of religion requires more dynamic modelling of the mind to appreciate its own political involvement.

We need therefore to 'extend' the range of our conceptual platform for a greater critique of our thinking and recognise the extraordinary range of debate and new insights in this complex and ever-developing field. Cognitive science is, therefore, neither good nor bad – it is just good old-fashioned modelling – but there is good and bad modelling within cognitive theories (of religion), which relate to an unawareness of what shapes the modelling. The problem is that those who model reality are unaware of the embedded nature of their practices within the political-economic order and the dangerous totalitarian nature of such systems of thinking when the social order uncritically receives and welcomes such thinking. This unawareness is a result of the fact that models easily slide beyond 'modelling' to become 'political ideology' (prior to the scientific testability), which in turn gives those who model a disturbing inflation about their activity, especially when dominant social and political groups use calculative logic to make humans more efficient. There will always be those cognitive scientists who refuse to hear the social echo of complex extensions (because of claims about 'scientific' truth), but abstract modelling is only the precursor of a scientific endeavour.[4] The danger is when the model becomes greater than the testable premises it rests upon, when its philosophical logic becomes uncritically celebrated and when, in its encounter with cultural realities, it oversteps an examination of its own object. It is time to make cognitive science the *object* of analysis. But first I want to make a few preliminary comments to locate my thinking in the political displacement of thinking about cognition.

First, cognitive theory is a discourse in flux, which spirals back and forth to old philosophical debates in its very imagining of new ones (as the two quotations at the beginning of this chapter indicate). The various shifts in modelling in the last 20 years are evidence that the ground is far from stable, immersed in disciplinary amnesia (see Chapter 2), and far from conclusive. In this context, we need to ask why the theory in the cognitive science of religion remains conceptually and, in my view, politically, unimaginative. The very fact that cognitive science offers increasingly diverse models of the mind is cause for reflecting why some ideas are dominant and others are not. Rather than reduce this to 'cognitively optimal representation' (Whitehouse 2004: 328), we might want to take the transmission of ideas out of our brains and into the systems those brains interactively created; into the transmission of ideas in electronic networks and capital exchanges.[5]

The technical ability to construct and develop a range of mental models is now with us, but the political climate of technological innovation remains under-theorized. This raises important questions in the history of science and how and why forms of modelling emerge at any point of time. The emergence of cognitive modelling has distinct historical foundations, but what is even more alarming is why, when ever-more complex models are available, there is a social persistence in using isolated and individualistic models of cognition, which deny the environment of brains and the philosophical problems of such mind-brain discourse. John Shotter is, in this sense, correct in his appraisal that 'isolation of everything from everything typifies cognitivism' (Shotter 1997: 322), but this does not have to be the case. For, as Wilson (2004: 148) indicates, isolation and individualism are 'not the only game(s) in town' in either cognitive science or the political world; even if theories in the cognitive science of religion and the knowledge economy would appear to suggest otherwise.

The problem is that the contemporary political-economic conditions of thinking are supporting this order of the *same* – that which increases disciplinary isolationism, reduces the self-reflexive politic of discourses, sustains individualistic categories of thought and supports the knowledge economy. This order of the *same* is particularly found in cognitive theories of religion and it prevents primary philosophical questions being posed to the discourse. The confusing aspect of cognitive science is that it presents itself as an inter-disciplinary subject, including such areas as philosophy, anthropology and linguistics. However, this inter-disciplinary thinking is often not about opening thought to its outside, but rather returning thought to a single object of 'truth'. It thus reads all domains of thought through the vector of its own 'truth', becoming in effect an inter-disciplinary virus (to recall Sperber's (1985a, 1985b) epidemiological analogy), mutating all systems of thought into one domain (the domain of the knowledge economy or the empire of technological cognition). In my view, rather than holding hermeneutical complexity and responding to recent dynamic models of mind, it seeks a one-dimensional model of being human.

However, not all those working in the cognitive science of religion operate on the same ideology or remain restricted to simple '*encoding views* of mental representation', to use Wilson's (2003: 147) terminology. There are striking regimes of intellectual totalitarianism in mental representation (the dominant codified mode), but more dynamic ideas that open intellectual exploration and undercut this framing of the mind offer alternatives to how we think about thinking. My concern here is to carry forward my wider discussion of political-economy and psychology into the discursive formations of the cognitive science of religion. I want to frame questions of the politics of knowledge in cognitive readings of religion in terms of the knowledge-economy. Cognitive science and the knowledge-economy both came of age in the same political era of late capitalism and any philosophical critique of knowledge must seek to unravel the conditions of these systems of thinking; connected as they are through the metaphorical domination of the technological and electronic finance of the computer age.

The objects of religion, economy and cognition may appear to belong to such different orders of truth as to make little sense to those operating in each domain. Already one can see how displacing the structures of the cognitive science of religion (and their self-generating nomenclature), through an examination of the historical conditions of economic thought, we create voices of dissent, which leads to the immediate shutting down of interest in intellectual dialogue. The investments in certain models of cognitive science – financial, personal and professional – are too great to think otherwise for some, and the intellectual entrenchment is such that systems of thought become more important than open enquiry. Obsession, power, money and institutional orders all prevent dynamic complexity in thinking and it becomes easier for totalitarian short-cuts in any analysis to be entrenched.

The desire to know and control closes minds to the complexity at the edges of different orders of knowing. The cognitive science of religion, as I will show, suffers more than most from these plagues of thinking, because its dominant isolationist rationale (one dimensional truth[6]) always reinforces its own 'truth'.

I should add that I restrict myself to a discussion of examples in the cognitive science of *religion*, not only because of the limits of this presentation and my own specific disciplinary critique, but because I think there is a value to the 'science' within some discussion of computer technology, philosophical modelling and therapeutic application (even though these need to be critically examined for their own ideological misuse and are implicated in some of my wider concerns about cognitive modelling of reality and their metaphorical illusions). There are exciting developments of the extended and dynamic mind on the frontiers of cognitive science, which, as I will show, take us back to some very different ways of imagining ourselves and offer potential for an integrated and politically informed complexity of thought. The engagement with religion is also particularly fascinating, not only for its fundamentally conservative order, but because it makes all sorts of epistemological errors in its *invention* of the theological, religious, metaphysical and cultural object (see Carrette 2002, 2005c). The turn to the cognitive in religion is often so limited in its engagement that much remains an attempt to find a *scientific* justification for – at times – innovative taxonomies of anthropology.[7] The insights established are often not grounded in mind-stuff but rather classificatory orders long-established in the methods of anthropology and social science. The *cognitive* is thus a discursive formation introduced in abstract thinking that carries the ideological values of the social environment. In the knowledge-economy, the signification of *cognition* is a currency of *capital* and the rewriting of traditional projects in the history of religion in this contemporary language is an act of cultural translation into the logic of the technological economy.

My argument is that the category errors, epistemological problems and theoretical lacunae of the cognitive science of religion reflect an ideological shift, rather than scientific modelling of the mind, and the very fact they are often so limited to 'encoding' models only reinforces their political convenience. Much of the language of cognitive science of religion follows what Jones and Elcock (2001: 174) call 'knowledge production', an expansion of concepts in the knowledge economy. The highly elaborate concept formation in cognitive science is therefore – often unwittingly – part of the new capital. It is also important to realise that the very detachment of theory from the ethical-political order means that cognitive theorists often have little idea of how their thinking is embedded, nourished and supported by the knowledge economy. As Turkle ([1978] 1992: 242) insightfully reminds us: 'The politics of the theorist are not necessarily the politics of the theory'. It is therefore possible for modes of totalitarian thinking to appear within the texts of even the best-intentioned theorist, especially when the concepts and ideas are assumed to operate in a separate realm from the dominant ideology of knowledge.

Stages of making thought more complex

Given the assertions in my extended opening remarks, it is necessary to outline each step of my argument carefully. I have already explored some of my concerns in earlier reflections on Persinger's (1987) neuroscience of religion and Lawson and McCauley's (1990, 2002) 'cognitive' model of ritual. However, my aim in those examinations was to show how the language of neuroscience and the cognitive theory of religion evaporate under their own logic and how they hide the ideological and philosophical errors behind the rhetoric of science (Carrette 2002, 2005c).[8] What I wish to do here is establish a stronger link between the politics of knowledge and the cognitive science of religion by examining yet another key thinker in the field, the cognitive anthropologist Harvey Whitehouse. I take up his work, in the second part of this chapter, because there has been a lot of contemporary interest in his studies in the field of religion and because some of his work clearly reflects a number of my key ideological and epistemological concerns about codified cognition and the knowledge economy. I should add at the beginning that I have great respect for his anthropological insights and fieldwork, but I think he is fundamentally mistaken to adopt and read these insights in terms of the language of codified cognitive science and, indeed, his work would have a different order of value if he had a wider reading of cognition and its ethical-political context. Although, as I will show, his turn to codified cognition becomes part of the reason why his thinking is culturally and intellectually transmitted. I should also add that I prefer to focus on one thinker in detail to demonstrate my argument, rather than the so-called emergent new field of cognition and religion as a whole, because the slippage in thinking takes slightly different forms in different thinkers; although the ideas I discuss will touch upon wider concerns in the literature and are applicable to much of the emerging theory (see Andresen 2001; Slone 2006).[9]

Let me restate my argument to keep the reader with me as far as possible, because complexity can often be read as confusion, especially when discursive rules are stretched. My thesis in this chapter is that the cognitive science of religion holds patterns of thought that make it easy to embed in the dominant economic order and that this increases its social transmission and receptivity in the knowledge economy. Behind its mask of scientific rhetoric, however, there are profound philosophical errors and ethical-political problems. The philosophical errors persist unchallenged because of the appeal of the coginitive science of religion to the (culturally pervasive) scientific materialistic ground of the brain and the economic forms of codification. These provide it with a cultural cache that enables it to flow within those forms of institutional apparatus that give it influence, the appeal to a language of brains and science concealing its ethical-political affiliations. Even more alarming is the fact that its links with certain forms of codification in the knowledge economy reveal a totalitarian edge (a single economic model) to such thinking.

I will now, again for the purposes of clarity, summarise the stages of my argument. I will follow four steps. First, I will briefly overview the social conditions of cognitive thinking; second, I will briefly reiterate how the codification of cognition is linked to the knowledge economy, which I have already discussed in the first section of this book. I will then, third (and not dependent on the first two steps of my argument), show how appeals to the brain allow for philosophical bad practice and how a cognitive hygiene of concepts returns us to the body and enables us to return to some forgotten insights of William James and to reflect on more recent complex models of cognition. This third stage of my argument needs addressing even if the first two seem problematic, but the blind persistence of the errors would seem to add support to the first two steps of my argument. Finally, I will show how these arguments have a bearing on Whitehouse's study of the object of religion. Here I will examine Whitehouse's work in some detail in relation to models of the knowledge economy and seek to reveal forms of closure in his thinking, the limited models of memory and his individualistic constructs of mind. I will also show how his language of transmission is part of the cognitive knowledge economy. My critique is therefore necessarily multi-faceted in order to show that no single dimension of thought can be isolated from another. The problem I will be seeking to show is that thought reduced to an isolated cognitive ground is both mistaken philosophically and ideologically problematic; above all, the concepts are often not grounded in science or philosophical reasonableness and thus become more sinister for their hidden adaptation to the dominant political environment. I fully accept that most codified cognitive theorists will wish to remain in the comfort zone of imagining 'concepts' as science and that they will suspend critical thought in the 'machine dream' (Mirowski 2002) by denying the ethical-political value of dynamic minds. But let us be clear, the knowledge economy offers its own rewards for the codified mind. Theory is always and necessarily ethical-political in both construction and application. It is therefore necessary that critique walks against the dominant trend to identify what is not being thought and what is unseen in each age of metaphorical modelling, because this will reveal the values of the time.

The sociology of cognition and the question of religion

The history and social emergence of cognitive science is important in locating how ideas and concepts shift and how they carry different registers of meaning. History demystifies the scientific pretensions of thought, because it reveals the errors, inadequacies and mistakes of an evolving set of experimental thoughts. In this context, recognising that the signifier 'cognitive' does not always mean the same thing at all times and periods is significant in terms of what it reveals about the contemporary field of use. I can only map the general contours of the history for my argument, but there are many more details that others have drawn out and which could add to my discussion (see Gardner 1987; Anderson 1995; Dupuy 2000; Descombes 2001; Harnish 2001). Often forgotten in practice, it is important to reiterate that mind and thinking/cognition have carried different registers of meaning from ancient Greece to artificial intelligence. The conceptual frame of reference is 'mobile', according to 'the army of metaphors' – to recall Nietzsche ([1873] 1976: 46–7) – available to establish meaning. The meaning of cognition therefore shifts according to its use and purpose within different disciplinary contexts and, we might add, the political environment.

   The idea of cognition is thus a multi-layered reality and we need to differentiate a number of stages of its function and operation, especially between the 'cognitive' in its pre-and post-computer age of modelling, and even between simple and complex cognitive modelling in more recent years. The history of philosophy, for example, has a much-valued tradition of 'cognitive' thinking. Indeed, Descartes's 'cogito ergo sum' ('Je pense, donc je suis') in his *Discourse on Method* (1637) holds an important register of cognitive meaning, but always one held within terms of an active subject thinking rather than an encoded machine; the difference between an open and closed system (even if, at another level of critique, the embodied mind is lost in Descartes). In the field of psychology, some early roots of cognitive science can be seen to go back to the group of Gestalt psychologists in Germany and with Jean Piaget in the 1920s and 1930s. However, most historical studies of cognitive theory will point to post-war developments for its formal emergence, either in 'cybernetics' (Dupuy 2000) or general developments in the 1950s, such as Alan Turing's ([1950] 1964) famous essay on machines and intelligence. These technological developments brought cognition into a new order of discursive operation, with very different registers of meaning. Indeed, many conceptual problems result as a consequence of employing cognition in both an old and a new sense (Bennett and Hacker 2003: 6). Cognitive theory was slowly institutionalised with the Cognitive Science Society and the establishment of the journal *Cognitive Science* in the mid-1970s. The field then spread out through the various institutional and disciplinary frameworks in computer science, philosophy and anthropology; having already become more explicit in the field of psychology with Ulric Neisser's 1967 *Cognitive Psychology*.

Post-war computer modelling of the mind brought a different epistemological order into the cognitive, as it was now associated with the driving edge of modern cultural developments. Cognition was no longer a dusty philosophical word, it was part of an expanding technological science; it was not human thought but the binary data of robotic dreams. The aura of cognition changed and the idea of modelling mind and machine became its discursive intention. Cognition did not simply mean to think or know, but prediction, calculation and control. The problem, which prevails to this day, is that there is confusion about what is metaphor and simile and what is scientific fact. The desire to know and control can easily reify an object and make us imagine we *are* machines. Much of the early euphoria of encoding was caught in this form of cognitive science; and it is this which is still dominant in the cognitive science of religion.

The imagination of the machine-brain in the new cognitive order has been discussed by Sherry Turkle in her illuminating sociological study, *The Second Self: Computers and the Human Spirit* ([1984] 2005). Here she seeks to assess the impact of the cultural shift of computer technology on our sense of self. Using over 400 interviews with adults and children, she assesses 'the cultural assimilation of a new way of thinking' (Turkle [1984] 2005: 305). She recognises that 'the computer makes a new contribution' to our self-understanding by providing us with a new 'object to think with' (Turkle [1984] 2005: 284; Turkle [1978] 1992: xvi). Computers 'offer new models of what it means to know and to understand' and give 'support to those who see human psychology in mechanistic terms' (Turkle [1984] 2005: 284). The rapid new developments since Turkle's study only increase the sense that in the Western technological world we cannot begin to think of the implications of what it is to model ourselves on computer technology, because the technology is shaping the very way we think about thinking.

Turkle explains that today computational metaphors now seem 'banal' and she argues:

> Cognitive science has developed far more sophisticated computational models of mental processes than were dreamt of two decades ago, and the Internet has opened up new paths for the exploration of self and sociability. However, with time grows a sense of familiarity. What was once exotic begins to seem 'natural'.
>
> (Turkle [1984] 2005: 6)

The social ground of the cognitive is part of our cyborg-identity and its discourse is now a part of who we are becoming (Graham 2001). It may now be impossible to think without recourse to the machine, but we still do not have to think we are machines, even if we are *like* machines. The network of concepts generated in cognitive science now extends beyond human manageability; we cannot think who we are without the conceptual apparatus of the machine. There is also an entire new nomenclature that has arisen with cognitive science and it requires razor-sharp scrutiny to show how use of language (the public space) tricks the mind (the mental space). Cognitive science today stretches across numerous fields of study and yet no one is asking sufficiently rigorous questions about the political-economic environment that makes this possible; although pretensions to read the 'socio-political history of our species' through cognitive science are desired (Whitehouse 2002: 312). Perhaps, before we read the socio-political history of our species, we should read the socio-political history of our discourses about minds.

In a slightly different context, Jerry Fodor (2001) captures something of this shift in signification in later cognitive theory when he makes distinctions between types of cognitive theory that utilise computational forms. He usefully illustrates that Chomsky bases his early nativism on a theory of knowledge, whereas Steven Pinker (1997) builds models of cognition from computational analogy in what Fodor calls 'New Synthesis psychological theories' (Fodor 2001: 11–13). Chomsky also expresses these concerns in his 1999 University of Siena lectures, when he raises a note of caution about developments in cognitive theory (Chomsky 2002). Understanding these shifts of meaning is also about registering 'investments' in modelling the self on computers and the language of computers – in distinction to those who hold to wider theories of knowledge or at least do not attempt to read *all* reality in these terms. Even the cognitive scientist falls in love, has physical addictions and faces death, but oddly enough at such a moment of the disappearance of his brain (the imagined place of thought) his ideas (sadly in some cases) continue beyond his death. Could thought be represented outside the brain? These problems raise important questions about the confusions made in the field between conceptual and empirical matters, between conceptual thought and scientific thought. There is much elision between the two, especially in an intellectual vacuum where the terms of debate remain hidden or where concepts are 'misconstrued, or misplaced, or stretched beyond their defining conditions of application' (Bennett and Hacker 2003: 1). Cognitive science is often unaware of the social apparatus that allows its articulations to move more easily in the corridors of influence and persuasion. As Turkle once again disturbingly illustrates:

> The computer culture is carried not only by ideas, not only by the writings of its theorists, not only by articles in magazines or programs on television, but by a machine that people bring into their homes, give to their children, use to play games, to write letters, and to help them in the management of time and money.
>
> (Turkle [1984] 2005: 307)

What Turkle does not sufficiently examine in her sociological account is the way post-1980 Western leaders embraced the knowledge-economy and electronic systems of finance. Could the success of cognitive science not only be linked to our mental processes but also be linked, in complex ways, to technological and economic developments? Could the deregulation of the market and the shift to computer finance during the Thatcher-Reagan years in some way be linked to the success of a way of thinking? Does the nature of exchange affect the transmission of cognition beyond minds? We will return to some of these questions, but in the ever-increasing expansion of models of computer-led thinking, 'religion', as an imagined object, would in time become the subject of this regime of thinking.

'Religion', cognition and the knowledge-economy

The cognitive revolution in the study of religion can be seen to go back to the French tradition of psychology and anthropology in the work of Jean Piaget (1926) and Lévy-Bruhl ([1910] 1985). Cognition for these writers was bound by an epistemic cognition, which Erica Burman's (1994) deconstruction of Piaget shows rested on the value of a 'male epistemic knower' and colonial models of representing thought. The full force of such a critique has yet to unsettle later disembodied thinking in the field of cognition, but it shows how the basic philosophical premises of thinking about thinking have yet to be understood. Nonetheless, Dan Sperber (1975, 1985a, 1996) developed the psychological and anthropological traditions of cognition that were to be carried into the study of religion. His early thinking about epidemiology provided the new metaphorical ground for imagining universal structures of the mind. *Rethinking Symbolism* challenged the inherited models of anthropology and provided, in what Segal (1978: 610) called a 'hopelessly sketchy' book, the prospect of a cognitive foundation to cultural forms.

The early use of cognition still retained a largely epistemic condition and was dependent on secondary supporting questions, such that Stewart Guthrie's (1980) discussion of cognition was concerned with intellectualist human models and anthropomorphism. The cognitive in these early texts had not been reified into its later codified form and still retained a wider field of coherence, with at least some echo of structuralism. More importantly they had not yet made 'religion' and other such related ideas into stable cognitive objects. However, these lines of thinking were taken up by a whole group of scholars in Bush senior's 'decade of the brain' (the 1990s), with some fascinating, but philosophically and politically naïve, theoretical models: including examination of ritual (Lawson and McCauley 1990), memory (Whitehouse 1995) and, subsequently, a whole range of religious concepts (see Slone 2006).[10] In these studies cognition is converted into the codified forms of the new economic logic and this increasingly isolated the discourse from wider epistemological concerns.

The studies proliferated not through brains alone, but through the medium of information and knowledge exchange, both in the old institutional and physical gatherings[11] of scholars and expansion of their resources in the ever-increasing nomenclature (systems of knowledge codification), which led to an increase in cognitive thinking about religion. The success was increased through important funding opportunities, showing that ideas do not generate themselves by codified cognition alone.[12] As with other applications of cognitive theory, the transmission, both within and outside the mind, established the area within institutional locations, but as we shall see below, much remained at the level of codified theory and the more dynamic models remained restricted, or, at best, marginally acknowledged, because such ideas threatened the imperialistic potential of fixed objects for transmission in the knowledge economy.

Dynamic thinking and codified religion

The machine-encoding model of mental representation largely determined the developments in the cognitive science of religion, but the wider field of cognitive modelling evolved in far more complex ways. It is not possible to discuss adequately all these very technical developments in computational modelling in a single chapter and all I can do is highlight the key epistemic shifts, which obviously related to new technological developments, in order to show the general sense of an opening to ever-greater contexts. Following the early models emerging from the 1950s, new and more complex models of computational modelling were developed in the late 1980s and 1990s that started to examine the connections or neural networks (Churchland (1995)). Knowledge in these systems is not directly encoded but exists in the relation or connections. As Bem and De Jong (2006: 183) clearly summarize:

> The knowledge of the network is usually *distributed* over many connections; unlike the so-called classical approach with its discrete symbols and data structures, the content of the system's belief cannot be localized in discrete symbol structures or program statements.

While it is still questionable these can simulate brains, there was a sense of the organisational and inter-related aspects of thinking. This was followed by another development known as 'dynamicism' (Port and Van Gelder 1995; Bechtel and Abrahamsen 2002; Bem and De Jong 2006: 190ff). This work first emerged from 'mobots' (mobile robots) and returned theorists to key questions of the environment in cognition. In these theories, cognition was linked to the *interaction* with the environment and significantly these models questioned the need for 'representational' structures, because it did not rely on simple input or output signals, something Turing ([1950] 1964) had long recognised.[13] Thought was now 'embedded' in interaction and environment. We must not forget that these ideas are surrounded by much ongoing research, discussion and debate, but the direction in thinking is important. Significantly, they led to ideas of the 'extended mind' (Clark and Chalmers 1998), which returns cognition to its wider environment. According to Bem and De Jong (2006: 216), the 'fierce' reaction against behaviourism undervalued behaviour and action in theoretical discussion, even though earlier thinkers like James and Dewey had held mind, body and action together. While computational theory has driven forward some creative and alternative modelling in its experimentation, large parts of cognitive science still remained caught in an idea of 'mind as a logical reasoning machine connected to a continually growing database' (Bem and De Jong

(2006: 216). This early model of cognitive thinking still dominates, not least in the cognitive science of religion. Nonetheless, new modelling does open up important potential for thinking beyond ideas of the knowledge economy and its allegiance to codified thinking.

Robert Wilson's (2004) insightful study *Boundaries of the Mind*, as we saw in Chapter 2, is one examination that offers ways to correct implicit assumptions in the field and, more importantly, his work opens ways to recognise how ideology shapes the conceptual. His concern, as we noted, was to challenge the individualistic errors in cognitive science and – reflecting the spirals of thinking in the field – returned to late nineteenth century models of the group mind to counter individualistic assumptions. His challenge to individualism in what he calls the 'fragile sciences' (Wilson 2004: 8–9) recognises the historical nature of thought. As Wilson rightly points out:

> Neither psychology as a discipline nor mind-laden individuals as the subject matter of that discipline are givens. The discipline has not always existed, and there is a history or genealogy to the formation of the discipline that has involved constructing individuals and minds in different ways at different times.
>
> (Wilson 2004: 29)

If models of the mind change over time it is important to recognise the interests that are served within the cognitive order of reality. Important for our purposes here is that Wilson's work principally explored the individualistic bias in cognitive computational studies and questioned the idea that 'they were or must be individualistic' (Wilson 2004: 144). He argues that individualism is maintained and shapes the field because of cognitive science's connection to representational theory (assuming representation exists between perception and behaviour). This view is maintained because of what Wilson – as we noted – calls an 'encoding view' of mental representation, a view that closes off wider analysis (which we can call simple modelling). However, in his study, he engages the alternative models in recent modelling and opens up wider areas of analysis (Wilson 2004: 148ff). Wilson exposes how 'innate assumptions' are made about computers and the world, which can be and are challenged. Indeed, he importantly argues that certain assumptions are '*exploited* by our computational mechanisms, rather than innate in our cognitive architecture' (Wilson 2004: 163). Wilson's critical thinking about cognition dislodges the representational and computational assumptions to create a space for an 'externalist' view of cognition and the mind. He provides a way to return cognition to a 'situated, embedded, and embodied' reality and reveals that more complex thinking (higher cognition) leads to ever-greater location in the physical and social world, as cognition is shown to register with environments (Wilson 2004: 185ff). As Wilson summarizes his complex position:

> I will argue that many cognitive capacities in symbol-using creatures, far from being purely internal, are either *enactive bodily* capacities, or *wordly-involving* capacities. These capacities are not realized by some internal arrangement of the brain or central nervous system, but by embodied states of the whole person, or by the wide system that includes (parts of) the brain as a proper part.
>
> (Wilson 2004: 188)

Wilson develops what he terms a 'wide psychological' or 'wide cognitive' view that opens knowledge up to its outside. Understanding cognition as 'worldly-involving' may just rescue us from destroying the environments that sustain them and recognise the overlapping and social nature of cognition. What Wilson does not do is examine why individualistic assumptions and cognitive closure occurs, but by blending his critical perspective with a reading of the knowledge-economy we might understand how some of our thinking about cognition is saturated with individualism and computational frames of reference. Enculturing the mind may not only be a necessary part of philosophy and the history of scientific psychology, but also an ethical-political challenge to the reading of religion.

Although the cognitive science of religion as a discursive space does not entertain the politics of its own knowledge – something impossible according to the rules of an aspiring science – it is not unaware of the 'cultural' location of cognition, especially given the concerns of anthropology that inform the observation and making of the religious object. However, as I will show with Whitehouse, while professional lip-service is paid to the social environment, codified models of cognition find useful rhetorical devices to by-pass the problem and refuse complexity. There are, however, interesting fusions emerging between those concerned with cultural anthropology and theories of the extended or dynamic mind. Mathew Day is one critical reader whose creative intuition established these important links. As he writes, in critique of Whitehouse's cognitive theory and referring to Hutchins's (1995: 360) *Cognition in the Wild*: 'In the case of religious thought and behaviour, for instance, it is odd that so few people have underscored how we customarily find computationally relevant representations of agency – such as statues, icons, and masks – outside of our heads in a "culturally constituted material environment" of our making' (Day 2004: 248). Boyer (2005) has also, again in critique of Whitehouse, established an opening to increase the variables in examining cultural phenomena. He writes referring to various appeals to supernatural agencies:

> We could then specify political conditions under which each of these is more likely, and measure the success of such predictions against observed institutions. More generally, what we could do is gradually *add factors* to the general likelihood function of religious concepts and norms, and measure to what extent each addition reduces the overall behavioral variance to explain.
>
> (Boyer 2005: 7–8, emphasis added)

Boyer, of course, is talking about religion and not himself or other cognitive scientists at this point, but in making Boyer and other cognitive scientists the subjects of observation, in a self-reflexive analysis we need to *add* political-economy in assessing the conditions of their *thinking about cognition*. It is thus necessary to extend *thinking about cognition* to the political order in a dynamic and complex mind, remembering that it, like religion, is a natural occurrence. It is time not only to bring our supernatural gods back to humanity, but our sciences back to the politics of concept-formation; for our language of mind is always formed by the changing historical environment of our minds. This takes on new dimensions when the knowledge economy saturates all systems of thinking.

The links between codified cognitivism and the knowledge economy are striking, because once we explore wider embedded interactions we appreciate the political nature of their assumptions in the 'machine economy' (Mirowski 2002). This makes 'complex' inter-disciplinarity a vital point of resistance against a codified world. Putting cognition back into complex worlds will be a necessary critical task for cognitive thinking about religion. If Wilson's work constitutes what we can call the mental-individualistic fallacy, then it is worth marking out other key fallacies that maintain the codified mental models in the study of religion. This critique is necessary in order to identify the continuing philosophical errors that hide behind the bright light of scientific endeavour.

Cognitive science, as an arena for the study of religion, is now with us and by its nature it will always be confused and fused with actual developments of computer technology. There are important insights to be taken and much to be learnt, but much is lost in the conceptual labyrinth of a new world with all the uncritical celebration and dreams of a world of prediction, control and mastery of minds, covering a fear of unpredictable bodies and their fluid political environments. In a world where technological power drives social and economic practices, the notion of information processing and machine orders saturates the language, imagination and the thinking about thinking. As all cultural reality comes under the signification of the technological-economic power, so all discourses will be read in terms of the discourse that carries the values of that technological-economic order in the knowledge economy.

As explored in the earlier sections of this book, the knowledge economy is based on knowledge production generating finance and not simply information reproduction (Foray 2004: 1). Computer-led innovation is the central model of such knowledge production, because of its efficiency. Codification of knowledge, in terms of the technological structure, thus provides an ease of distribution and a capacity to self-generate. The concepts of cognitive science can replicate sufficiently and efficiently, they migrate well by translating all knowledge into cognitive processes. Codified cognition, in its computational discursive formation, becomes part of the logic of contemporary thought. These operations – gestures of authority – become possible because the field of use is sustained by political-economic agencies and institutions, which require a specific form of calculation to facilitate the 'cultural flows' within a society. The 'cultural flow' in a neo-liberal environment requires conceptual modelling that works on the definable mathematical orders of computational logic. Hence models that assist the dominant order (in this case financial transactions) will be reinforced by the system. As Valerie Walkerdine (1988: 211) states in her assessment of developmental and cognitive psychology:

> It is my contention that the modern order is founded upon a rational, scientific, and calculating form of government, government which claims to describe and control nature, according to natural laws. Thus mathematics can be understood as absolutely central to the production of this order.

Cognitive science of religion embeds itself in a calculating order by stabilising definite mental operations – indisputable orders of the mind (based on a mind-brain fallacy and a concept-science fallacy). The calculus of cognition in its post-1980s statement is qualitatively different from that of the pre-1980s, as the field of use holds a more abstract set of associations allowing the impression of greater precision in connections and networks. Let us be clear at this point that the economic environment does not create the discourse in a conspiracy theory model. Rather, as I have already stated, the dominant social order of finance capital takes over other domains of knowledge and enables a flourishing of models that reinforce its environment. Cognitive science, in its computational mode, is therefore the conceptual capital for a model of being human in a neo-liberal environment, because it makes *subjects* objects for order. Indeed, they easily become 'commodified' by being reduced to a possible mathematical equation.

Models of the mind in the technological age of computers and artificial intelligence mirror each other because of the conceptual capital behind it. The dream of the financial machine is that humans become *efficient*. Efficiency is maximised in a calculating order of representation, thus (again) models of the mind that service the calculus of capital will flourish. Cognition is the acceptable order of innovation to make us into something for profit. The cognitive science of religion is therefore a discourse of its age and rather than ask about its truth-value we should rather ask about its political value, because irrespective of its 'truth' it is now a political reality of the knowledge economy. However, before we see the ideology, we need to contextualize and question the claims to be a 'science' without a politics of concepts.

Amnesia and avoidance: elisions of the cognitive brain

Sustained by a wider political environment, the cognitive science of religion is able to articulate a range of statements with little critical examination. Jensine Andresen (2001), in her edited collection of papers on the subject, is aware of the problems of generating concepts without sufficient analysis or empirical support and calls for urgent work, but the slippage continues in the euphoria of a new 'science' and a supporting political climate. I want to take three central fallacies (in addition to Wilson's mental-individualistic fallacy above) that we need to address in the cognitive science of religion in order to return it to its ideological environment: first, the fallacy of stable religious objects; second, the mind-brain fallacy; and, third, the concept-science fallacy. When we examine these problems we re-enter the realms of philosophical and political contestation. I introduce a series of central fallacies here to dislodge the cognitive closure of thought and allow space for a greater complexity in interactive worlds. William James dealt with some of these problems over 100 years ago, but, as I have shown, disciplinary amnesia is part of the way fields of knowledge cover over logical errors and I will return to James at certain moments (even though some other aspects of his thinking have been seen to be problematic).[14] It is not my aim or desire to give a full and comprehensive account of these questions, but rather to draw together some of the theoretical concerns in order to show that, at least, some caution and concern is required and that the elisions within theory are sufficient to warrant a socio-political analysis.

It would be wrong to think I am trying to eradicate the cognitive field of knowledge. I am rather attempting to find the political ground of concepts and to make thought more complex by locating it within the prevailing social apparatus. Indeed, I can appreciate Dan Sperber's (1996: 38, 43; 1997) bold assertions to step out into theory and the embrace of his 'bias', through weak and strong assertions, for as long as we meet in the wrestling of ideas between the mental and the public representations, we can at least open a door to the politics of knowledge and recognise the interacting worlds (which at times he appears to acknowledge). Within Sperber's more epistemic openings there is at least an honest will-to-power and a struggle to assert his 'more basic' position. The problem is when the rhetoric of 'science' in the codified cognitive study of religion throws out other orders of truth-making in the dogma of the 'basic' understanding of the cognitive. Before we can establish grounds for exchange, let us, as Sperber (1996: 37, 43) suggests, do some 'conceptual house cleaning'.

The stable religious object fallacy

At the outset, cognitive science is always trapped inside the making of its 'religious' object, because the conceptual modelling requires a stable domain for its articulations and thus requires that religion and its objects are distinct, otherwise there would be no subject for examination. This problem is not so much found in writers such as Sperber, who largely avoids specificity of religious objects (perhaps reflecting his French context), referring instead to symbols and beliefs. However, it is a defining feature of the emergent field of religion and cognition (Slone 2006). Indeed, for its all philosophical technicality and empiricism, it is remarkable how unaware those working in the area of cognition are about the philosophy of language, the history of psychology and the debates about the category of religion in the last 20 years, revealing the nature of disciplinary amnesia.[15] Lawson and McCauley (2002) never resolved their own 'manufacturing' of the ritual object of *religion* and in the end, after much irritation, conceded to suspend the idea of religion into a general functioning of the mind. 'Instead', they argue, 'it is only a theory about actions that individuals and groups perform within organised communities of people who possess conceptual schemes that include presumptions about those actions' connections with the actions of agents who exhibit various counter-intuitive properties' (Lawson and McCauley 2002: 9).

William James ([1902] 1960: 26) had been aware of many of these errors of definition that late modern scholars stumble over in their amnesia. He is aware, for example, in his own study of 'religious experience' that 'the word "religion" cannot stand for any single principle or essence, but is rather a collective name'. As James continues with a profound insight for later psychological thinking: 'The theorizing mind tends always to the over-simplification of its materials'. James was also aware that just as there was no essence to 'religion' there was also no distinct 'religious' faculty within the mind. For James there were only feelings, sentiments and thoughts 'directed to the religious object' (James [1902] 1960: 27). The psychological state is only made religious according to the context and categorization of the object. Indeed, I have made the point elsewhere that James is more of a social psychologist in his discussion of religious emotion than might at first be realized (see Carrette 2005b).

However, forgetting James, 'ritual' (Lawson and McCauley), 'god-concepts' (Barrett) and the 'supernatural' (Boyer) are all variously isolated in the cognitive science of religion from wider historical, linguistic and theological scholarship to make religion a stable cognitive object for analysis; although Boyer (1994) at least recognises the need to naturalize. For example, in order to make a series of assertions about God (real or not), Barrett and Keil (1996) boil down exceedingly complex and nuanced traditions of hundreds of years, stating: '*Unfortunately*, the canonical texts of Western religions do not simplify matters much' (emphasis added). Nonetheless, years of complex and highly debated concepts, with diverse cultural and historical variations, are made into easily manageable and reducible forms for easy programming and conceptual modelling. The key words in their analysis are 'recast' and 'basic', which covers many an ideological leap and jump (Barrett and Keil 1996: 118). The problems of understanding God are 'recast' in terms more accessible to cognitive analysis.

The cognitive science of religion does not study religion it rather *makes* a new object, which only exists in its own formation and which can be reduced to quantifiable outcomes. Critique needs to suspend this order of simplification, because once we start looking behind all the complex statistical performances we find only meaningless objects, or common sense responses, dressed in the clothes of science. These moves enable us to see that the cognitive science of religion strategically uses the imagined objects of religion in order to support its rhetorical operations and adjust reality for the knowledge economy (see the Introduction to this book;

Proudfoot 1985). It is the recasting of religion for the calculated logic of contemporary knowledge production that generates its new income. Huge amounts of knowledge are produced in the cognitive science of religion, but experimental data so reduced that the researchers can only conclude that 'many questions remain' (Barrett and Keil 1996: 142). Indeed, many questions remain and it is not just scholars of religion, as Andreson (2001) rightly argues, that need to 'familiarize themselves with cognitive science's key orienting concepts and methodologies', scholars of cognitive science need to show a greater technical respect for studies in the history of religion and the philosophy of religious language before the simple 'recasting' of an object for the knowledge economy. But let us go precisely into the entangled world of the philosophy of science to unsettle a few more dogmas of the cognitive science of religion.

The mind-brain fallacy (in the knowledge economy)

The power of the knowledge economy is such that highly complex technical disputes in the history of ideas are easily ignored in the commodification of concepts. Nuanced thinking is resisted in the binary modes of the knowledge economy; even as complexity theory tries to add some wisdom to the one-dimensional thinking of the market. However, we can perhaps save wisdom by taking support from Bennett and Hacker in their balanced and careful reading of cognitive neuroscience from the position of Wittgenstein's philosophy of language; even if Sperber (1996: 37) will resist here, we can at least debate in the space of philosophy and politics without pretensions to science. Bennett and Hacker document how scientists confuse philosophical thinking in their grand assertions. For example, the scientist Susan Greenfield claimed during her television series on the brain that positron emission tomography enables us to 'see thoughts' (Bennett and Hacker 2003: 70, n.11; see also Greenfield 2000).

Bennett and Hacker realise that in an atmosphere of growing consensus (supported I would argue by wider orders of knowledge management) 'one is prone to be swept along by enthusiastic announcements – of new fields of knowledge conquered' (Bennett and Hacker 2003: 70). They raise important questions in the philosophy of language to contextualise confusing statements. Their work reveals how after the euphoria of the 1990s 'decade of the brain' the claims of science need philosophical correction and contextualisation. For example, they point out that while we know what it is for human beings to experience, reason and pose questions, we do not know 'what it is for *a brain* to see or hear, for *a brain* to have experiences, to know or believe something'. They develop the 'mereological fallacy' to counter attempts to attribute psychological attributes to the brain, other than as metaphor (and metaphors have a funny way of becoming the real thing in cognitive 'non-science'). The mereological fallacy is the 'neuroscientists' mistake of ascribing to the constituent *parts* of an animal attributes that logically apply only to the *whole* animal' (Bennett and Hacker 2003: 73).

Before I am accused of confusing issues in cognitive neuroscience with cognitive science, I should add that the rhetorical power of both cognitive science and its modelling is grounded on the central appeal to the brain; as if to give the statement greater material and scientific 'truth' when in reality it is swamped in philosophical ambiguity. Discourses of the brain provide a kind of safe-harbour for ungrounded concepts, but such concepts are philosophically at sea. Such that Harvey Whitehouse (2002: 293 emphasis added) can write: 'Patterns of mental activity, *rooted in the biology of brain functions* and the contexts in which these develop, have direct effects on the elaboration of all domains of human culture'. But the biology of brain function has not been shown 'scientifically' to carry his cognitive concepts; rhetoric and the ideological ground of the knowledge economy enable scholars 'to boldly go' where no scientist or philosophy has been. Of course, James had already done his homework on these matters for the study of religion and the fault-lines of the past replicate in the disciplinary remaking of the subject.

James ([1902] 1960) made it clear, for example, that all states of mind have an organic basis in his attack on the 'medical materialists', but this has little value in understanding the taxonomy of religion. There is nothing surprising about physiological processes shaping life, but it is a qualitatively different order of statement to jump from social discourse to cognitive modelling to brains. 'Scientific theories', as James ([1902] 1960: 16) argues, 'are organically conditioned just as much as religious emotions are ...'. Here we see the importance of making cognitive science or neuroscience the object, rather than religion, to see the tricks of analysis (see Carrette 2002). Why is it that the organic chemicals of the believer's brain are subject to the organic chemicals of the scientist's brain and not the other way round? Perhaps, it is not just about chemicals but also politics. It is not what is going on in the brain or the heavens, but how we are living together on earth that matters. Here we come again to what James ([1902] 1960: 42, 40) wonderfully called the 'bugaboo of morbid origin'. He, like Bennett and Hacker, recognised that the importance of an idea was '*the way in which it works on the whole*' that matters, the fruits not the roots. As James makes clear to the medical materialists, we should make clear to cognitive scientists:

> To plead organic causation of a religious state of mind, then, in refutation of its claim to possess superior spiritual value, is quite illogical and arbitrary, unless one has already worked out in advance some psycho-physical theory connecting spiritual values in general with determinate sorts of physiological change. Otherwise none of our thoughts and feelings, not even our scientific doctrines, not even our *dis*-beliefs, could retain any value as revelations of the truth, for every one of them without exception flows from the state of its possessor's body at the time.
>
> (James ([1902] 1960: 36)

We learn slowly and circle back to old debates – is this James against Spencer again? Are old ideas replayed for the new theories to yet again be reminded, in their desire for conquest and power, that knowledge and understanding are complex and not reducible to our will for simple theories? However much we wish to 'recast' complex thought into a simple programme our interacting and categorising nature will always return us to the politics of logical errors and the way we give order to things prior to their analysis. The question is always how long the socio-economic conditions will permit such errors and which errors facilitate the practical logic of the time.

The concept-science fallacy

It has been a major part of my argument, following the work of Bennett and Hacker, to underline that *concepts* within the models of cognitive *science* are not innately *scientific* by virtue of their discursive domain, as some clearly imagine. I want to return to this fallacy, because of the ideological cover within the scientific claims of some cognitive theory. As Bennett and Hacker (2003: 2) indicate: 'When a conceptual question is confused with a scientific one, it is bound to appear singularly refractory'. The continuing problem, as Bennett and Hacker go on to point out, is that conceptual questions are not open to empirical verification just as problems in 'pure mathematics' are not 'solvable by the methods of physics'. The fact that conceptual problems are not open to scientific investigation by logical definition returns us to the nature of language and meaningful articulations.

In James's discussion of psychology and philosophy he recognised that when psychology was taken as a natural science the phrase 'states of mind' was taken as data (James [1892] 1985: 329). He recognises that the problem begins when we become metaphysical and he rightly asks what we mean by 'corresponds' in relation to statements of mind and brain. Concepts bring us back to philosophy; and cognitive science is full of concepts. I agree with James, but I want to go further. I want to bring psychology back into philosophy and philosophy back into the politics of embodied exchanges in living environments.

It is acknowledged by those within cognitive science of religion that greater philosophical scrutiny of its concepts is required and once we can return it to this domain we can then begin to see the investments behind the disputes. Philosophy does not have the means of resolving all conflicting assertions, one can believe one set of arguments or another, but in the end there are different ways of looking at the same problem. Of course, philosophy becomes passionate in the struggle to assert one set of meanings over the other. I am happy with these unresolved disputes, because they bring us to the joy of irresolution in conceptual argumentation, especially when imagining who we might be and become. Human thought and social activity are about debate and exchange of ideas, the danger is when we run into intellectual fundamentalism rather than holding complexity – the blight of our present age of thinking.

Conceptual modelling is a valuable exercise, but misapplication and misunderstanding are made easier when there is a prevailing climate of opinion validating certain conceptual models for the market of technology, which is driving our economic world. If we are to appreciate the nature of theoretical modelling, cognitive science cannot be innocent of political economy. Philosophy is always involved in assertions of truth-power as well as trying to work out statements of fact, but statements of fact and empirical verification should not be confused with a political will-to-power.[16] The history of psychology reveals these problems of conceptual modelling, especially when they persist with their errors. To return to James again:

> The fundamental conceptions of psychology are practically very clear to us, but theoretically they are very confused, and one easily makes the obscurest assumptions in this science without realizing, until challenged, what internal difficulties they involve. When these assumptions have once established themselves (as they have a way of doing in our very descriptions of phenomenal facts) it is almost impossible to get rid of them afterwards or to make anyone see that they are not essential features of the subject.
>
> (James [1890] 1983: 148)

We have now set the complex ground to examine the politics of knowledge within the quasi-empirical vision of the cognitive science of religion and we must now turn in detail to the work of Harvey Whitehouse.

Two modes of imagining religiosity

Harvey Whitehouse (1995, 2000, 2005a) developed an original 'cognitive' theory of two modes of religiosity from his ethnographic observation of the Pomio Kivung community in Papua New Guinea. He identified two 'contrasting politico-religious regimes' (the mainstream and splinter group) and marked them out according to a 'doctrinal' (frequent semantic memory) and the 'imagistic' (infrequent episodic memory) patterns. Such a dichotomy, as he admits, is not new, but found in the history of the sociology of religion in Weber's ([1904–5] 2001) 'routinized' and 'charismatic', Gellner's (1969) urban and rural religious syndromes, Goody's (1968) rigid-literate religions and mutable non-literate religions, Turner's (1974) fertility rituals and political rituals, to mention a few of his identified correlations (Whitehouse 1995: 5, 2000: 3). The key difference is his attempt at '*recasting* the problem in the light of recent findings of cognitive psychology' (Whitehouse 1995: 5, 194, 203, emphasis added) and his creation of a 'single theory' for all the features identified in the existing literature (Whitehouse 2000: 4).

What is particularly interesting about Whitehouse's theory is its evolution in each of his three monographs on the topic and the increasing application of the signifier *cognitive* into his discursive regime. In the first book *Inside the Cult* (1995: 194) he 'mak[es] use' of the cognitive and cushions his thinking with Weber's 'ideal types' (Whitehouse 1995: 207). The cognitive findings are almost an appendage in the last chapter to the rich ethnographic study in the first seven. However, in the second book, *Arguments and Icons* (2000: 1), he extends his assumptions to the wider historical developments in Melanesia and religious forms originating in Europe. The cognitive register increases its discursive function and power to order 'universal' features and the work is seen as discussing 'certain "cutting-edge" theories of cognitive psychology' (Whitehouse 2000: 4, 5, 11). The language also takes a stronger force referring to 'cognitive dimensions', 'principles of cognitive processing' and 'cognitive underpinnings', even though he insists the model is developed according to '*tendencies*' and 'they remain tendencies and nothing more'.

By the third book, *Modes of Religiosity* (2005a), these processes are developed and further 'embedded' in a 'hard and factual' cognitive apparatus in a desire for empiricism – an empiricism without philosophical analysis of the *a priori* assumptions and one that also continues the dream of context-free science (Whitehouse 2005a: 169). This can be seen in the way the theory is embellished in restricted cognitive concepts, as the codified foundations are 'substantially enriched and extended' (Whitehouse 2005a: 1).[17] Although some concessions to context are added to the work and a caution against computer modelling of the mind is offered, the cognitive still operates on limited codified forms that are concealed by the focus on the object of religion and an 'enclosed' discussion with other cognitive theorists (Whitehouse 2005a: 22). There is nothing wrong with subsequent clarification and development of a theory and idea, but what is fascinating about his approach is the way the unexamined rhetoric of *cognition* functions in his texts and how this language mirrors the social apparatus of the political world precisely as he employs strategies to underplay the ideological against the cognitive. Let me explain these strategies in more detail.

The cognitive functions in Whitehouse as a politically neutral concept and in his own readings of memory he believes his position is counter to the political and ideological work of such writers as Maurice Halbwachs (1925, [1950] 1992). For example he writes contrasting himself with such thinking:

> The central thrust of my argument goes in the opposite direction. Instead of asking how political organization and ideology help to mould people's memories, I am asking whether universal features of human memory, activated in different ways, might be said to mould political organization.
>
> (Whitehouse 2000: 5)

The *cognitive* is then used as a scientific strategy to preclude it from the ideological and political. Following Sperber (1985b: 79), he makes a similar point: 'Political, religious, and economic institutions cannot be said to affect each other without *first* affecting people's minds' (Whitehouse 1995: 194, emphasis added).[18] This is a clever device of deflection, because it isolates minds by an appeal to origins and limits any extension. It is a genetic fallacy, explaining something by a false appeal to origins. Obviously, *there is no question that human agents create social systems from their own given capacities but to suggest that we can separate the cognitive from its own representational order is to suggest cognitive scientist can step outside of time, language and culture to reveal an original cognition beneath their own ways of representing that cognition.* Concepts of cognition and thinking about ourselves are not preserved from extraneous influence. The genetic fallacy also entails the concept-science fallacy (discussed above) in the same move, because the cognitive is not a given order, even as Whitehouse uses the term without question. Concepts of cognition are not given *a priori* with the physical brain, although that assumption frames the writings of cognitive science as we have seen.

This appeal to an imaginary space of cognition is supported by an appeal to psychological 'truth' outside anthropological ethnographical practice, to the 'crucial' findings of cognitive science (Whitehouse 1995: 194). The appeal to another discipline and sets of research is always a false insulation of argumentation, because it never brings into question the supporting discourse and its formation (something common to studies in the science of religion). Whitehouse's starting point is the 'psychologist', but the psychologist, as this book has repeatedly shown, is caught in a wider politic of knowledge formation. The cognitive then functions as an externally valid concept imported to read the object of culture or religion without philosophical analysis. It functions as the *a priori* ground of experience and behaviour like the concept of *experience* in Proudfoot's (1985) study.

To extend the insight of Proudfoot (1985), discussed in the introduction, the *cognitive* acts as a placeholder (the unquestionable ground) for a certain type of utterance outside the political (and implicitly against the political). It carries a cultural order of meaning in Whitehouse's work along the lines we have already examined. It becomes, as Whitehouse acknowledges, a way of 'welding' knowledge together in a 'unified theoretical framework' and of reading the intellectualist and sociological in terms of the psychological (Whitehouse 1995: 218, 220). But the extraordinary function of the cognitive placeholder is that this overriding of other discourses, and the prioritizing of psychological-cognitive 'truth' over all other forms of perspective on 'truth', is never perceived as 'ideological'. The *cognitive* then becomes a protected concept, presumably on the assumption it does not require qualification, but as we have shown it is an historically volatile and theoretically unstable concept, carrying all sorts of assumptions about individualism, science and ideologies of codification. Whitehouse's work is littered with references to 'encoded' and 'codification', but what metaphorical order of power do these words carry?

The ideology of codification

Whitehouse's ethnographic work is concerned with socio-political realities. Indeed, he confirms, 'the two modalities of codification may be linked to some extent with divergent political trajectories' (Whitehouse 2000: 50). Whitehouse is also clear when discussing Christian missionary activity in Melanesian society that the memory of rituals and anonymous identities had political significance. 'The political implications of this cannot be underestimated' (Whitehouse 2000: 40). His work on the Pomio Kivung is also concerned with nationalist agendas and millenarian expectations

(Whitehouse 1995: 203). The politic was on transmitting ideas in these contexts, but what Whitehouse never considers is the politics behind his own transmission of *cognitive* ideas. What is the value of 'recasting' socio-cultural realities (*vis-à-vis* the imagined object of *religion*) into the discourse of codification? Or we might add, what is the mind-stuff doing to transform Whitehouse's taxonomy of cultural transmission and why does that transmission depend on limiting *cognition* to the mind?

Let me make the rhetorical and ideological structure clear by reading 'routinized religion' (Whitehouse 2000: 112) in different ways. In discussing the issue of Christian missions, Whitehouse talks of the way Christian missions attempted to 'routinize worship far more extensively than was usual in the lives of church-going Europeans during the same period' (Whitehouse 2000: 39). He discusses daily 'habits' and routines at the mission station and children chanting to remember – or 'encode' as Whitehouse prefers – knowledge more deeply. Now first – and here I go back to James and the question of 'naturalization' that later cognitive theorists, like Boyer, rediscovered – there is nothing different about *religion* and any other forms of educational practice of learning and remembering. They are the same human processes. So removing Whitehouse's work from the religious object fallacy, we are returned to questions of memory itself and the mind-stuff of cognition. How does it help to use the term cognition? The term appears to 'anchor' the discovery in some way beyond the taxonomical 'observation'. The hypothesis is that there is some place – one assumes the brain – which is determining this memory process, but why is the abstract notion of *cognition* closed and confused in this way? What does Whitehouse want in this appeal? What cause does it serve? The danger is always, to recall Shotter (1997) again, the 'isolation-from-everything-else' of this approach and it is at this point we see the ideology of cognition very clearly.

The logic of Whitehouse's position is to argue that everything we do is determined by cognitive processes of codification, which shapes institutions, political orders and ritual behaviour. In this process it is interesting to note how he shifts the Weberian language of 'routinize' into the 'cognitive' as a device of reordering. 'Routinization is *directly connected* to the style of codification' (Whitehouse 2000: 9, emphasis added) And later, he writes 'rituals are highly routinized and *therefore* cognized as general schema' (Whitehouse 2000: 51, emphasis added). It is not that he is providing evidence of Weber's position, because Weber only argues for an 'ideal type' not an empirical reality, but Whitehouse seeks to 'recast' everything in the cognitive order.

The language of making the *cognitive* operates by deflecting enquiry into an *a priori* structure, but this concept-fallacy masks how its own reality is 'manufactured' in the very discourse. We can see this in relation to the idea of memory. Whitehouse's work is built on the foundation of 'types' of memory. 'Modes' are 'encoded' in 'types of memory'. What is striking about this is that the 'mode' is imagined, created or invented – it even has a certain 'arbitrariness' (Whitehouse 2000: 3) associated with its characteristics. Thus before the hypothesis of 'encoded memory', there already exists a postulated *mode* that is rooted in the memory, which makes it possible to have all sorts of memory by imagining all sorts of modes. The codified is dependent on the second order creation of a thing or mode being memorized. I have discussed this problem in relation to McCauley and Lawson, 'such that where Ritual Act "A" is abstractly equated with Cognition "B", B=A, irrespective of the politics of theory construction X, Y, and Z' (Carrette 2005c: 247). This circular logic is part of a way of preserving the cognitive from all other factors of influence. It is also important to note that the way we think about *memory* today, in an age of non-human extended memory in the computer, is different to how we imagined memory in ages prior to machines (see Carruthers 1992; 1998). Whitehouse thus uses the word 'memory' without qualification, because he frames it in terms of a hidden individualistic cognitive model and not in terms, for example, of Wilson's social memory (Wilson 2004: 189–98). As Wilson insightfully remarks:

> 'Memory', like 'cognition', is something of a catch-all term, and the phenomena it refers to are ubiquitous in our mental lives: in language acquisition and use, the performance and learning skills, communication and socializing, daily routines, and any form of employment. If memory is externalized, then so too is much of our cognitive life.
>
> (Wilson 2004: 197)

We can characterise Whitehouse's shift in thinking to the cognitive as a 'syntax precedes symbolic argument', but syntax never exists in some isolated domain. It is always a specific historical and social operation and always both in and outside the brain (as in the written, printed or electronic text). Syntax only makes sense in its symbolic operation, as they are inter-dependent. It is always both mental and public and the syntax-symbolic power then has the capacity to regulate the operation of the mental capacity. I can imagine and create many different things according to the same rules of syntax, but to want to isolate syntax reveals nothing about the symbolic values of living. I can also use the same syntax to talk of 'remembering' and 'encoding', but the symbolic power of such references reveals a vastly different order of representation about 'thinking' or 'cognition' and a pre- and post-computer metaphorical modelling of ourselves.

Whitehouse is, at least, aware of the problems of transferring his model to other regional and historical contexts (Whitehouse 1995: 160), but this does not stop him from making 'universal' claims with the signification of *cognition* and then mapping his model according to the literate and non-literate societies, a frame which would appear to undermine the necessity to talk of *cognition* (Whitehouse 2000: 5, 11, 160ff). The key to the isolationist politic is the word 'linked'. Whitehouse notes that 'codification' is linked to 'group formation', 'dynamics of social organization' and 'divergent political trajectories' (Whitehouse 2000: 49, 50), but submerges these 'links' by elevating the 'cognitive' as *the* primary order of importance. It is also, somewhat bizarrely, an approach that is both 'less obvious' and 'common sense' (Whitehouse 2000: 50, 118), such subtle shifts reveal the ideological desire to take what we know (observe) and make it more than it seems (the innate). The move from observation to scientific fact is nothing new. As Goldenberg (1979) and others have noted, Carl Jung moved easily over time from original taxonomical patterns to biological fact in his theory of archetypes (see Carrette 1994) in a very similar way to Whitehouse; although Whitehouse's reading rests on wider technological shifts in society.

What we have therefore in Whitehouse's work is an introduction of the language of cognition, codification and transmission into the language of thinking, remembering and communicating. The former language is far from neutral as a scientific 'truth', as we have shown with the concept-fallacy discussion above. How then are we to make sense of it and where might we find this 'mode' of discourse operating in the contemporary Western world? The point becomes clearer if we follow again the word 'routinized' in Whitehouse's discourse. If Weber's world was shaped by industrial metaphors, the language of computer technology overlies Whitehouse's language. The fundamental difference, however, is that Whitehouse's language rests on a 'scientific' register rather than the descriptive order of 'ideal types', but we have already seen that this appeal to the 'scientific' is not conclusive or by any means certain.[19] It is then worth considering Whitehouse's language in relation to the literature of the knowledge economy to make my point, but before that, perhaps we can make cognitive science the object of examination by exploring some other critical voices of Whitehouse's work – both within and outside of the area of cognitive science.

Critical extensions

There is no doubt that Harvey Whitehouse's choice to read his anthropological fieldwork in terms of cognitive science has attracted a lot of critical attention and for that alone it has value in creating enormous debate. While few have considered his model from the perspective of its location within the conditions of the knowledge economy, there have been those who question his isolationist logic.[20] Three useful critical voices are important in my attempt to extend Whitehouse's theoretical discourse to economics and the political culture.

First, Gregory Alles's (2004) critical essay is one of the few to examine Whitehouse's work from economic theory. He seeks to 'complement' or 'intersect' models of cognition with economic variables of repeated and term exchange and, although I would want to question forms of cognitive-economic theory, he uses these to at least counterbalance Whitehouse's selectivity. Importantly, Alles recognises the 'extended' context of cognition when he concludes: '[T]he world is not something that we merely conceptualize and remember; it is a place where we live. Organisms do not cognize the world for the sheer pleasure of doing so; they cognize the world in order to live in it' (Alles 2004: 286). Alles, rightly in my view, wants to widen Whitehouse's model, but he never questions the discursive order of cognition inside the politics of Whitehouse's knowledge.

A second argument that is nearer to this position, is put forward by Mathew Day (2004). Day, anticipating the moment when scholars versed in 'Geertzian thick descriptions of local cultural arrangements' start approaching cognitive research, offers a 'primer' for future debates. In his critique of Whitehouse he puts the case (as I have mentioned earlier in this chapter) for an 'embedded cognition', which he believes will only succeed if established on 'modest lines' that resist Mithen's (1997) thesis of material forms 'beyond the capacity of the mind' (Day 2004: 253). While Alles and Day are concerned to offer methodological critiques in examining the object of 'religion' and my concern is with the discourse of 'cognition' in reading 'religion', it is still worth exploring some of Whitehouse's very revealing responses to their work as a way forward to my concern with the conditions of meta-cognition in the knowledge economy.

Whitehouse's response to Alles is to return to the safety of the 'generalizable variables' and to question Alles's speculation of the 'possible'. But after underlining these points, in his response to Day, he is emphatic about his support for a 'complex array of processes that unfold through the development of organisms-in-environments' (Whitehouse 2004: 330). One can admire Whitehouse's modesty in his expectations at this point, but not his ethical-political will or desire to think in complex ways. Whitehouse is right to question the 'reification' of social institutions, but wrong to assume that 'active agents' do not 'reify' concepts for political purposes and then support them by creating institutions to sustain and propagate such concepts, especially when the concepts close down a wider social analysis (which would reveal the ethical-political nature of knowledge). It is also striking that in response to Day's critique, Whitehouse refers to an article outside the main corpus of his writings on cognitive modes of religiosity. In this article, Whitehouse (2001: 170, 179) is clearly open to an argument, following Hutchins (1996), that cognition is 'distributed' and he clearly argues for a 'combination' approach. What is not clear is how far this is carried out in the *practice* of his theory, because of the inability to capture the infinite variables.

Here, and in his later work (Whitehouse 2005a: 22–4, 27, 174), Whitehouse, under increasing pressure from critical voices, does acknowledge the importance of the environment, but this is never fully theorized because of his 'empirical challenge' to establish a discourse of measurability and the blindness to the fact that his own *cognition* about cognition is subject to the same criteria (Whitehouse 2005a: 157–70). Whitehouse (2005a: 16, 22–4) can argue for the importance of 'religion' as a 'distributed' and 'context dependent' phenomenon, but he does not apply this to his own discursive formations. In the later work, he even moves towards a middle position between 'fixed generic device' and 'organic structure' but is too entrenched in his own position to think dynamically about cognition in the ways Wilson (2004) has articulated. The problem is, however, not just about cautious scientific accounts (for which he must be commended), but an unwillingness to widen the remit of investigation by sufficiently unpacking what the *context* and the idea of a *dynamic* mind means for empirical 'science' of the mind itself, which bring us to a third critical voice of Whitehouse's work.

Boyer (2005: 23, 17–18), sensitive to the issues of an 'empirical discipline', wants to open up Whitehouse's work to a wider set of variables and to claim his modes of religiosity are 'bundles-of-features' or a 'description of features that fit together'. He believes Whitehouse would benefit from examining social stratification. What is even more striking is that Boyer (2005: 18), as we noted earlier, shows an appreciation of economic and political factors informing the reading of the doctrinal mode. Boyer (2005: 18–22) then locates these within a discussion of 'religious guilds' – 'a group that derives its livelihood, influence, and power from the fact that it provides particular services'. Boyer's reading of the cultural practices in terms of market control and brands is a striking – and refreshing – development for a cognitive theorist. It reveals the importance of complex and integrated levels of reading. As Boyer, uncharacteristically, writes against Whitehouse's view of doctrinal modes: 'The conflict is a political and economic one between individuals located in different niches of the religious market'.

Boyer's turn to the wider environment, rather than isolating cognitive theory, is an important development against cognitive imperialism. Such a move then gives us an opportunity to read cognitive science in the same terms. What specialist services do cognitive scientists offer in a niche market of the knowledge economy? And what might we find with a 'more historically specific version of cognitive understandings' not just of religion but of cognitive theory? Could it be that Whitehouse's own model is part of the social stratification of the knowledge economy? Alles, Day and Boyer open up a valuable critical context by widening the intellectual space for thinking about cognitive patterns of religion and, although they may be a little uncomfortable with my extension, by the same rules they enable us to return this critique back on cognitive science. In the light of these reflections, let us examine how the discourse of cognitive science operates in Whitehouse's work and explore how it mirrors thinking in the knowledge economy. In addition, if we are to take seriously Whitehouse's (2005a: 174) later concession that the 'causes of religion reside not only in mechanisms of human thinking but in the contexts of their activation' then this must be no less true of psychological theory. While Whitehouse may want to keep to the safety of empiricism, the 'context of activation' in the knowledge economy reveals the ideological basis of his empirical vision.

Whitehouse in the neo-liberal knowledge economy

In his study of the knowledge economy the French knowledge management theorist Dominique Foray, whose work we discussed in Part I, explores the reproduction of knowledge. In this discussion he uses the language of 'codification' and examines the 'role of codification in the context of our knowledge-based economies' (Foray 2004: 73). He notes the nature of costly reproductions of what Polanyi called 'tacit' knowledge; knowledge that 'cannot be expressed outside the action of the person who has it'. However, 'codified' knowledge is more efficient because it can be reproduced at 'low marginal costs'. As Foray writes:

> Knowledge can, however, be codified; that is to say, it can be expressed in a particular language and recorded on a particular medium. As such,

it is detached from the individual, and the memory and communication capacity created is made independent of human beings.

(Foray 2004: 74)

In discussion of written societies and knowledge storage Foray also makes reference to Jack Goody's *The Domestication of the Savage Mind* (1977) and underlines the importance of written material in social orders and the economic function of modes of 'traditional' *codification*. So far we may appreciate the shared language and understanding with Whitehouse on knowledge transfer and the techniques of oral and, also following Goody's (1977) work, literate societies. But then Foray takes us into another question of the 'evolution of knowledge modelling', where he notes that the 'type of code has cognitive implications' (Foray 2004: 79). From lists, tables, formulae to software languages, simulation technology and the World Wide Web, there are different orders of knowledge modelling. This shows that the 'tools' we create for memory change memory and the language about memory, but also that these are economically driven. Foray, like Whitehouse, is thus caught up inside his own logic of representing knowledge inside an evolving set of metaphors about knowledge. He is, for example, using the language of codification and cognition as sub-parts of his discussion of knowledge, because knowledge-management emerges out of the technological age.

However, the key part of Foray's argument to note at this point, is the *link* he makes between codification and economic costs. Any form of codification is linked to an economic benefit (a resource distribution question) and the needs of adaptation to specific economic contexts (cognitive in the extended sense). 'Thus, the economic analysis of the choice to codify concerns only that which is *codifiable* in a given historical context' (Foray 2004: 83, emphasis added). Here we see the ideological tension and paradox in Foray, because the language of the knowledge economy *codifies* knowledge for the technological age of the global market. The situation is reinforced when the codification of cognitive science also appears at the heart of neo-liberal economic theory. 'The key underlying philosophical commitments of mainstream mathematical economics', as economist John Davis (2003: 89) argues, 'are those of early cognitive science which models individuals as mathematical or computational machines'.[21] The ideology of networked *mathesis*, as we saw in Chapter 2, sustains knowledge management, cognitive science and contemporary economics and is exploited for efficiency. The force of my argument here needs a little unpacking for the purposes of greater clarity.

The discourses of 'knowledge economy' and 'cognitive science' emerge out of, *and subsequently contribute to*, the economic environment of a network society. They are relatively new discourses (or rather new mutations) arising from the fact that technological innovation provides new language options for thinking about knowledge, which in turn provides new forms of knowledge for technological development. Thus computers increase the language of 'codes' by providing a new environment for efficient coding, which then feeds back into the public environment to create yet more new languages in a resource-technology evolution and increased resources for modelling the mind.

Codification is the language of codes in a computer age and its development by cognitive science and, in turn, by knowledge management, offers opportunity for new forms of knowledge-production in terms of the new language. The key factor is the mutual imbrication of knowledge, environment, resources and language that generate ever-new possibilities in every age. Foray's question, borrowing from Nelson and Winter (1982) is: 'how do economic agents decide whether or not to codify "codifiable but not yet codified knowledge"?' (Foray 2004: 82). We could rephrase this by asking when do traditional and modern forms of knowledge – like discourses of ritual and religion – become translated into the new discourses of the cognitive-knowledge economy of late modernity? The answer is when there is a market potential for such translation. As Foray highlights by quoting Steinmueller (2000): 'Codification has become the very essence of economic activity' (Foray 2004: 90). What this means is that systems of thinking that 'codify' knowledge through the discourses of either cognitive science or the knowledge economy reflect and generate themselves in the present order of capital production. Thinking about thinking in terms of codified cognition is generated by economic demand or at least sustained by efficiency and the technological economic environment. The symbolic orders of ideology drive the language for thinking about structure; or, to put it simply, there may be given structures but how we represent them changes. Theory takes place in a political environment, even theory about thinking. Is it possible that we could place the order of cognitive science of religion back into its socio-political environment?

It is my contention that Whitehouse unwittingly takes the codified cognitive language of the Western knowledge economy into the descriptive politic of Papua New Guinea and his other expanding 'universal' contexts. He 'transmits' *cognitive* orders from and through the technological age and produces 'concepts' for the expanding representational market – to echo Boyer's specialist analysis. Cognitive concepts have a currency because they are the dominant ideological language of the market and they therefore flow through the social apparatus more easily. Whitehouse's work therefore is part of the *translation* of reality into the language of a different economy. Whitehouse can take all those ideas of Weber, Goody and Gellner and 'recast' their modernist descriptions into the language of *codification*, into the language of the individualised computer-mind, and indeed confer upon them the ideology of *science*. The ethical-political responsibility is clouded when concepts are isolated from the political environment that shapes and receives them and, even, portrays them as a neutral science.

The desire to rightly overcome 'essentialized institutions' has mistakenly led to a theoretical blindness about political economy and knowledge (Whitehouse 2005a: 173). What is extraordinary about this move is that Whitehouse's new capital of cognition establishes a 'community' of scholars built around a set of continuing fallacies. This community is established not through cognitive patterns of memory, but the human imagination of binary technological machines and the operational errors within the field. Cognitive theorists are unaware of their environmental modelling, but the machine-language of the economy functions efficiently on this basis and provides ample un-theorized, and under-theorized, support.

Inside the technological order of capital, Whitehouse's cognitive remaking of anthropology holds greater cultural receptivity. Whitehouse is a scholar of his time, using the tools of the dominant scientific-political order. He never has to question his language or its cultural location, because to do so would then turn his work into the very object of his own analysis and make his 'isolationist' power of cognition unravel in the rhetorical and political environment. It is precisely this *environment* of cognitive thinking that he has to underplay and under-theorize to retain his individualistic codified mind (his own hidden *ideology*), which he reads – in terms of the conceptual fallacy – as the neutrality of *science*; generating empirical realities of imagined entities within the brain. In postulating a universally given mind, he has forgotten the dynamic mind of his contextual apparatus that enables him to represent the idea of that mind.

It is necessary to employ additional strategies of 'isolationist' philosophy to dis-*credit* my own argument and maintain the *market-value* of cognitive science. I am, however, not seeking to prevent cognitive theory, that would be foolish, but I am trying to extend its environment in a self-reflexive political move. I want to show how knowledge is not simply codification but also about the dynamic mind of how we live together in ethical-political worlds of knowledge. Our ability to represent the mind as both *codified* and as *dynamic* reflects how our ideas can be used for different political effect and how there must be some ethical account of how we think, what we think about and how we exclude categories.

Cognition and capital

The critique I have put forward in this chapter has to be addressed at its different levels and disagreeing or agreeing with parts of the argument does not mean other aspects are unproblematic, because the critique comes from both within and outside the field. At the very least there needs to be some conceptual clarity within cognitive theories of religion, but that is nothing new, as I have already argued.

The next question is whether the evolving theoretical space of cognitive science can continue to open the field sufficiently to counter its imperialistic and totalitarian modes. If Boyer (2005) is right, there is a possibility to open the field outward rather than close it down. But beneath all of this is my sharper critique of turning cognitive science back on itself through its own extensions. Here the resistance will be stronger, because the economic loss is greater and knowledge resists losing its coherence to historical change and ideological struggle. The scientist never likes to dirty empirical concepts with political economy. It is however imperative, as Roazen suggests of intellectual inquiry more generally, to question the relations of knowledge and power behind scientific rhetoric.

> The duty of the intellectual, as I understand it, entails a commitment to resisting power. This principle amounts to the proposition that it behoves freethinkers to oppose, as a matter of principle, whatever current fashion might dictate. It has always appalled me how, both in academic life as well as in the outside world, most people seem so apt to worship blindly that which is currently established. This sort of enslavement may make some sort of sense for those who stand to gain, in terms of self-interest, by following the dominant trends in society. But for individuals who are supposed to be devoted to the life of the mind, uncritically endorsing any aspects of the *status quo* amounts to a special sort of degradation.
>
> (Roazen 2000: 99)

The resistance to the totalitarian drive within all thought must constantly open thinking to its outside. This will entail the ability to hold complexity, but this is not for the intellectually faint-hearted who wish to build empires of knowledge. It requires resisting the order of the *same*, in order that we can begin to think again at the point we open and close thought in each movement of time. It requires rescuing the cognitive science of religion from the devotional acolytes. We need to re-imagine the cognitive science of religion by questioning the terms of its formulation, its misplaced assumptions and its lack of extended theorization of its own discourse.

Let us return to the philosophy of concepts and let us understand the value of *science* and the limits of *science*. Thinking can isolate itself in the rhetoric of science and shelter its concepts from the environment of concept-formation, but the knowledge-economy disrupts our innocence by making thought a production of economy, especially thought that offers the same ideology of closure in the democratic pretension to be a science. It is these closed thoughts that will be transmitted into the heart of the knowledge economy as the capital for reducing ourselves to the measurable. While connection and extension are useful metaphors for future resistance against such regimes of knowledge, the dangers of reification and totalitarianism are never far behind our new imaginations. The problem that thought presents to itself is not only how we think, but also why we close and open our minds – why we close further relational dynamics to build empires in the closure of knowledge. In the desire to know we limit the scope of knowing to the efficiency of knowledge and to the dangers of total knowledge, rather than imagining thought as a relational processes of complexity with ever-extending environments.

Conclusion

Critique and the ethics of not-knowing

> The so-called drive for knowledge can be traced back to a drive to appropriate and conquer: the sense, the memory, the instincts, etc. have developed as a consequence of this drive. The quickest possible reduction of the phenomena, economy, the accumulation of the spoils of knowledge (i.e., of world appropriated and made manageable).
>
> Friedrich Nietzsche [1883–8] (1968) *The Will to Power*,
> Vintage Books, p. 227

In the history of the psychology of religion there have been many intriguing conceptual insights, such as Stanley Hall (1890) reading conversion as part of adolescent development; James (1902) reading individual religion in terms of the sick and healthy mind; Freud (1914) reading the experience of the devil, in the seventeenth century painter Christoph Haizmann, as a neurosis; Jung (1934) reading images of God as archetypes; Erikson (1974) reading the life of Luther in terms of his personal cycles of life; Piagetian scholars using models of development to read religious education (Goldman 1964); object relation theorists reading transitional objects as the space of religious experience (Winnicott [1971] 2005); neuroscientists reading the temporal lobes as locations of the God-experience (Persinger 1987); cognitive scientists reading rituals as forms of mental codification (Lawson and McCauley 1990). In each of these cases the creativity and invention of the psychological hermeneutic has produced a way to make experience, but the authority of the theory depends on an epistemic closure that silences the institutional conditions of its statements. It requires restricting the scope of enquiry to its self-enclosed articulations and masking the ethical assumptions and conditions of political economy. Making such links does not diminish the theory, but rather reveals the ground of its articulation, it makes it more rationally coherent and provides the force of its fragile and feeble disguising of concepts – it reveals its ethical will-to-power.

The problem results from the fact that stabilizing the statements in the narrow logic of disciplinary, and inter-disciplinary, thought demands a restriction of thought, because the complexity of multiple domains and inter-related objects of political concern are seen to threaten the articulation by revealing its assertion of value. But now, as the ethical-political network of knowledge becomes transparent in the excess of economy, such charades of the human sciences have the opportunity to reveal those hidden values behind the 'instincts' of knowledge.

While many of the psychological ideas listed can be linked to complex and at times nuanced readings these are often closed down in the desire for fixed objects of value. Such interpretations are all moments of theoretical closure that have a particular use-value for the social orders of the late nineteenth, twentieth and twenty-first centuries. They mirror and inform in the mobile space of shifting institutional exchanges. Each reflects a particular ordering of experience according to modes of individualism-collectivism and reflects a closed-open ethic of knowledge. The rhetoric of science is employed throughout the history of the psychology of religion, but intriguingly questioned by later generations of scholars as non-scientific; time upsetting the authority of each successive age in the movement of authority and institutional support. The statements of psychology make experience not according to science, but through the discursive power of science, in the process of reifying the objects of invention through the trickery of empiricism and the blind imagination of fact. Values dressed as calculations. They all reflect a peculiar moment in the evolution of human thought and imagination, a moment when thought read itself in terms of the desire to measure the self for political economy and not for life. Economy invested in (pseudo-) science and (pseudo-) science invested in economy, because of the inability to think of the self outside measurement, outside control and inside imagination.

Each of the above systems of psychological thought hold within them the potential to become fluid articulations at the moment when its statements become at once both a model of self and an articulation of social orders, when the human sciences return to the ethical practice of living at the interface of knowing and not-knowing, between given reality and philosophical assumption, between essence and construction. But in our thinking we are often too afraid to acknowledge that we may not know or that our knowing is supported by our not-knowing. The desire to know limits us to the measurable and prevents us from realising that we are always more than we imagine, more than we can measure, more than we can capture in our languages and patterns of evaluation. Knowledge is leaking across its artificial boundaries and the controlled mind is constantly finding ways to hide its vulnerability and errors. In such a time, Western thought is always in danger of explaining human beings in terms of the known order of domination, rather than respecting the unknown, and in doing so it feeds the totalitarian impulses to control life. The nightmare of life in the knowledge economy is that we think we know the unknown by networking all the measurements of human thought in the rational economy. Economics, psychology and religion are all built on the shifting sands of philosophical aspirations and values; and history is constantly revealing these temporary models of our given natures – a given nature that exists on the edges of its own impossible knowing inside the paradox of its cultural, linguistic and political orders of representation.

Following the lines of argument in this book, we can represent – as a way of summary and as a temporary holding of categories to evaporate in the movement of thought – the ethical-politic of psychological knowledge (including forms of government and types of modern experience registered under the category of 'religion') in a diagram. The diagram holds multiple points of tension across two binary schemes – in the attempt to overcome them and reveal the politic of either/or in the dictatorship of knowledge about the self, forms of belief/practice and political structures. Each quadrant reveals the interplay of forces that map knowledge in the human sciences and it enables us to see how we model knowledge on a set of desires to establish either mobile or controlled models of the self, which are embedded in, arise from and inform the process of open and closed systems that support such statements. Figure 6.1 attempts to illustrate the values behind knowledge along two indexes. It shows how knowledge is organised according to a hidden ethical dynamic, even if it is articulated in other terms. Indeed, most thought is ignorant of its underlying desire and impulse, especially when it is rationalised according to the economy of discipline. The values hidden in the individual-social and the open-closed binary structure form the key ground of orientation for self-knowledge and it enables us to see the motivations of thought in areas not open to a natural science method. Humans are driven according to these dynamics and build systems of knowledge according to their desire to control or open themselves to the other in dynamic relation.

I want to argue that knowledge is faced with a sharp and painful predicament, which is ever increasing in the knowledge economy; and which becomes simultaneously more acute and less visible. Human thought pivots on two impulses[1] (both a survival instinct and a developed ethical attitude) in the desire to know, impulses that are at the heart of political struggle and conflict: first, the desire to control, close and contain and, second, the desire to free, open and move, which we can call simply the desire for controlled-

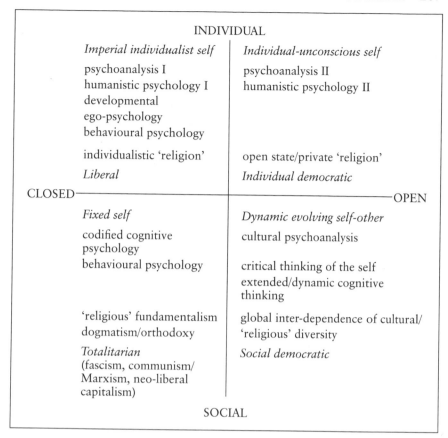

INDIVIDUAL

Imperial individualist self	*Individual-unconscious self*
psychoanalysis I humanistic psychology I developmental ego-psychology behavioural psychology	psychoanalysis II humanistic psychology II
individualistic 'religion'	open state/private 'religion'
Liberal	*Individual democratic*

CLOSED ———————————————————— OPEN

Fixed self	*Dynamic evolving self-other*
codified cognitive psychology behavioural psychology	cultural psychoanalysis critical thinking of the self extended/dynamic cognitive thinking
'religious' fundamentalism dogmatism/orthodoxy	global inter-dependence of cultural/ 'religious' diversity
Totalitarian (fascism, communism/ Marxism, neo-liberal capitalism)	*Social democratic*

SOCIAL

Figure 6.1 Modes of knowledge in open and closed systems

separation and the desire for fluid-connection. They form two dispositions of being in the world. Both are necessary for surviving in unknown environments and organising social actions, but in the regimes of the totalitarian control of knowledge they become restricted to the dimension of control in an over-determination that becomes destructive.

Figure 6.1 shows how knowledge of political-economy, 'religious' organisation and models of self cluster around types of knowledge instinct/ attitude. This is simultaneously an instinct/attitude of survival and an ethical attitude because it brings us into a certain subject relation to the world and knowledge of the world. As I have shown in the preceding chapters, psychoanalysis, humanism and cognitive science can be marked by both an openness or closure, they are not inherently restrictive or limited, but the ethical ground of thought upon which they operate can hold fundamentally different orders of value. What I hope to show in Figure 6.1 is that each method of thinking can, with some exceptions, organise itself according to different ethical-political instincts/attitudes of knowledge (for example, we can find different versions of the same type of psychological knowledge, as indicated by I and II, or in the newly constituted forms in the bottom right quadrant, which often lose their identifying mark in the dynamic position).

The dynamic of the individual-collective politic is, as we have seen, a central ethical-political force of social order, because it is always written across the closed-open system. Indeed, it is constituted by it, in so far as closed systems create the individual as a closed atomistic form and the collective positions establish a fluid relation between individuals as collective beings. The interaction of these registers is the site of knowledge about being human in so far as it reflects an instinct/attitude for a certain socio-economic-self in the individual-public management of life. We think in relation to and with a view to someone or something and this movement of thought as *relation* itself rests on the desire to control or open those relations. Knowledge in the human sciences, in this sense, is not containable, because it emerges in the relational dynamic that constantly evolves and shifts. We make experience through these instincts/attitudes by stablizing them in the social institutional order, so they can be layered as given – empirical truth – through the discursive regime of that institution. We hide the given nature of the underlying instincts/attitudes of knowledge – those philosophical assertions of the ethical will-to-value. We need to remember, at this point, Nietzsche's ([1883–8] 1968: 169) attempt to jolt our senses to the rude awaking of knowledge:

> Over immense periods of time the intellect produced nothing but errors. A few of these proved to be useful and helped to preserve the species: those who hit upon or inherited these had better luck in their struggle for themselves and their progeny. Such erroneous articles of faith, which were continually inherited, until they became almost part of the basic endowment of the species, include the following: that there are enduring things, that there are equal things; that there are things, substances, bodies; that a thing is what it appears to be; that our will is free; that what is good for me is also good in itself. It was only very late that such propositions were denied and doubted; it was only very late that truth emerged – as the weakest form of knowledge.

Nietzsche spoke of the condition of knowledge in the late-nineteenth century at the advent of the disciplinary formations. His gesture might not apply to all subsequent forms of knowledge, but it takes on a sharper edge in the value-laden human sciences. The positioning of my argument, in line with a Nietzschean tradition, also indicates my own instinct/attitude towards an open and relational system of thinking. The openness recognises that the givenness of the world is covered with our circulating multiple desires about the world, into which we become embedded and, simultaneously, engage, resist and embrace. The instinct/attitude of open knowledge takes itself to relations outside the disciplinary subjects of control – it gathers, makes complex, evolves – and it takes us to the ethics of knowledge itself. The danger is always, of course, that the tendency of control leads us to build new empires, new mutated subjects, to perpetuate a new order of knowing. It is, however, only by embracing the not-knowing in our knowing that we can prevent new forms of fascism emerging in our knowledge and in our life. It is the holding of flux and movement that allows us to be constantly transformed by knowledge as relationship. As Naomi Goldenberg (1979: 71) poetically, but no less sharply, writes: 'If we must indeed have some creeds in an age of new gods and new possibilities, I hope that they will be written on water and open to life'. Knowing that is fluid is more expansive and less fearful – it is the most difficult form of knowing because it holds not-knowing in the act of knowing.

Knowing becomes limited by its utility, limited to the captured parts, the things that can be grasped and calculated, rather than the things that are vague and evaporate. Easy thinking is thinking that can be controlled or asserted as given, but the human spirit lives and relates at the points of not-knowing or not-controlling in order to know and relate. This is not to diminish what we know in the natural sciences (which I am not specifically addressing at this point or the importance of knowledge about the physical world), rather I question what we know in the human sciences, the sciences that pretend to be 'natural' sciences in the act of hiding the ideologies of living behind their fragile utterances.

In the face of this situation, it may be that we have reached a point in the history of knowledge when the saturation of thought and the aspiration to know demands that we cultivate the ethics of not-knowing. It is part of a necessary *strategic scepticism*, as Nietzsche ([1883–8] 1968: 221) recognised, 'toward all inherited concepts'. This scepticism is not against 'science', but against the pretension of all thought to be 'science' – indeed the pretension to imagine 'science' is a fixed, closed, value-neutral practice – in the world of *networked mathesis*, the sign of the knowledge economy. It is to champion an ethics of provisionality and mobility as a way to dissolve the growing, and largely unseen, totalitarian forms of knowing in our time.

It is not to restrict assertions, which we must always make, but rather to test their ability to dissolve and critically evaluate their use-value for a society. This does not take us to some post-modern quagmire of relativism – that imaginary creature of the non-readers – but to the ground of a political struggle for justice inside our capacity to think in the space of not-knowing. We miss the given of not-knowing in the obsession of knowing the given, but not-knowing is the recognition of the complexity of inter-relation, coupled with the dynamic of time. It requires that we honour the values and leakages behind all forms of knowing, not in some self-confession, but in recognising the instincts/attitudes of our knowledge. It requires that we make critique an ethical duty to expose the values of our thinking through an examination of our binary distinctions, our protected categories and our unconscious *a priori* assumptions. It requires us to acknowledge how we fiercely defend our ways of knowing, and what we know, because such things matter to the values we uphold.

Critique opens knowledge to its hidden values. It opens thought to its unthought, to what a discipline or regime of thinking does not want to think, but which a claim for greater justice demands of thought. Critique is about opening thought to its outside in order to challenge its internal arrangement and return thought to the communal quest to find ways of living beyond oppression. When terms dissolve in social critique they show their ethical-political value and the ideology of subjectivity. In the realm of the nineteenth-century invention of the psychology of religion and its correlate disciplines, we find the disappearance of the *subject* in the leakages across disciplinary boundaries. We open thought to its fluidity as a political strategy in the practice of eradicating forms of totalitarian thinking about the self and the world. We extend thought and make it more complex than those who wish to limit knowledge for control. It is a question of who we might be and who we might become. Useful-knowledge for the economic regime and useful-knowledge for the social and environmental order is not necessarily the same thing, but survival of the latter is necessary for the former, which may suggest we have our values about knowledge and the environment the wrong way round (Heilbroner 2000: 290).

In the collapse of human sciences into the philosophical values of being human we can see the ethical order of thought. Thought and concepts become ethical practices and not detached 'sciences'. The fact-value illusions mask the drive to stabilize knowledge in the fragile spaces of knowing, which always simultaneously embrace the philosophical art of not-knowing. Knowledge leaks because it is always more than the frame we create to capture the process of life. This requires that we see theory as part of our ethical imagination and that we create models of being in the world to assist our understanding, not to control it, especially in thinking about who we are as human beings. Understanding has so many different orders of value and judgement that it is difficult to claim certainty in the uncertainty of our imagination. In the knowledge economy, knowledge control often means capital gain, but the gaining of capital is reducing what we know and the richness of our living.

Nicolas Rescher (1989: 6–7), in his own study of the economics of knowledge, rightly indicates that the 'need for knowledge is part and parcel of our nature'. The human spirit aspires to know and, as Rescher also rightly indicates, knowledge 'brings benefits too'. More importantly, he points to the fact that the 'discomfort of unknowing is a natural component of human sensibility'. The ethic of not-knowing is not about inducing anxiety, but about preventing false ambitions of knowing and overcoming the limits of knowledge in the creation of isolated domains of thought. What we seek to know and what we do not want to know is also part of the equation; and thus knowing and not-knowing become ethical-political categories that can be used in different ways.

Not-knowing, in the sense I want use it here, is not about political mystification and oppression, it is not about getting individuals to accept regimes without thinking, it is rather a strategic and creative move to question total systems of knowledge and government; something Hayek (1945a) recognised, but sadly could not see in the operations of the totalitarian market that came about from his attempts to protect against governmental totalitarianism. I thus reject Hayek's own appeal to an 'unknown' in his binary system, because it is framed by a confused neo-liberal capitalistic knowing (see Chapter 2.) To embrace knowing we must extend knowing to the ethical-political value of what is known, the failure to do so only becomes a way of masking the fragility of what we know by stabilizing knowledge in some imagined space of priority or transcendence. To embrace not-knowing is to respond to the desire to know as a *relation* and not a dogma, to embrace not-knowing is to start to know in all the rich complexity of the world and hold not-knowing as a way of sustaining the justice of humility, something Hayek (1945a: 32) also put forward to guard against totalitarian ways of thinking.[2] It is only when knowledge becomes relationship, rather than ownership, that we can overcome the totalitarian impulse.[3]

It becomes imperative in the new climate of the knowledge economy to establish critique and an ethic of not-knowing, as part of this critique, in order to demand of our knowledge (on the edges of knowing and not-knowing) an articulation of its values. Critique brings us to the justice of free, open and mobile thought. In systems of control this demands entering many paradoxical realms of thinking to jolt and resist any closure. As Giorgio Agamben ([1978] 1993: 23) insightfully comments: 'Thus anyone proposing to recover traditional experience today would encounter a paradoxical situation. For they would have to begin first of all with a cessation of experience, a suspension of knowledge'. To suspend knowledge in the mobility and fluidity of thinking needs careful reflection. It takes us to the heart of how we think and to the nature of life and death. As the feminist philosophy of Grace Jantzen (2004: 10) makes clear, our concepts and models reflect not simply a fear of death – the final mark of the desire to control – but our fear of life. It is our openness to the vitality of movement, change, fluidity and relation that alters the potential of knowledge:

> The habitus of western society is a disposition towards the enactment of death and its concomitants, especially anxiety and a drive to control, to exert mastery over anything perceived as threatening. Natality, creativity and beauty have been displaced, despised or ignored; at best seen as an unnecessary if pleasant extra to the real business of living.

This should not be recourse to exclamations of undermining rationality or the value of science, or even the value of theoretical assertions, it should rather be an opportunity to acknowledge our values inside such creations. It is about making our values visible. It is about extending the rational framework to account for the embeddedness of all our thinking and the limits of all thought, not to reduce all thought to construction, but to embrace how we surround the given with our desires.

It seems appropriate at this point, in a book that began with a critical reflection on William James's decision to 'ignore the institutional branch entirely' in his study of the psychology of religion, to return to his own philosophical concerns. James ([1902] 1960: 484–90) concludes his *Varieties of Religious Experience* by noting that the 'most interesting and valuable things about a man (sic) are usually his over-beliefs' and that these are necessary 'as long as they are not intolerant'. When knowledge becomes 'intolerant' we need to return to an appreciation of the 'More' and it is this ethics of knowledge James shares with Foucault ([1969] 1991: 76); in appreciating how the 'More' marks the limits of knowing and experience. The ethic of the 'more' demands something of the not-knowing of knowledge, that which can so easily be silenced in the professional ambition, the disciplinary structure, the theory and the social order.

Not-knowing demands the 'more' behind economy, psychology and religion; it demands we overcome our intolerance and return thought to the humility of the unknown. In this move, we end the innocent of our theories in the face of what we ethically and politically assert and desire to be. It may be that as a result we have to watch and hear the sad tears of the once pure realms of knowledge, that purity with such great claws of aggression and exploitation. The silent laugh of philosophy will watch these words be put in order. Let them wrestle and juggle, but in the end let us struggle for the justice of knowing and not-knowing and search for an ethics of knowing in the face of not-knowing. The mystery of what we might be can only be found in our capacity to open ourselves to the values inside our binary knowledge and to the paradox of our not-knowing. This is the beginning and end of all critique.

Notes

Preface

1 See, for example, Jantzen (1989), Lash (1990), Zaleski (1993/4) and King (1999).
2 I locate the beginning of a critical psychology of religion within feminist critical perspectives. See, for example, Goldenberg (1979) and Jonte-Pace (1997).
3 Note that Hayek's (1976) excursion into theoretical psychology is trapped inside a disciplinary isolation of knowledge. As he writes: 'A great deal of explanation would be necessary were I to try and justify why an economist ventures to rush in where psychologists fear to tread' (Hayek 1976: v). I hope to show how economics and psychology can be united in a critical epistemology and, in turn, overcome Hayek's anxiety of leaving his own field of study.
4 See also Mokyr (2002: 221). I am grateful to Joel Mortyr's work for originally drawing me to this notion, although I am not following Mokyr's description of this idea, in so far as he links it to the example of language. I am rather attempting to show how knowledge holds a self-organizing quality in decentralized forms of the knowledge economy.
5 For a useful introductory account of the relation between science and the social world see Williams (2000). I am not opposed to 'science', but rather seeking to make 'scientific' theory more complex in addressing the nature of being human and the ethical foundation of our knowledge. I am seeking to raise a set of philosophical concerns in the complex construction of knowledge and its categories prior to testability and address a set of questions that are closed when applying empirical, mathematical and laboratory experimental methods. Much of the appeal to science is a rhetorical practice employed to instigate the institutional authority of statements. The human sciences often aspire to the values of the natural sciences not only in order to legitimate knowledge and indulge an obsession to find 'truth' only in this register, but because it offers the greatest level of control of the subject; it is also forgotten that the best science begins with not-knowing and an examination of its preliminary categories and innate obscurities. My choice of strategy, as will become clear in the book, is to expose the application of mathesis (the calculated order) as valid knowledge and its extended use within the network society. My aim is to build an appreciation of the 'fragile' theory surrounding knowledge of the human being and its political and economic embedded nature as an ethical question. It is to question the certitude of those who employ the rhetoric of science in order to ground all knowledge of what it is to be human in the ethical will-to-power. I will, therefore, take knowledge to its most 'fragile' edges in inter-disciplinary thinking and in the conceptual construction of the individual-social to show the implicit values of knowledge in the understanding of being human, which makes

it fundamentally different from objects in the extended natural world. For a useful discussion of the problem of psychology as a science and the question of ontology in relation to James's work see Shamdasani (2005).

Introduction

1 As Drucker ([1968] 1969: 248) argues: 'The emergence of knowledge as central to our society and as the foundation of economy and social action drastically changes the position, the meaning, and the structure of knowledge'. The argument of my book will link experience to knowledge and social institutions. I will examine Drucker's ([1968] 1969) notion of the knowledge economy in more detail in Chapter 2.

2 Simmel draws attention to the central aspects of differentiation in groups by referring to the social orders of Quakers. According to Simmel (1908b: 258), 'the Quakers are individual only in collective matters, and in individual matters, they are socially regulated'. The paradoxical dimension of sociality and individuality in the history of Quaker life has enabled me to think through the central ethical focus of the individual-social binary in my own life and thought, but as Simmel shows it has much wider relevance. Rawls's (1971) own study of justice, outside communitarian ethical systems, holds the same binary politic in a different way. I hope to clarify these issues in a more specific study of ethics, but the scope of critical thinking here is limited to a reading of economics, psychology and religion.

3 See Chapter 2. In my view, the academy often reproduces traditions of knowledge in the human sciences in order to prevent any thought reaching outside the ever-increasing micro-realms of professional success, making intellectual knowledge either redundant as excessive wastage for self-glorification in professional circles or a form of latent ideological support for the dominant militarily backed economic regime. Indeed, even to 'think differently' is no longer possible in a world of the trademarked slogan, where thinkers are turned into marketed icons and gurus, rather than political companions to change. At the same time, knowledge and thought are no longer protected from the illusion of neutrality, but swamped inside the iron-cage of instrumental rationality. It is precisely at this point that we can begin a critical analysis of knowledge in the knowledge economy.

4 Sharf (1998: 113), for example, takes on board the wider critical reading of experience when we writes: 'The category experience is, in essence, a mere placeholder that entails a substantive if indeterminate terminus for the relentless deferral of meaning. And this is precisely what makes the term experience so amenable to ideological appropriation'.

5 The category of religion has opened itself to the waves of post-war philosophical scholarship. The historical-socio-political rendering of the category in European and colonial histories has been well-argued by scholars of 'religion', including insightful works by McCutcheon (1997), King (1999), Fitzgerald (2000), Kippenberg (2002) and Masuzawa (2005).

6 Jantzen (1989) and King (1999) embrace some aspects of this by examining James's 'psychologism' of mysticism, but they are not concerned with the wider issue of psychological theory.

7 There has been greater critical awareness of the problems of anthropology in relation to the construction of religion, not least because of its assimilation into colonial and post-colonial analysis, see King (1999). There has also been useful, but theologically narrow and limited, critical reflection on the assumptions of sociology, see Milbank (1990).

8 My argument supports such future lines of argument, but departs from McCutcheon's modernist rendering of knowledge precisely at the point he domesticates Foucault in the will-to-a-science-of-religion. As McCutcheon (2003) honoured my earlier work enough to discuss it, kindly supported publication of conference discussions of my work and showed me even greater honour by reinterpreting/misreading it for his own purposes, I am indebted to his support and thus cannot but acknowledge the value of some of his work by offering this footnote as a political invitation to read again, even as I do not share the philosophical nature of his work in its entirety. I share with McCutcheon a Chomsky-inspired political concern about knowledge and the state and a reading of religion according to a Foucauldian taxonomy of knowledge (something which he generously acknowledges), but he misreads the conclusions of my work – in modernist fashion – to assume fixed objects of knowledge rather than strategic openings. The central problem is that he reads Foucault principally from a rhetorical-discursive (archaeological) model, rather than in terms of an institutional-power (genealogical) model, and simultaneously assumes a science of religion paradigm rather than a model of the history of ideas. I am less concerned and trapped by the question of 'religion'. He thus ignores how my reading of Foucault uses religion as a counter-discourse against the human sciences, which is neither imagining a fixed object of religion or an original tradition, but is rather showing how the relations operate across religious and nation-state institutions. Religion is always set up within discourse and such strategic application can easily be read as essentialism, especially when it requires a subtle and nuanced reading to appreciate writing that concludes at the 'edge of the sea'; as my first book on Foucault concluded. In the same way that it would be an error to read Foucault's use of the word 'sexuality' as essence, when his interest is always in the 'deployment' (dispositif) of 'sexuality' within the social world, so it is an error to read my reading of Foucault according to the certainty of modernity; a corrective point I have already articulated (Carrette 2001b). To accuse me of misreading Foucault is like accusing Nietzsche of being too systematic in his critique of Western philosophy. Like Foucault (1969: 17), I am not where you think I am, but over there laughing (or are they tears for the loss of political energy?), as the modernist police try to put my papers in (dis)order. Of course, the clever trick of the thought-police is to set up divisions within intellectual camps and map out territory rather than allow coalitions against the oppressive political orders, but then it is never clear whether academics really want political change or professional success. And so I invite new readings, new political understanding and new forms of broad alliance, because the stakes are far higher than we can ever imagine and academics have yet to imagine how they can become an effective political force in or against the new knowledge economy. Such a struggle will always and necessarily have to leave the narrow corridors of disciplinary knowledge and examine all those unseen assumptions written on the changing tides of 'science'.

9 See Dreyfus and Rabinow (1982: 49, 59). I am grateful to my colleague Laurence Goldstein for his useful clarifications on Wittgenstein's work.

10 As I have indicated elsewhere, we can add to Foucault's play on 'subjection' (power) and 'subjectivity' (sense of self) with the idea of 'subject' discipline (see Carrette 2000).

11 See Carrette (1993/4, 2001a).

12 For a more updated discussion of the theory of emotion see Williams (2001).

13 Proudfoot does not read James's theory of emotion beyond the classic 1884 James-Lange statement that emotion is the perception of a bodily change. I have written elsewhere about James's model of emotion and shown that James gradually acknowledges cognitive aspects and, indeed, shows awareness

of a social dimension (see Carrette 2005b: 79–93). Proudfoot likes James's intellectual 'instinct' if not his theory and is aware that James does not identify specific 'religious' feelings and understands the 'secondary products' of religion (Proudfoot 1985: 156ff). He is also able to provide an excellent reading, along with Otto's language, of James's mystical discourse. I agree with Proudfoot (1985: 157) about the importance of James's philosophy of religion, but it is precisely this philosophical contribution that has the potential to offer a corrective to much later psychological theory, see Carrette (2005a).

14 Proudfoot 1985: 28–9. However, Wittgenstein's critical discussion of psychology has far greater potential than Proudfoot offers, see Harré and Tissaw (2005).

15 See references to the 'conditions' (Proudfoot 1985: 123, 125, 178, 184, 235) and 'context' (Proudfoot 1985: 100, 108, 160, 185, 219, 223–6) of experience.

16 Although I know he will not be happy with my conclusions, I am grateful to Laurence Goldstein for clarifying such a distinction between Wittgenstein and Foucault.

17 As I explained in Carrette (2001a: 124), I develop the idea of disciplinary amnesia 'from Foucault's argument that positivistic psychology in founding a discipline that excluded the difficult and problematic areas of human experience, fatally provided Western consciousness with the "ability to forget" (Foucault 1962: 87). I use the phrase "disciplinary amnesia" to refer to the procedure through which discourse is able to function by suppressing issues and problems that undermine its coherence'. I further develop this idea in relation to Abbott's idea of a disciplinary 'axis of cohesion' in Chapter 2.

18 The reference to physical processes of amnesia and myopia echoes for me the sense of how ideas are always ways of embodying. As Judith Butler has made clear, we make things 'matter'; thought becomes the way 'matter' is lived and explored, see Butler (1993).

19 Stephen Frosh (2000: 3) rightly argues: 'Critical psychology is not a specific thing'; although it can have a functional value.

20 Critical psychology emerged from 'counter cultural movements, the anti-psychiatry movements, the New Left, Civil Rights and Women's Movements' (Walkerdine 2001: 9). It subsequently embraced work in the sociology of knowledge and post-structuralism from 1968, most vividly portrayed in the journal *Ideology and Consciousness* (1977), which was captured in an important collection of pieces by Henriques *et al.* ([1984] 1998).

  The first attempts to formulate a critical psychology, including the pioneering *International Journal of Critical Psychology* (2001) and Tod Sloan's (2000) useful collection of international essays on the subject, embrace a diversity and multiplicity of concerns. In these works we find a whole array of issues, but broadly a concern about 'value commitments' (Sampson 2000: 1, cf. Sampson 1983), 'injustice' (Fox 2000: 21); and a 'disenchantment' with traditional psychology (Ussher 2000: 7). Within this overall set of primary issues we find more specific concerns, often overlapping, about the problem of positivistic scientific methods (Schraube 2000), a questioning of the status quo (Prilleltensky (2000) an ethical critique of psychology (Lira 2000) an arena for appreciating cultural diversity and post-colonial theory (Nsamenang 2000, Mama 2001), a platform for social action (Montero 2001); a post-Marxist theoretical space (Maiers 2001), post-structuralist theory (Gulerce), a political critique (Montero 1997; Parker 2001), a concern about social, political and economic oppression (Oropeza 2000) and a concern with institutional practice (Cabruja and Gordo-López 2001). In the late 1980s and the early 1990s there were a number of critical works in two key series of publications that brought together many existing strands of critical thinking in psychology, the *Critical Psychology* series (Routledge) and the *Inquiries in Social Construction* series (Sage). Works within these two series of books established the climate for the so-called 'critical psychology' movement as a distinct set of ideas within academic psychological theory. These works drew together existing critical discourses from feminist, gay, lesbian theory, race and post-colonial studies and established a radical arena for psychological study (see Fox and Prilleltensky 1997). In these works 'critical psychology' re-established the critical link between the individual and the social that had been seen through the twentieth century in wider traditions of psychological and social theory, such as the *Kritishe Psychologie* of Berlin in 1968 (Tolman 1994) and the Frankfurt School in Germany (see Jay [1973] 1996); the anti-capitalist work of Deleuze and Guattari in France ([1972] 1984) and the anti-psychiatry movement in the UK (Laing [1960] 1965). These debates resurfaced in new discourses of cultural and political analysis. The studies from this period covered a range of themes from social constructivist thinking (Shotter and Gregen 1989; McNamee and Gregen 1992), discourse dynamics (Parker 1992), psychology and post-modernism (Kvale 1992) modernity and the psyche (Sloan 1996), embodiment (Bayer and Shotter 1998) feminism (Ussher 1989; Squire 1989) and specific critiques of different types of psychology, including developmental (Burman 1994; Morss 1996), and cognitive psychology (Walkerdine 1998). There has been little appreciation in these studies of the psychology of religion, but critical thinking has occurred in the area from a number of critical perspectives, such as feminism (Goldenberg 1979) and post-structuralism (Carrette 2001a; Lee and Marshall 2002; 2003; Blackman 2001). There have also been a range of other works addressing the theme of psychology and religion under a more general idea of critical psychology (see Wulff 1992; Watson 1993; Browning 1987).

21   Jones and Elcock (2001: 3–4) identify two 'coarsely defined groups' within critical psychology. First, the 'political critical psychology', which is concerned with issues of social justice, welfare of communities, and changing the status quo of society and psychology; and, second, the 'metatheoretical critical psychology', concerned with addressing the adequacy of theory, method and practice within psychology. This set of distinctions is problematic as it is determined principally by its 'subject-discipline' formation and neglects the wider politics of knowledge. My own work resists the closure of knowledge within the discipline of psychology, or the field of the psychology of religion, because it covers over deeper philosophical problems. I see the attempt to make critical psychology a disciplinary sub-area as a way of ignoring the epistemological errors of formation.

22   Such a concern is also echoed by 'Voice B' in the discourse unit discussion from members of the Manchester Metropolitan University, UK, which wanted to 'dispel some of the myths and anxieties' and 'political and professional guilt' that surrounds critical psychology (Durmaz *et al*. 2000: 148): 'I suspect "critical psychology" is seen by some as a tactical move to disturb the hegemony of mainstream psychology without necessarily challenging the concept of psychology itself and where any overt challenge might result in being marginalized in academia'.

23   It should also be noted that Teo's conjunction of 'ethical-political' is a grouping of themes taken from the nomenclature of the critical literature. He rightly notes that he uses the terms *critical psychology* and *ethical-political* 'interchangeably', because of the focus of the literature from Marxist, feminist, post-modern and post-colonial perspectives. I, however, use the conjunction of *ethical-political* in the context of showing how the binary individual-social can be read in the context of psychological and economic thought to reveal the ethics of all knowledge. In this sense, all knowledge is at once ethical *and* political in the sense of it being caught in the impossible problem of the individual-social binary and, importantly, both terms rest equally within and across both sides of the

binary. I am grateful to Teo's (2005) work for enabling me to clarify a number of theoretical problems in our creative differences within and outside the discipline. I am grateful to Naomi Goldenberg for also drawing my attention to my elision of ethical and political and requiring me to think through this problem. I now see how my use of the word 'political' reflected my attempt to show how *a priori* values operate across the individual-social binary.

24 Teo (2005: 182), for example, clearly acknowledges that his approach to the ethical-political domain is to 'offer a heuristic tool, conceptual toolbox, that *enables psychologists* to think about these issues' (my emphasis).

25 I use the capitalized form here, following Richards (1996), to give emphasis to the discipline rather than to the topic before the discipline came into existence.

26 Browning (1998: 40) writes: 'Psychology, in all its forms, is first of all a hermeneutic discipline. By this I mean that psychology begins its investigations into the psyche by being first shaped by culturally or historically mediated images of the human ... These historically mediated images of the human shape us as individuals long before we begin to reflect critically on their meaning, character, and nature. They form and shape us prior to beginning more systematic investigation of human nature as psychologists and behavioural scientists'.

1 The ethical veil of the knowledge economy

1 Fleischacker (2004: 84) rightly notes that Smith's *The Wealth of Nations* is wrongly read as simple self-interest governing human relations.

2 The problem with studies of James is that the psychological, philosophical and religious readings of James tend to be separated, see Carrette (2005a).

3 I use the metaphor of 'leakage' in echo of James ([1892] 1985: 400).

4 I am not accepting Foucault's *episteme* at this point, but rather trying to map an institutionally constructed order of power that frames disciplinary knowledge.

5 This type of knowledge can be seen at the foundation of the sciences of economics, psychology and religion as they were developed in the late nineteenth century. In the study of religion, this is usefully explored by Kippenberg (2002).

6 We may note the popular story that when an air hostess was asked why she was not smiling by a business man in first class she replied: 'Can you smile for me?'. The businessman dutifully smiled, and then she said: 'Now hold that for 24 hours, that's why I am not smiling!'. There is also an important gendered dimension to this scenario of bodies, economy of emotion and social pleasure.

7 Barbalet ([1998] 2001) questions Hoschschild's analysis, because it fails to take into account other types of work, which may have negative emotional outcomes as a control for the study. There is, as Amy Wharton shows, no way of knowing if emotional labourers are more likely to suffer from emotional exhaustion than anyone else, which seems more to do with job autonomy and job involvement than anything else. But Barbalet also questions Hocshchild by asking whether emotion can be a 'product' as such, because the situation which directs the emotion changes the emotion. Barbalet is here making a distinction between object and agency, which means that people 'have feelings about their feelings'. We have feelings about the emotions we are asked to produce, which for Barbalet, in turn displaces the emotion as a product. As Barbalet states: 'Emotions themselves are never finished objects, but always in process'. As he continues: 'They retain their pre-commodiefied quality because they continue to be possessed by those who have the conscience, the honor, or the pleasing smile' (Barbalet [1998] 2001: 179–82).

8 Simon Williams (2001) also picks up this question in his study *Emotion and Social Theory* when he remarks: 'Commodities entice us in numerous ways, including their aesthetic appeal, their sensual qualities, their status or prestige

value, and the fantasies with which they are imbued by consumers and advertizers alike: a mutually reinforcing dynamic' (Williams 2001: 113). The contemporary discussion of emotion has seen a creative engagement with the wider aspects of sociology and politics, see Harré and Parrott (1996), Barbalet (2002) and Ahmed (2004).

9 As Menger writes: 'The *historical* sciences have to examine and describe the individual nature and the individual connection of economic phenomena' (Menger [1883] (1996): 195).

10 Intriguingly, Hayek (1976) was also concerned with theoretical psychology and although not making any direct links with his economic theories there is still some common assimilation of epistemological structures in both discourses. See Ebenstein (2003: 147–52).

11 Waterman (2004) provides an important historical account of the relation between political economy and theology before, what he calls, the 'estrangement'. As he writes: 'Until well into the nineteenth-century the political thinking of all save a tiny minority of Europeans and Americans was deeply influenced, if not wholly formed, by the theology of Western Christianity' (Waterman 2004: 1). There have been contemporary attempts to return economics to theology, but any simple reconnection of the subjects easily ignores how theological language is already mutated in the contemporary world and that traditional theology is transfigured as much as classical economics in new political orders of knowledge, see, for example, Long (2000).

12 The significance of the non-economic can also be seen in Polanyi (1944), where he recognises how economic systems are always 'embedded' in the social system. The detachment of economic thinking from the social and ethical values of a society dangerously leads towards a hidden form of economic totalitarianism.

13 In Arestis and Sawyer's (2000) *A Biographical Dictionary of Dissenting Economists*, Heilbroner (2000: 287) describes the argument in his *Behind the Veil of Economics* (1988) as follows: 'My argument is that behind the veil of conventional economic rhetoric we can easily discern an under-structure of traditional behaviour – trust, faith, honesty and so on – as a necessary moral foundation for a market system to operate, as well as a concealed superstructure of power in the characteristic allocation by the market of a disproportionately large share of the social product to owners of the means of production. From various perspectives, the book examines these and other ambiguous boundaries of the economy, and of economics itself'. Heilbroner (2000: 290) concludes his personal reflection about his work in economics by noting that economics needs to sustain the social order upon which it depends. He believes this is best realized through 'socio-political adaptability' rather than on 'scientific and depoliticizes rigidity, of a capitalist system'.

14 Peters and Besley (2006) offer very useful overviews of the literature and valuable critical insights, but because of their educational concern they obviously concentrate on such related matters in reviewing the literature. As a corrective they usefully refer to 'knowledge cultures' to counter the neo-liberal ideology assumptions and even, somewhat more confusingly refer to 'knowledge socialism' as opposed to 'knowledge capitalism'. This move is still caught in much Cold War rhetoric and the Marxist agenda masks the quest for justice beyond concepts of Right and Left. We can no longer return to the past political blocks of ideology and as Left and Right collapse as useful terms we now require new forms of political thinking for rethinking oppression and injustice in new worlds of the knowledge economy.

15 Cognitive science, as we shall see in Chapter 5, brings together anthropology, philosophy and linguistics, amongst other disciplines. One reaction to codified knowledge is to read truth in terms of other privileged categories, as seen in

forms of late modern theological knowledge which reacts against modernist knowledge. This can be seen in academic groups such as Radical Orthodoxy, which like contemporary forms of fundamentalist discourse, are forms of late capitalist discourse. It functions in a similar way, privileging a category by reading knowledge according to historical moments of theological value. See Milbank (1990) and Milbank *et al.* (1998).

16 I am indebted to the late Grace Jantzen for keeping the question of who benefits from certain forms of knowledge at the forefront of my work, see Jantzen (1998) and (2004).

17 There are different forms of historical inter-disciplinary exchange. There is some economic value in the institutional structural persistence of old disciplines in the university. It allows for some traditional inter-disciplinary thinking and consists of excursions that do not threaten the individual discourses; such that forms of social psychology do not threaten sociology. This has been the sign of twentieth century confusions of inter- or multi-disciplinary debate and it relates to the bio-politic of the human sciences. We also find new constellations of subjects in late capitalism such as business studies, cultural studies or environmental studies that merge subjects around critical issues or social objects of concern. This has led to new institutional structures driven by economic utility, but predominantly these are still operating across nineteenth century forms of knowing. I am concerned with a new form of subject blending in the knowledge economy.

18 As I made clear in the preface, this aspect of my argument is crucial and one that will be questioned by those who imagine the human can be measured. I, however, locate psychology within philosophy rather than physiology and argue that the central epistemological confusion results from trying to make psychology into a biological science. There is, of course, some crossover, but these remain, as James (1890) makes clear, only the 'possibility' of a science of psychology. It becomes clear from the epistemological problems of the self that psychology requires too many *a priori* assumptions to make it into a science; something I will explore in Chapter 5.

2 Binary knowledge and the protected category

1 Contemporary psychology tries to deal with such dilemmas in the development of 'positioning theory' (Harré and Van Langenhove 1999; Harré and Moghaddam 2003).

2 For an account of introspection, see Lyons (1986).

3 I am grateful to Adrian Cunningham for first enabling me to see the problems of the location of the psychology of religion as a field of study, trapped as it is between other disciplinary spaces. In the UK, there are few specific positions in the psychology of religion and it has become a largely North American enterprise, which in itself raises a number of socio-political problems.

4 Parker (1997a: 111) notes Bettelheim's ([1983] 1986) concern about the translation of this text, which is better translated as 'The uneasiness inherent in culture'. He also notes how the cultural dimensions of Freud's texts were 'filtered out in the process of translation into English' (Parker 1997a: 107).

5 For an excellent biographical study of Hayek, see Ebenstein (2003).

6 According to the biographer Alan Ebenstein (2003: 97), quoting from Hayek's autobiographical notes, some of the essays in this volume offer his 'most original contribution' to theory in economics. This underlines the importance of a closer reading of some of these texts to reveal Hayek's own values.

7 The binary tension leads Hayek to set up a foundational distinction between 'individual-ism' and 'social-ism' (Hayek 1945a: 3). My own position rejects models of Left-Right in a global context, on the grounds that these reflect

nation-state politic operations of the Cold War. It is important to reject such distinctions in order to talk of different forms of 'democracy' and models of 'justice' across a range of international institutions, such that a fundamental 'break' has occurred relegating the nation-state to a cipher or mediator of global market processes.

8 See Carrette (2004a) for a discussion of the problem of 'spontaneity' and 'control' in Mestrovic's (1997) discussion of manufactured post-emotion.

3 Religion, politics and psychoanalysis

1 See, for example, Henriques *et al.* ([1984] 1998), Parker (1997a), Blackman (2001) and Carrette (2001a).

2 The feminist critique of psychoanalysis began to emerge strongly in the 1970s, not least with Juliet Mitchell's ([1974[1990) formative critical reading. Within the field of the psychology of religion, Naomi Goldenberg (1977, 1979) was one of the first to establish key critical links across subject domains. I regard Goldenberg's work as one of the first critical psychological readings of religion, because it questions the political structure of the categories of knowledge. For an overview of the material see Jonte-Pace (2001).

3 In this study, I do not examine the social and political thinking of Klein and Jung. I have decided to omit these because the economic question is never made explicit in their primary discourses, and certainly not as it is in Reich and Fromm. Even though the secondary literature surrounding these thinkers has extended discussion to the socio-political world, the psychoanalytical discourse of Klein and Jung is never brought under particular economic analysis. My inclusion of Lacan is to explore an economic-cultural difference between France and the USA. For a discussion of Kleinian psychoanalytical politics see Frosh (1999: 120–38). There have been some useful attempts to use object relations work to read social and religious contexts (see Jacobs and Capps 1997; and Jones 2002), but these do not establish a self-reflexive critique or make suggestions of how psychological discourse may itself be part of the political problem. In a different approach to the one I am developing here, Andrew Samuels (1989), (1993) and (2001) has explored political aspects of Jungian psychology, largely from a clinical perspective. There are useful insights scattered in these works (not least on economy and Jung's psychology of nations), but his investment in a psychotherapeutic hermeneutic prevents a critical-political reading of psychological discourse that marks my own hermeneutic of suspicion. Nonetheless, while I am suspicious of uncritical investments in psychological discourse, those works establishing links with the political are significant and creative attempts to think along the edges of disciplinary limits.

4 The psychoanalytic study of religion was first created according to the historical process of individualism in the Western world, established at least from the Enlightenment, but arguably from the Protestant Reformation, which removed religion from the public to the private world. It was secondly caught within a political order of science, which attempted – albeit unsuccessfully – to police the 'religious subject' and remove it from the interference of nation state politics. Third, the capitalist university produced ever-greater 'specialism' and restricted the scope and application of its insights, which in turn created an 'inflated' sense of its internal importance by feeding imaginary inner worlds for the 'feel-good' spirituality and consumer value (see Carrette and King 2005). The psychoanalytical discourse of religion thus provided an important social and intellectual *habitus* for individuals to create 'therapeutic' identity-communities within the new economy.

5 The Rev. J.C.M. Conn, the minister of Kelvinside Old Parish Church in Glasgow, stands out for his informed and critical examination of the new psychology. In his fascinating work *The Menace of the New Psychology* in 1939, Conn questioned the foundations of psychology. He was certainly well read on the subject, having studied with R.H. Thouless, who wrote the first British textbook on the psychology of religion in 1925 and having a friendship with the psychoanalytical thinker W.R.D. Fairbairn. While Richards sees Conn's work as 'highly unrepresentative of mainstream Christian attitudes', it does skilfully highlight the limits and flaws of the new subject (Richards 2000: 58). While I agree with Richards's assessment, Conn's concerns are revealing, because they provide an insight into the anxieties within the church about the rise of the new psychology, before psychology was adopted and embraced so enthusiastically. Due to his wish to identify the broad themes of the inter-war period, Richards never sufficiently draws out Conn's argument which shows the dangers beneath the surface of psychology. While Conn's concerns are with theological purity, according to his conservative agenda, his strategic identification of the lacunae in psychological knowledge is worth noting, because once the church and society have adopted psychology these fractures of psychological history are buried in the 'disciplinary amnesia' of the subject. The purpose of Conn's book, *The Menace of the New Psychology*, graciously supported with Prefaces by the Very Rev. Daniel Lamont and the Rev. D. Martyn Lloyd-Jones, was 'to vindicate the claims of religion against the challenge of some of the new theories of psychology' (Conn 1939: 7). Although conceding some usefulness of the new psychology, he does, nonetheless, in his more extreme moments, believe that psychology is 'the most dangerous menace to the Christian view of life of the present hour' (Conn 1939: 9). The alliance between theology and psychology since 1939 has shown that this prediction was perhaps exaggerated, for psychology, in part, enhanced Christian spiritual life in overcoming aspects of personal suffering, while also assimilating itself into a wider political process. Conn's estimation that psychology was a 'dangerous "ally" to religion' is correct in so far as there were advantages and disadvantages to this new alliance (Conn 1939: 21). The strength of Conn's work is not his overt anxiety about theological purity but his clever interrogation of psychological knowledge. He questions the basis of psychology and undermines its ambitions as a new force for understanding the world. Conn makes four important critiques of psychology, each supported by comments from leading psychologists of his time: (1) the diversity of the field, (2) boundary and limits of the subject, (3) technical vocabulary, and (4) confusion within the subject. Conn, first, questions the unity of the subject, remarking: 'Actually and paradoxically, there is no such thing as "psychology" but only a multitude of psychologies; and the number continues to increase' (Conn 1939: 21). This realisation of the diversity and conflict within the field, reflects the way psychology merges within different structures, but Conn did not, or was unable, to articulate the political nature of such diversity. Conn, as a theologian, was however more concerned with the way psychology went beyond its limits as a subject. This is interesting in so far as psychology was unclear about its subject matter – whether it was a physiological science, a philosophical discipline or a politics of self-knowledge – what it could not integrate was the fact it played with all three. As Conn stated: 'Frequently, with ill-judged enthusiasm, it ventures beyond its subject-matter, and encroaches on the problems and on the methods of other studies. It threatens to dominate the whole of life' (Conn 1939: 23). Conn's fears of domination were to some extent justified, especially as psychology filtered into all domains of life. Conn supported his comments by refering to the great British psychologist William McDougall and his 1934 *The Frontiers of Psychology* which stated: 'Psychology claims an enormous

territory but is in effective occupation of very little of it. Its frontiers are ill-defined and nowhere delimited properly' (quoted in Conn 1939: 23). One of Conn's major concerns was the nature of technical vocabulary. Words, such as defence mechanism, displacement, complex, projection. etc. which we take for granted today were extraordinary inventions in Conn's time and ones we need to be suspicious of in our construction of reality or, at least, understand their genealogy as metaphors from physics and mechanistic models of energetics. Conn was suspicious that such terms could not be translated into everyday language, which echoes the regimes of power-knowledge of such professional discourses (Conn 1939: 23). As Conn goes on to state: 'How this parade of weird terms has intrigued the popular mind! Psychological jargon turns up everywhere. Nurse-maids are familiar with its lispings, and Sunday-School teachers with its prattlings. Far too much psychology is being dispensed, both from the pulpit and in the vestry, by ministers who are endeavouring to be up to date' (Conn 1939: 23–4).

6   I am grateful to David Wulff for explaining his omission of Reich. His avoidance is explained in terms of his obscurity as a figure and lack of relation of his ideas to the 'psychology of religion', but Wulff is caught in a wider disciplinary silence of political-economy that makes Reich obscure and hides his psychology of religion. Rieff ([1966] 1987), at least, shows how it is possible to move beyond such easy dismissal in a different imagining of the psychology of religion. I will explore Rieff ([1966] 1987) below.

7   According to Chasseguet-Smirgel and Grunberger (1986: 9): '"organism" turned out to be a misprint by an absent-minded typist or a prudish producer; it ought to have read "orgasm" of course'.

8   See also McLaughlin (1998a) and (1998b) for a sociology of knowledge approach to Fromm's intellectual exclusion. Cf. Roazen (2000: 99–123) for an appreciation of his intellectual courage.

9   There have been few biographical studies of Fromm, see Burston (1991) and Funk (2000).

10 The limits of space and the focus of my particular argument do not permit me to develop a more detailed reading of Lacan at this point. For a discussion of Lacan's Marxism and Žižek's use of Lacan see Valente (2003). The broader nature of Lacan's thinking has been applied to political thought in Yannis Stavrakakis's (1999) study. Stavrakakis usefully draws out the problems of using Lacan's concepts within political thinking, but nonetheless finds Lacan useful in overcoming 'traditional fantasmatic politics' and establishing a ground for 'radical democracy' in overcoming utopianism (Stavrakakis 1999: 120–1).

11 I am grateful to Jacob Belzen who has drawn attention to the lack of French members of the European Association of the Psychology of Religion.

12 See Lacan [1966] 2006: 235–47; Lacan [1974] 1998. There has been some theological reflection using Lacan's work outside France, see Wyschogrod *et al.* (1989). Cf. Leupin (2004) and passing comments in Shepherdson (2003: 140–1) and Luepnitz (2003: 228–9). In French, see, Fouilliaron (1986).

13 For a location of Lacan's thought see Roudinesco (1997), Macey (1988) and Borch-Jacobsen (1991).

4 Maslow's economy of religious experience

1   See Foucault ([1979] 1997: 135–52). This central relationship between self and nation-state was realised, as we noted in the introduction, by McCutcheon (2003: 261) in his study of religion.

2   As we saw in the last chapter, there is a general harmonious relationship between psychology and Christianity, see, for example, Graham Richards (2000: 57–84).

3 I use the word 'spirituality' according to all its vagueness and as a term reflecting the privatization of religious ideas and practice, see Carrette and King (2005: 14–45)

4 I have documented these political-economic shifts with Richard King in Carrette and King (2005).

5 See the discussion of 'critical psychology' in the introduction to this book and Carrette (2001a).

6 James develops the ideas of the 'More' and 'over-beliefs' to preserve a mystery and refuse a closure on the religious subject. See James ([1902] 1960: 484ff).

7 For a discussion of the psychological construction of the mystical see Jantzen (1989; 1995) and King (1999; 2005). These works show how James's ([1902] 1960: 366–413) definition reshapes the understanding of mysticism in the twentieth century.

8 See Danziger's (1990) important discussion of the professionalism of psychology.

9 Foucault ([1976] 1980, 1982b) uses the same technique in showing how confession in early monasticism helped to reconfigure modern psychoanalysis according to a hermeneutics of self.

10 As we saw in the introduction, the idea of 'religion' and its relation to culture has been critically examined in recent years. See King (1999) and Fitzgerald (2000). William James recognised the problem with the idea of religion, see James ([1902] 1960: 26).

11 See James ([1902] 1960: 484ff; [1896] 1903).

12 The individual-social division in Maslow reveals his underlying values, see also Maslow (1971: 207–19).

13 Vitz ([1977] 1994).

5 Cognitive capital and the codification of religion

1 Whitehouse (2005a: 23) is caught in a theoretical tension between 'universal features of cognitive organisation' and the contextual 'operations' and it is precisely here that the meta-cognitive organisation of thought enters the political-economic ground of debate. The central problem is that there is always an interaction between the 'given' nature and the 'variable' perception. This easily becomes a battle for which is 'more basic' (Sperber 1996: 37) and thus it loses the dynamic interactional nature. I am, thus, not interested in trying to solve the binary nature or nurture debate, but rather to examine the values of the 'extended' space between both as – in part at least – informed by political-economy.

2 I will point out later that there are exceptions and some evidence of more recent openness, see Boyer (2005). However, most pay lip-service to such ideas and continue to carry out a restricted codified analysis.

3 Whitehouse (2005a: 26–7, 2005b: 221) does seem to concede this point, but is unable to theorize what it might mean for his work or even turn the question to his own language of cognition. The object of religion masks any potential enquiry about his own meta-representational politic.

4 See my discussion of 'science' in the Preface and related footnotes.

5 Whitehouse (2001: 169) does appear to recognise the importance of technological developments for religion, but again is unable to theorize it implications for cognitive theory. There is, however, no appreciation of economic factors in relation to cognitive theory.

6 I am aware this term links with Marcuse's ([1964] 1991) idea of 'one-dimensional man', but I am not using it specifically with this sense in mind, rather showing how thought isolates itself in the desire for truth-power.

7 Boyer's (2005) critique of Whitehouse's modes of religiosity reflects something of the attempt to find a scientific ground for a taxonomy or 'bundles of features'.

8 It will also follow that the key areas of analysis mentioned in my previous work (Carrette 2005c: 245) still pertain to my argument: (1) the social codification of the cognitive science of religion; (2) the recycling of old ideas, or disciplinary amnesia; (3) the process of metaphorical mutation and reification; and (4) the mechanistic modelling of the mind.

9 My overall tactic of reading cognitive science in terms of its own logic is employed to make it the object of analysis rather than religion. I want to place the discourse of cognition within a socio-political order of modelling and conceptual thinking. Rather than return the socio-political to cognition/minds, I want to reverse the political power order and question the grounds for such a move in the first place and, in turn, highlight alternative voices working in the wider area of cognitive theory. This removes religion as object (making a thing out of a taxonomy) and returns the cognitive to the position of the object of analysis. I am here, in turn, suspending the order of domination of cognitive science and the errors of its conceptual ideas. It should be reiterated at this point that my aim is not to salvage religion against science or cognition, for such an object has already evaporated as a political formation in my schema, but rather my aim is to make thought aware of its embodied political context (or, to repeat again, for those so inclined, to put brains back into the interacting environment of their bodies). My concern is, therefore, with the nature of abstract theory in psychology and the politics of representation in the knowledge economy.

10 For a different overview of the history of the cognitive science of religion see Barrett (2000), Martin (2004) and McCauley and Whitehouse (2005).

11 Not least, the subject received increased disciplinary visibility at the International Association of the History of Religions (IAHR) conference in Durban, South Africa, 2000.

12 Acknowledgement of direct funding institutions are given in published work, but non-specific institutional funding can also be seen in the neo-liberal university funding structure to support forms of research adopting the ideology of the knowledge economy.

13 Turing ([1950] 1964: 27) poignantly remarked: 'It will not be possible to apply exactly the same teaching process to the machine as to the normal child. It will not, for instance, be provided with legs, so that it could not be asked to go out and fill the coal scuttle. Possibly it might not have eyes. But however well these deficiencies might be overcome by clever engineering, one could not send the creature to school without the other children making excessive fun of it'.

14 Bennett and Hacker (2003: 396) claim that James is one of the few philosophers noted by neuroscientists, but without being specific they claim that 'grave flaws' inform his work. Obviously, James's thinking needs some updating from the philosophy of language, but his theory of the limits of the scientific method that I am discussing here are in line with Bennett and Hacker's own critical perspective, which obviously does not discuss James's work on religion and the neurological method.

15 Whitehouse (2005a: 1–3, 10, n.1) does acknowledge some of the literature, but does not conceptualize its implications for his theory. I think there is a genuine attempt in Whitehouse (2005b) to account for some problems in his work, but the theoretical limits and commitments of his project already mean that he is unable to think outside his codified model.

16 Many of my gestures towards Sperber are to play and appreciate his thinking on this edge of dispute; and just, perhaps, we can here have an ethically and politically informed dialogue about cognitive *science*. Once we are able to make

a distinction between mental and public representations, as Sperber does, we can at least acknowledge the political environment of the knowledge economy and the nature of technology creating an environment/ecology for cognitive models to thrive and be transmitted (even if he wishes to make this statement stronger than I by returning to a cognitive ground). Then, at least, we can out those unaware neo-liberal ideologues of cognitive science.

17 I have chosen not to discuss this last volume in detail, because it is in my view an embellishment of the earlier creative insights and thus a practice of knowledge consolidation for extending the lines of intellectual transmission. It, therefore, continues all the errors of the previous work, with perhaps some concession to environmental factors, which I note in the main body of my text. What is striking about this final text is his attempt to acknowledge some wider contextual aspects, but without any substantial change of theoretical direction. It is interesting to see that his inter-disciplinary appeal does not include the history of economics or political theory (never mind critical thinkers within these disciplinary spaces), which confirms the philosophical limits of his theory (Whitehouse 2005a: 170).

18 Sperber (1985b: 79) asserted that: 'For economic infrastructure to affect religion, it must affect human minds', but we can now rephrase it by saying: 'for cognitive theory to affect religion, it must first affect the ethical *values* of economy that shape the *representation* of human minds'.

19 I would argue that the *cognitive* has the aura of 'science' by its conceptual apparatus inside the misleading brain-mind hypothesis and by order of the knowledge economy, which sustains this discourse.

20 Whitehouse's work has been the subject of many conferences and subsequent special editions of journals, including *Method and Theory in the Study of Religion* (2002, vol. 3) and *The Journal of Cognition and Culture* (2005, vols. 1–2). See also Whitehouse and McCauley (2005). His work has also inspired a book series *Cognitive Science of Religion Series* (Alta Mira Press) and led to the establishment of his own Institute of Cognition and Culture, at Queen's University, Belfast, Northern Ireland, UK.

21 What Davis (2003) reveals is that forms of individualism are implicit within cognitive theory and economics, something confirmed by Wilson (2004) in his study of cognitive science. These hidden ideological forms of individualism and restricted ways of modelling reveal the values behind a science.

Conclusion

1 In my conclusion, I am following a Nietzschean reading of knowledge and at the same time attempting to develop an ethical framework of knowledge. For a clear summary of Nietzsche's idea of instincts and its relation to psychology see Shamdasani (2003: 192–4). Shamdasani makes the important point that Nietzsche's thinking on instincts and drives should be seen in a 'cultural-historical context'. Drives and instincts are shaped by cultural systems and thus I seek to hold a tension between an embodied biological reading of knowledge and a cultural-historical ordering of this physical order of knowledge. This links with my own desire to read across essentialist and constructivist positions. My representation of the two impulses as both 'instinct/attitude' is to hold this tension and to recognise that at the ethical attitude end of the problem I am seeking to build a framework for knowledge, but one existing upon a layered ground of embodied yearnings. I am thus trying to articulate an embodied form of knowledge.

2 I agree with Hayek's wish to over come totalitarian thinking, but not his final answer to find this in the free-market, which becomes a new form of non-governmental totalitarianism (see Chapter 2).

3 While Hayek could not make the links between economics and psychology, Hayek's (1976: 185–94) own study of theoretical psychology shows an appreciation of the 'limits of explanation' and the impossibility of comprehensive knowledge of the mind and thus rightly guards against totalitarian thinking in psychology. The problem for Hayek (1976: 185) is that he is unable to see *how* economics and psychology can be linked and thus does not see how concepts of the self order social life. He thus undermines the sociology of knowledge, which at least attempts to address the ideological link. Even if the models of interpretation hold value judgements and only 'aim at an explanation' there is the beginning of an ethical practice in reflecting on the political and economic context of science and thinking about self and world. I, nonetheless, share an appreciation of 'limits' with Hayek, but it is precisely at the limits of knowing that we have to be critically aware of the ideology of knowing and its totalitarian forms, particularly with statements about the market and the mind.

Bibliography

Abbott, A. (2001) *Chaos of Discipline*, Chicago, IL: University of Chicago.

Agamben, G. [1978] (1993) *Infancy and History: Essays on the Destruction of Experience*, London: Verso.

Ahmed, S. (2004) *The Cultural Politics of Emotion*, Edinburgh: Edinburgh University Press.

Allen, N.J. (2000) *Categories and Classifications: Maussian Reflections on the Social*, New York, NY: Berghahn Books.

Alles, G.D. (2000) 'Exchange' in Braun, W. and McCutcheon, R.T. (eds) *Guide to the Study of Religion, London: Cassell,*, pp. 110–24.

—— (2001) 'Religious Studies After Foucault: Comments on Carrette' in *Culture and Religion*, 2(1), pp. 121–6.

—— (2004) 'Speculating on the Eschaton: Comments on Harvey Whitehouse's *Inside the Cult* and the Two Modes of Religiosity Theory' in *Method and Theory in the Study of Religion*, 16(3), pp. 266–91.

Allport, F.H. (1924) *Social Psychology*, Boston, MA: Houghton Mifflin.

Althusser, L. (1971) *Lenin and Philosophy, and Other Essays*, London: New Left Books.

Althusser, L. and Balibar, E. [1968] (1979) *Reading Capital*, London: Verso.

Anderson, J.R. (1995) *Cognitive Psychology and its Implications*, New York, NY: W.H. Freeman & Company.

Andresen, J. (ed.) (2001) *Religion in Mind: Cognitive Perspectives on Religious Belief, Ritual and Experience*, Cambridge: Cambridge University Press.

Arestis, P. and Sawyer, M. (2000) *A Biographical Dictionary of Dissenting Economists*, 2nd edn, Cheltenham: Edward Elgar.

Auden, W.H. (1940) 'In Memory of Sigmund Freud' in *Another Time*, New York, NY: Random House.

Augustine [c. 420] (1988) *De Trinitate: Nicene and Post-Nicene Fathers*, 1st series, vol. 3, Edinburgh: T&T Clark.

Backhouse, R.E. (2002) *The Penguin History of Economics*, London: Penguin.

Bakan, D. (1967) *On Method: Towards a Reconstruction of Psychological Investigation*, San Francisco, CA: Jossey-Bass.

Barbalet, J.M. [1998] (2001) *Emotion, Social Theory and Social Structures: A Macrosociological Approach*, Cambridge: Cambridge University Press.

—— (ed.) (2002) *Emotion and Sociology*, Oxford: Blackwell.

Barrett, J.L. (2000) 'Exploring the Natural Foundations of Religion' in *Trends in Cognitive Sciences*, 4(1): pp. 29–34.

Barrett, J.L. and Keil, F.C. (1996) 'Conceptualizing a Nonnatural Entity: Anthropomorphism in God Concepts' in Slone (2006), pp. 116–48. (Originally published in *Cognitive Psychology*, 31(3), pp. 219–47.)

Barry, F.R. (1923) *Christianity and Psychology: Lectures Towards An Introduction*, London: SCM.

Barrows, S. (1981) *Distorting Mirrors: Visions of the Crowd in Late Nineteenth-Century France*, New Haven, CT: Yale University Press.

Bayer, B.M. and Shotter, J. (1998) *Reconstructing the Psychological Subject: Bodies, Practices and Technologies*, London: Sage.

Beer, D. (2002) *Foucault: Form and Power*, London: Legenda.

Bechtel, W.B. and Abrahamsen, A. (2002) *Connectionism and the Mind*, 2nd edn, Oxford: Blackwell.

Beck, U. and Beck-Gernsheim, E. (2002) *Individualism: Institutionalized Individualism and its Social and Political Consequences*, London: Sage.

Belzen, J.A. (2005a) 'Methodological Concerns in the Psychology of Religion: Continuities, Losses and Transforming Perspectives' in *Religion*, 35(3), pp. 137–65.

—— (2005b) 'The Varieties, the Principles and the Psychology of Religion: Unremitting Inspiration from a Different Source' in Carrette (2005a), pp. 58–78.

Bem, S. and De Jong, H.L. (2006) *Theoretical Issues in Psychology: An Introduction*, London: Sage.

Bennett, M.R. and Hacker, P.M.S. (2003) *Philosophical Foundations of Neuroscience*, Oxford: Blackwell.

Birken, L. (1999) 'Freud's "Economic Hypothesis": From Homo Oeconomicus to Homo Sexualis' in *American Imago*, 56(4), pp. 311–30.

Bettelheim, B. [1983] (1986) *Freud and Man's Soul*, Harmondsworth: Peregrine.

Blackman, L. (2001) *Hearing Voices: Embodiment and Experience*, London: Free Association Press.

Bleicher, J. (1982) *The Hermeneutic Imagination: Outline of a Positive Critique of Scientism and Sociology*, London: RKP.

Borch-Jacobsen, M. (1991) *Lacan: The Absolute Master*, Stanford, CA: Stanford University Press.

Bourdieu, P. [1980] (1990) *The Logic of Practice*, Cambridge: Polity.

Boyer, P. (1994) *The Naturalness of Religious Ideas*, Berkeley, CA: University of California Press.

—— (2005) 'A Reductionistic Model of Distinct Modes of Religious Transmission' in Whitehouse, H. and McCauley, R.M. (2005a), pp. 3–29.

Brinkley, I. (2006) *Defining the Knowledge Economy: Knowledge Economy Progress Report*, London: The Work Foundation.

Brennan, H.G. and Waterman, A.M.C. (eds) (1994) *Economics and Religion: Are They Distinct?*, Boston, MA: Kluwer.

Browning, D. (1987) *Religious Thought and Modern Psychologies*, Philadelphia, PA: Fortress Press.

—— (1998) 'Can Psychology Escape Religion? Should it?' in Imoda, F.A. (ed.) *Journey into Freedom*, Leuven: Peeters.

Bulkeley, K. (ed.) (2005) *Soul, Psyche, Brain: New Directions in the Study of Religion and Brain-Mind Science*, New York, NY: Palgrave Macmillan.

Burman, E. (1994) *Deconstructing Developmental Psychology*, London: Routledge.

Burr, V. (2002) *The Person in Social Psychology*, Hove: Psychology Press Ltd.

Burston, D. (1991) *The Legacy of Erich Fromm*, Cambridge, MA: Harvard University Press.

Butler, J. (1993) *Bodies That Matter: On the Discursive Limits of 'Sex'*, New York, NY: Routledge.

Cabruja, T. and Gordo-López, A.J. (2001) 'The Un/State of Spanish Critical Psychology' in *Critical Psychology*, Issue 1, pp. 128–35.

Campbell, K. (2004) *Jacques Lacan and Feminist Epistemology*, London: Routledge.

Caputo, J.D. (2004) 'On Not Knowing Who We Are: Madness, Hermeneutics and the Night of Truth in Foucault' in Bernauer, J. and Carrette, J., *Michel Foucault and Theology*, Aldershot: Ashgate, pp. 117–39.

Carnoy, M. (2000) *Globalization and Educational Restructuring*, Paris: International Institute of Educational Planning.

Carrette (1993/4) 'The Psychology of Religion: Re-Examining the Psychological 'Subject', *Journal of the Psychology of Religion*, vol. 2/3, pp. 171–99.

—— (1994) 'The Language of Archetypes: A Conspiracy in Psychological Theory', *Harvest: Journal for Jungian Studies*, vol. 40, pp. 168–92.

—— (2000) *Foucault and Religion: Spiritual Corporality and Political Spirituality*, London: Routledge.

—— (2001a) 'Post-Structuralism and the Psychology of Religion' in Diane Jonte-Pace and William Parsons (eds) *Religion and Psychology: Mapping the Terrain*, London: Routledge, pp. 110–26.

—— (2001b) 'Foucault, Strategic Knowledge and the Category of Religion: A Response to McCutcheon, Fitzgerald, Alles and King' in *Culture and Religion* (Spring 2001) 2(1), pp. 127–40.

—— (2002) 'The Return to James: Psychology, Religion and the Amnesia of Neuroscience' in the Special Centenary edition of William James's *The Varieties of Religious Experience*, London: Routledge.

—— (2004a) 'Religion and Mestrovic's Post-Emotional Society' in *Religion*, 34(4), pp. 271–89.

—— (2004b) 'Foreword' in Fromm, E., *The Dogma of Christ*, London: Routledge.

—— (ed.) (2005a) *William James and the Varieties of Religious Experience*, London: Routledge.

—— (2005b) 'Passionate Belief: William James, Emotion and Religious Experience' in Carrette (2005a), pp. 79–93.

—— (2005c) 'Religion Out of Mind: The Ideology of Cognitive Science and Religion' in Bulkeley (2005), pp. 242–61.

—— (2007) 'William James and Emotion' in Corrigan, J. (ed.) *Oxford Handbook on Religion and Emotion*, Oxford: Oxford University Press.

Carrette, J. and Keller, M. (1999) 'Religions, Orientation and Critical Theory: Race, Gender and Sexuality at the 1998 Lambeth Conference', *Theology and Sexuality*, Issue 11, September, pp. 19–41.

Carrette, J. and King, R. (2005) *Selling Spirituality: The Silent Take Over of Religion*, London: Routledge.

Carruthers, M. (1992) *The Book of Memory: A Study of Memory in Medieval Culture*, Cambridge: Cambridge University Press.

—— (1998) *The Craft of Thought: Meditation, Rhetoric, and the Making of Images, 400–1200*, Cambridge: Cambridge University Press.

Castells, M. (1999) *The Rise of the Network Society: The Information Age: Economy, Society and Culture*, Volume 1, Oxford: Blackwell.

Chasseguet-Smirgel, J. and Grunberger, B. (1986) *Freud or Reich? Psychoanalysis and Illusion*, London: Free Association.

Chomsky, N. (1999) *Profit Over People*, New York, NY: Seven Stories Press.

—— (2002) *On Nature and Language*, Cambridge: Cambridge University Press.

Churchland, P.M. (1995) *The Engine of Reason, the Seat of the Soul*, Cambridge, MA: MIT Press.

Clark, A. and Chalmers, D. (1998) 'The Extended Mind' in *Analysis*, 58(1), pp. 7–19.

Conn, J.C.M. (1939) *The Menace of the New Psychology*, London: Inter-Varsity Press.

Corrington, R.S. (2003) *Wilhelm Reich: Psychoanalyst and Radical Naturalist*, New York, NY: Farrar, Straus & Giroux.

Cox, R. (1987) 'Afterword: The Rich Harvest of Abraham Maslow' in Maslow, A.H. [1954] (1987), pp. 245–71.

Cullenberg, S., Amariglio, J. and Ruccio, D.F. (2001) *Postmodernism, Economics and Knowledge*, London: Routledge.

Danto, E.A. (2005) *Freud's Free Clinics: Psychoanalysis and Social Justice, 1918–1938*, New York, NY: Columbia University Press.

Danziger, K. (1980) 'The History of Introspection Reconsidered' in *Journal of the History of the Behavioral Sciences*, 16, pp. 241–62.

—— (1990) *Constructing the Subject: Historical Origins of Psychological Research*, Cambridge: Cambridge University Press.

David, P.A. and Foray, D. (2003) 'Economic Fundamentals of the Knowledge Society' in *Policy Futures in Education*, 1(1), pp. 20–49.

Davis, J. B. (2002) 'Collective intentionality and individual behavior' in Fullbrook (2002), pp. 11–27.

—— (2003) *The Theory of the Individual in Economics: Identity and Value*, London: Routledge.

Day, M. (2004) 'The Ins and Outs of Religious Cognition' in *Method and Theory in the Study of Religion*, 16(3), pp. 241–55.

Deleuze, G. and Guattari, F. [1972] (1984) *Anti-Oedipus: Capitalism and Schizophrenia*, London: Athlone.

Derrida, J. (1978) *Writing and Difference*, London: RKP.

Descombes, V. (2001) *The Mind's Provisions: A Critique of Cognitivism*, Princeton, NJ: Princeton University Press.

Devine, J.G. (2003) 'Psychological Autism, Institutional Autism and Economics' in Fullbrook (2003), pp. 212–20.

DiCenso, J.J. (1999) *The Other Freud: Religion, Culture and Psychoanalysis*, London: Routledge.

Dow, S. (1994) 'The Religious Content of Economics' in Brennan and Waterman (1994), pp. 193–204.

—— (2003) 'The Relevance of Controversies for Practice as well as Teaching' in Fullbrook (2003), pp. 132–4.

Dreyfus, H.L. and Rabinow, P. (1982) *Michel Foucault: Beyond Structuralism and Hermeneutics*, London: Harvester Wheatsheaf.

Drucker, P.F. (1939) *The End of Economic Man: A Study of the New Totalitarianism*, London: William Heinemann Ltd.

—— [1968] (1969) *The Age of Discontinuity: Guidelines to our Changing Society*, London: Heinemann.

—— (1993) *Post-capitalist Society*, Oxford: Butterworth-Heinemann Ltd.

Dumont, L. (1986) *Essays in Individualism*, Chicago, IL: University of Chicago.

Durkheim, E. [1895] (1982) *The Rules of Sociological Method*, London: Macmillan.

Dupuy, J-P. (2000) *The Mechanization of the Mind: On the Origins of Cognitive Science*, Princeton, NJ: Princeton University Press.

Durmaz, H. *et al.* (Discourse Unit, Manchester Metropolitan University) (2000) 'Critically Speaking: Is it Critical?' in Sloan (2000), pp. 147–58.

Eagleton, T. [1984] (2005) *The Function of Criticism*, London: Verso.

—— (2003) *After Theory*, London: Allen Lane.

—— (2006) 'Your Thoughts are no Longer Worth a Penny' in *The Times Higher Educational Supplement*, 10 March 2006.

Ebenstein, A. (2003) *Friedrich Hayek: A Biography*, Chicago, IL: University of Chicago Press.

Ellen, R. (2006) *The Categorical Impulse: Essays in the Anthropology of Classifying Behaviour*, New York, NY: Berghahn Books.

Elliott, A. and Lemert, C. (2005) *The New Individualism: The Emotional Costs of Globalization*, London: Routledge.

Erikson, E. [1958] (1962) *Young Man Luther: A Study in Psychoanalysis and History*, New York. NY: W.W. Norton & Co.

Esquicie, C.C. (2000) 'Critical Psychology or Critique of Psychology?' in Sloan (2000), pp. 211–22.

Evans, D. (2001) *Emotion: The Science of Sentiment*, Oxford: Oxford University Press.

Fischer, N. (1979) *Economy and Self: Philosophy and Economics from the Mercantilists to Marx*, Westport, CT: Greenwood Press.

Fitzgerald, T. (2000) *The Ideology of Religious Studies*, Oxford: Oxford University Press.

Fleischacker, S. (2004) *On Adam Smith's 'Wealth of Nations': A Philosophical Companion*, Princeton, NJ: Princeton University Press.

Fouilliaron, J. (1986) 'Lacan and Religion' in *Soins Psychiatry*, May, (67), pp. 21–2.

Fox, D. (2000) 'The Critical Psychology Project: Transforming Society and Transforming Psychology' in Sloan (2000), pp. 21–33.

Fox, D. and Prilleltensky, I. (eds) (1997) *Critical Psychology: An Introduction*, London: Sage.

Fodor, J. (2001) *The Mind Doesn't Work That Way*, Cambridge, MA: MIT Press.

Foray, D. (2004) *The Economics of Knowledge*, Cambridge, MA: MIT Press. (Originally published as *L'économie de la connaissance*, Paris: Editions La Decouverte.)

Forgas, J.P. (ed.) (1981) *Social Cognition: Perspectives on Everyday Understanding*, London: Academic Press.

Foucault, M. [1962] (1987) *Mental Illness and Psychology*, Berkeley, CA: University of California.

—— [1966] (1991) *The Order of Things*, London: Routledge.

—— [1969] (1991) *The Archaeology of Knowledge*, London: Routledge.

—— [1970] (1972) 'The Discourse on Language' in *The Archaeology of Knowledge*, New York, NY: Pantheon, pp. 215–37.

—— (1975) *Discipline and Punish*, London: Penguin.

—— [1976] (1980) 'Truth and Power' in Gordon, C. (ed.) *Knowledge/Power: Selected Interview and Other Writings 1972–1977*, Hemel Hempstead: Harvester Wheatsheaf, pp. 109–33.

—— (1978) 'Sexuality and Power in Reason' in Carrette, J. (ed.) *Religion and Culture by Michel Foucault*, London: Manchester University Press/Routledge, 1999, pp. 115–30.

—— [1978] (1997) 'What is Critique?' in Lotringer, S. (ed.) *The Politics of Truth*, New York, NY: Semiotext(e), pp. 23–82.

—— [1979] (1999) 'Pastoral Power and Political Reason' in Carrette, J. (ed.) *Religion and Culture by Michel Foucault*, London: Manchester University Press/Routledge, pp. 135–52.

—— [1980] (1999) 'About the Beginning of the Hermeneutics of the Self' in Carrette, J. (ed.) *Religion and Culture by Michel Foucault*, London: Manchester University Press/Routledge, pp. 158–81.

—— (1980) 'On the Government of Living' in Carrette, J. (ed.) *Religion and Culture by Michel Foucault*, London: Manchester University Press/Routledge, 1999, pp. 154–7.

—— (1982a) 'Afterword: The Subject and Power', in Dreyfus, H.L. and Rabinow, P. (1982), pp. 208–26.

—— [1982b] (1999)'The Battle for Chastity' in Carrette, J. (ed.) *Religion and Culture by Michel Foucault*, London: Manchester University Press/Routledge, pp. 188–97.

Frank, R. H. (1988) *Passions Within Reason: The Strategic Role of the Emotions*, New York, NY: W.W. Norton & Company Inc.

Frager, R. (1987) 'Foreword: The Influence of Abraham Maslow' in Maslow, A.H. [1954] (1987), pp. xxxiii–xli.

Fullbrook, E. (ed.) (2002) *Intersubjectivity in Economics: Agents and Structures*, London: Routledge.

——— (ed.) (2003) *The Crisis in Economics: The Post-Autistic Economics Movement; The first 600 days*, London: Routledge.

Funk, R. (2000) *Erich Fromm: His Life and Ideas*, London: Continuum.

Freud, S. [1912–13] (1985) 'Totem and Taboo' in *The Origins of Religion*, vol. 13, The Pelican Freud Library, London: Penguin, 1984, pp. 43–224.

——— [1915] (1984) 'The Unconscious' in *On Metapsychology*, vol. 11, The Pelican Freud Library, London: Penguin, pp. 159–222.

——— [1916–17] (1986) *Introductory Lectures on Psychoanalysis*, vol. 1, The Pelican Freud Library, London: Penguin.

——— [1921] (1985) 'Group Psychology and the Analysis of the Ego' in *Civilization, Society and Religion*, vol. 12, The Pelican Freud Library, London: Penguin, pp. 91–178.

——— [1923] (1984) 'The Ego and the Id' in *On Metapsychology*, vol. 11, The Pelican Freud Library, London: Penguin, pp. 339–407.

——— [1923] (1961) 'A Seventeenth-Century Demonological Neurosis' in *The Standard Edition*, vol. 19, London: The Hogarth Press and Institiue of Psycho-Analysis, pp. 67–105.

——— [1924] (1984) 'The Economic Problem of Masochism' in *On Metapsychology*, vol. 11, The Pelican Freud Library, London: Penguin, pp. 409–26.

——— [1930] (1985) 'Civilization and its Discontents' in *Civilization, Society and Religion*, vol. 12, The Pelican Freud Library, London: Penguin, pp. 243–340.

Fromm, E. [1930] (1963) 'The Dogma of Christ' in *Dogma of Christ and other Essays*, London: RKP.

——— [1941] (2001) *The Fear of Freedom*, London: Routledge.

——— [1950] (1978) *Psychoanalysis and Religion*, New Haven, CT: Yale University.

——— [1955] (2002) *The Sane Society* London: Routledge.

——— [1961/6] (2004) *Marx's Concept of Man*, London: Continuum.

——— [1962] (1989) *Beyond the Chains of Illusion*, London: Abacus.

——— [1963] (2004) *The Dogma of Christ and other Essays*, London: Routledge.

——— (1968) *The Revolution of Hope: Toward a Humanized Technology*, New York: Harper and Row.

——— (1970) *The Crisis of Psychoanalysis: Essays on Freud, Marx and Social Psychology*, London: Penguin.

——— (1973) *The Anatomy of Human Destructiveness*, New York, NY: Holt, Rinehart and Winston.

——— [1976] (1999) *To Have or To Be?*, London: Abacus.

——— (1993) *The Art of Being*, London: Constable.

——— [1994] (2005) *On Being Human*, London: Continuum.

Frosh, S. (1999) *The Politics of Psychoanalysis*, 2nd edn, London: Macmillan. (Originally published in 1987.)

——— (1991) *Identity Crisis: Modernity, Psychoanalysis and the Self*, London: Macmillan.

——— (2000) 'In Praise of Unclean Things: Critical Psychology, Diversity and Disruption' in Sloan (2000), pp. 55–66.

Galbraith, J.K. (1958) *The Affluent Society*, Penguin: London.

Gardner, H. (1987) *The Mind's New Science: A History of the Cognitive Revolution*, New York, NY: Basic Books.

Garvie, A. (1930) *The Christian Ideal for Human Society*, London: Hodder & Stoughton.

Gellner, E. (1969) 'A Pendulum Swing Theory of Islam' in Robertson, R. (ed.) *Sociology of Religion: Selected Readings*, Harmondsworth: Penguin.

Goodchild, P. (2002) *Capitalism and Religion: The Price of Piety*, London: Routledge.

Goody, J. (1968) 'Introduction' in Goody (ed.) *Literacy in Traditional Societies*, Cambridge: Cambridge University Press.

—— (1977) *The Domestication of the Savage Mind*, Cambridge: Cambridge University Press.

—— (1986) *The Logic of Writing and the Organization of Society*, Cambridge: Cambridge University Press.

Goldenberg, N. (1977) 'Jung After Feminism' in Gross, R. (ed.) *Beyond Androcentrism: New Essays on Women and Religion*, Missoula, MT: Scholars Press, pp. 53–66.

—— (1979) *Changing of the Gods: Feminism and the End of Traditional Religion*, Boston, MA: Beacon Press.

Goldman, R. (1964) *Religious Thinking from Childhood to Adolescence*, London: Routledge.

Graham, E. (2001) *Representations of the Post/Human*, Manchester: Manchester University Press.

Graumann, C.F. and Gergen, K.J. (1996) *Historical Dimensions of Psychological Discourse*, Cambridge University Press: Cambridge.

Greenfield, S. (2000) *Brain Story: Unlocking our Inner World of Emotions, Memories, Ideas and Desires*, London: BBC.

Gulerce, A. (2001) 'Toward a Critically Critical Psychology' in *Critical Psychology*, Issue 1, pp. 121–4.

Guthrie, S.E. (1980) 'A Cognitive Theory of Religion' in *Current Anthropology*, 21(2), pp. 181–203.

Halbwachs, M. (1925) *Les Cadres Sociaux de la Mémoire*, Paris: Presses Universitaires de France.

—— [1950] (1992) *On Collective Memory*, Chicago, IL: University of Chicago.

Hall, G.S. (1904) *Adolescence: Its Psychology and Its Relations to Physiology, Anthropology, Sociology, Sex, Crime, Religion and Education*, 2 vols, New York, NY: D. Appleton & Co.

—— [1917] (1923) *Jesus, The Christ, In the Light of Psychology*, New York, NY: D. Appleton & Co.

Harnish, R.M. (2001) *Minds, Brains, Computers: The Foundations of Cognitive Science – An Historical Introduction*, Oxford: Blackwell.

Harré, R. and van Langenhove, L. (eds) (1999) *Positioning Theory*, Oxford: Blackwell.

Harré, R. and Moghaddam, F. (eds) (2003) *The Self and Others: Positioning Individuals and Groups in Personal, Political, and Cultural Contexts*, Westport, CT: Praeger.

Harré, R. and Parrott, W.G. (eds) (1996) *The Emotions: Social, Cultural and Biological Dimensions*, London: Sage.

Harré, R. and Tissaw, M. (2005) *Wittgenstein and Psychology: A Practical Guide*, Aldershot: Ashgate.

Hayek, F.A. (1936) 'Economics and Knowledge' in Hayek, F.A. [1949] 1976, pp. 33–56.

—— [1944] (2001) *The Road to Serfdom*, London: Routledge, 2001.

—— (1945a) 'Individualism: *True and False*' in Hayek, F.A. [1949] 1976, pp. 1–32.

—— (1945b) 'The Use of Knowledge in Society' in Hayek, F.A. [1949] 1976, pp. 77–91.

—— [1949] (1976) *Individualism and Economic Order*, Chicago, IL: University of Chicago Press.

—— (1973–6) *Law, Legislation, and Liberty*, Chicago, IL: University of Chicago.

—— [1976] (2004) 'Introduction: Carl Menger' in Menger, C. [1871], *Principles of Economics*. Online edition. Auburn Alabama: Ludwig von Mises Institute. Available at www.mises.org/etexts/menger/principles.asp.

—— (1976) *The Sensory Order: An Inquiry into the Foundations of Theoretical Psychology*, Chicago, IL: University of Chicago. (Originally published in 1952.)

Heilbroner, R.L. [1953] (1983) *The Worldly Philosophers*, Penguin: London.

—— (1975) *An Inquiry into The Human Prospect*, Open Forum: Calders & Boyars.

—— (1985) *The Nature and Logic of Capitalism*, New York, NY: W.W. Norton & Company.

—— (1988) *Behind the Veil of Economics: Essays in the Worldly Philosophy*, New York, NY, W.W. Norton & Company.

—— (2000) 'Robert Heilbroner' in Arestis and Sawyer (2000), pp. 282–90.

Henriques, J. *et al.* [1984] (1998) *Changing the Subject*, 2nd edn, London: Routledge.

Herman, E. and Chomsky, N. (1995) *Manufacturing Consent: The Political Economy of the Mass Media*, London: Vintage.

Hirschman, A.O. [1977] (1997) *The Passions and the Interests: Political Arguments for Capitalism Before Its Triumph*, Princeton, NJ: Princeton University Press.

Hochschild, A.R. (1983) *The Managed Heart: Commercialization of Human Feeling*, Berkeley, CA: University of California.

Hodgson, G.M. (2001) *How Economics Forgot History: The Problem of Historical Specificity in Social Science*, London: Routledge.

Hoffman, E. [1988] (1999) *The Right to be Human: A Biography of Abraham Maslow*, New York, NY: McGraw-Hill.

Homans, P. (1989) *The Ability to Mourn: Disillusionment of the Social Origins of Psychoanalysis*, Chicago, IL: University of Chicago.

Houghton, J. and Sheehan, P. (2000) *A Primer on the Knowledge Economy*, Victoria: Centre for Strategic Economic Studies, Victoria University.

Hutchins, E. (1996) *Cognition in the Wild*, Cambridge, MA: MIT Press.

Infantino, L. (1998) *Individualism in Modern Thought: From Adam Smith to Hayek*, London: Routledge.

Jacobs, J.L. and Capps, D. (eds) (1997) *Religion, Society and Psychoanalysis: Readings in Contemporary Theory*, Boulder, CO: Westview.

Jacobs, K. (2002) 'Accounting for Ourselves: Accounting, spirituality and the Nature of Accountants' (unpublished paper).

Jacobs, K. and Walker, S.P. (2002) 'Giving an Account in the Iona Community: Exploring the Possibility of an Empowering Accountability' (unpublished paper).

Jacoby, R. (1975) *Social Amnesia: A Critique of Contemporary Psychology from Adler to Laing*, Boston, MA: Beacon Press.

James, W. [1890] (1983) *The Principles of Psychology*, Cambridge, MA: Harvard University Press.

—— [1892] (1985) *Psychology: The Briefer Course*, Notre Dame, IN: University of Notre Dame Press.

—— [1896] (1903) *The Will to Believe*, New York, NY: Longmans Green and Co.

—— [1902] (1960) *The Varieties of Religious Experience*, Glasgow: Collins.

Jameson, F. (1992) *Postmodernism; Or, the Cultural Logic of Late Capitalism*, London: Verso.

Jantzen, G. (1989) 'Mysticism and Experience' in *Religious Studies*, 25, September, pp. 295–315.

—— (1995) *Power, Gender and Christian Mysticism*, Cambridge: Cambridge University Press.

—— (1998) *Becoming Divine: Towards a Feminist Philosophy of Religion*, Manchester: Manchester University Press.

—— (2004) *Foundations of Violence: Volume 1: Death and the Displacement of Beauty*, London: Routledge.

Jay, M. [1973] (1996) *The Dialectical Imagination: A History of the Frankfurt School and the Institute of Social Research, 1923–1950*, Berkeley, CA: University of California.

—— (2005) *Songs of Experience: Modern American and European Variations on a Universal Theme*, Berkeley, CA: University of California Press.

Jevons, W.S. [1871] (1970) *The Theory of Political Economy*, London: Penguin.

Jones, D. and Elcock, J. (2001) *History and Theories of Psychology: A Critical Perspective*, London: Arnold.

Jones, J.W. (2002) *Terror and Transformation: The Ambiguity of Religion in Psychoanalytical Perspective*, London: Brunner-Routledge.

Jonte-Pace, D. (1997) 'New directions in the Feminist Psychology of Religion' Special section in *Journal of Feminist Studies in Religion*, 13(1), Spring, pp. 63–130.

—— (2001) 'Analysts, Critics, and Inclusivists: Feminist Voices in the Psychology of Religion' in Jonte-Pace, D. and Parsons, W. (eds) (2001), pp. 129–46.

—— (2001) *Speaking the Unspeakable: Religion, Misogyny and the Uncanny Mother in Freud's Cultural Texts*, Berkeley, CA: University of California.

Jonte-Pace, D. and Parsons, W. (eds) (2001) *Religion and Psychology: Mapping the Terrain*, London: Routledge.

Jung, C.G. (1933) *Modern Man in Search of a Soul*, London: Ark, RKP.

—— [1934] (1954) *Archetypes of the Collective Unconscious. The Collected Works of C.G. Jung, Volume 9, Part 1*, London: RKP, pp. 1–86.

Katz, S. (1978) 'Language, Epistemology and Mysticism' in Katz, S. (ed.) *Mysticism and Philosophical Analysis*, Oxford: Oxford University Press.

Kant, I. [1796] (1903) *Metaphysical Foundations of Natural Science*.

—— [1798] (1974) *Anthropology From a Pragmatic Point of View*, The Hague: Martinus Nijhoff.

King, R. (1999) *Orientalism and Religion*, London: Routledge.

—— (2005) 'Asian religions and mysticism: the legacy of William James in the study of religion' in Carrette, (ed.) (2005a), pp. 106–23.

Kemper. T.D. (1978) *A Social Interactional Theory of Emotions*, New York, NY: John Wiley & Sons.

Kippenberg, H.G. (2002) *Discovering Religious History in the Modern Age*, Princeton, NJ: Princeton University Press.

Komter, A.E. (1996) *The Gift: An Interdisciplinary Perspective*, Amsterdam: Amsterdam University Press.

Kusch, M. (1999) *Psychological Knowledge: A Social History and Philosophy*, London: Routledge.

Kvale, S. (ed.) (1992) *Psychology and Postmodernism*, London: Sage.

Lacan, J. [1966] (2006) *Écrits: The First Complete Edition in English*, New York, NY: W.W. Norton & Company.

—— [1974] (1998) *Encore, the Seminar of Jacques Lacan Book XX*, New York, NY: W.W. Norton & Company.

—— [1974] (2005) *Le Triomphe de la Religion*, Paris: Éditions du Seuil.

—— [1978] (1991) *The Seminar of Jacques Lacan: Book 2 The Ego in Freud's Theory and in the Technique of Psychoanalysis 1954–1955* (Miller, J-A. (ed.)), New York, NY: W.W. Norton & Company.

Laing, R.D. [1960] (1965) *The Divided Self: An Existential Study in Sanity and Madness*, London: Penguin.

—— [1967] (1984) *The Politics of Experience and the Bird of Paradise*, London: Penguin.

Lal, D. (1998) *Unintended Consequences: The Impact of Factor Endowments, Culture, and Politics on Long-Run Economic Performance*, Cambridge, MA: MIT.

Lal, V. (2002) *Empire of Knowledge: Culture and Plurality in the Global Economy*, London: Pluto Press.

Lane, R.E. (1991) *The Market Experience*, Cambridge: Cambridge University Press.

Laplanche, J. and Pontalis, J.B. [1973] (1988) *The Language of Psychoanalysis*, London: Karnac Books.

Lasch, C. (1980) *The Culture of Narcissism*, London: Abacus.

Lash, N. (1990) *Easter in the Ordinary: Reflections on Human Experience and the Knowledge of God*, Notre Dame: University of Notre Dame Press.

Lash, S. (1993) 'Pierre Bourdieu: Cultural Economy and Social Change' in Calhoum, C., LiPuma, E. and Postone, M. (eds) *Bourdieu: Critical Perspectives*, Oxford: Polity, pp. 193–211.

Lawson, E. and McCauley, R.N. (1990) *Rethinking Religion: Connecting Cognition and Culture*, Cambridge: Cambridge University Press.

—— (2002) *Brining Ritual to Mind: Psychological Foundations of Cultural Forms*, Cambridge: Cambridge University Press.

Lawson, H. (2001) *Closure*, London: Routledge.

Le Bon, G. [1895] (1995) *The Crowd*, New Brunswick, NJ: Transaction Publishers.

Lee, H. and Marshall, H. (2002) 'Embodying the Spirit in Pyshcology: Questioning the Politics of Psychology and Spirituality' in Walkerdine (2002), pp. 149–60.

—— (2003) 'Divine Individualism: Transcending Psychology' in *The International Journal of Critical Psychology: Spirituality*, Issue 8, pp. 13–33.

Lévy-Bruhl, L. [1910] (1985) *How Natives Think*, Princeton, NJ: Princeton University Press.

Lira, E. (2000) 'Reflections on Critical Psychology: Psychology of Memory and Forgetting' in Sloan (2000), pp. 82–90.

Long, C.H. (1986) *Significations*, Philadelphia, PA: Fortress Press.

Long, D.S. (2000) *Divine Economy: Theology and the Market*, London: Routledge.

Leupin, A. (2004) *Lacan Today: Psychoanalysis, Science and Religion*, New York, NY: Other Press.

Luepnitz, D. (2003) 'Beyond the Phallus: Lacan and Feminism' in Rabaté, J-M. (ed.) *The Cambridge Companion to Lacan*, Cambridge: University of Cambridge, pp. 221–37.

Lyons, W. (1986) *The Disappearance of Introspection*, Cambridge, MA: MIT Press.

Macey, D. (1988) *Lacan in Contexts*, London: Verso.

Maiers, W. (2001) 'German Critical Psychology at the Turn of the Millennium' in *Critical Psychology*, Issue 1, pp. 90–6.

Mama, A. (2001) 'Is Psychology Critical to Africa in the new Millennium?' in *Critical Psychology*, Issue 1, pp. 97–105.

Mansfield, N. (2003) 'The Subjectivity of Money: Critical Psychology and the Economies of Post-Structuralism' in *Critical Psychology*, Issue 8, Spirituality, pp. 129–46.

Marcuse, H. [1950] (1966) *Eros and Civilization*, Boston, MA: Beacon Press.

—— [1964] (1991) *One Dimensional Man*, London: Routledge.

Martin, L. (2004) 'The Cognitive Science of Religion' in *Method and Theory in the Study of Religion*, 16(3), pp. 201–4.

Marx, K. (1967) *Writings of the Young Marx on Philosophy and Society*, Indianapolis, IN: Hackett.

Maslow, A.H. [1954] (1987) *Motivation and Personality*, 3rd edn, New York, NY: Harper Collins.

—— (1962) *Toward a Psychology of Being*, Princeton, NJ: D.Van Nostrand Company, Inc.

—— [1964] (1976) *Religions, Values and Peak Experiences*, New York, NY: Penguin Books.

—— (1971) *The Further Reaches of Human Nature*, London: Penguin.

—— (1996) *Future Visions: The Unpublished Papers of Abraham Maslow* (Hoffman, E. (ed.)), London: Sage.

—— (2000) *The Maslow Business Reader* (Stephens, D.C. (ed.)), New York, NY: John Wiley & Sons.

—— with Stephen, D. and Heil, G. (1998) *Maslow on Management*, New York, NY: John Wiley & Sons. (Previously published as *Eupsychian Management: A Journal*, Homewood, IL: Richard D. Irwin Inc. and The Dorsey Press, 1965.)

Masuzawa, T. (2005) *The Invention of World Religions: Or, How European Universalism was Preserved in the Language of Pluralism*, Chicago, IL: University of Chicago Press.

McCauley, R.N. and Whitehouse, H. (2005) 'Introduction: New Frontiers in the Cognitive Science of Religion' in *Journal of Cognition and Culture*, 5(1-2), pp. 1–13.

McCloskey, D. [1985] (1998) *The Rhetoric of Economics*, Madison, WI: University of Wisconsin Press.

—— (2002) *The Secret Sins of Economics*, Chicago, IL: Prickly Paradigm Press.

—— (2003) 'Books of oomph' in Fullbrook (2003), pp. 125–7.

McCutcheon, R. (1997) *Manufacturing Religion: The Discourse of Sui Generis Religion and the Politics of Nostalgia*, New York, NY: Oxford University Press.

—— (2001) *Critics Not Caretakers: Rediscovering the Public Study of Religion*, Albany, NY: SUNY.

—— (2003) *The Discipline of Religion: Structure, Meaning, Rhetoric*, London: Routledge.

McDougall, W. [1908] (1912) *Social Psychology*, London: Methuen & Co. Ltd.

—— (1920) *The Group Mind*, New York, NY: Putnam.

McLaughlin, N. (1998a) 'Why do Schools of Thought Fail? Neo-Freudianism as a case study in the sociology of knowledge' in *Journal of the History of the Behavioral Sciences* 34(2), Spring, pp. 113–34.

—— (1998b) 'How to Become a Forgotten Intellectual: Intellectual Movements and the Rise and Fall of Erich Fromm' in *Sociological Forum*, 13(2), pp. 215–46.

McNamee, S. and Gregen, K.J. (eds) (1992) *Therapy as Social Construction*, London: Sage.

Menger, C. [1871] (1950) *Principles of Economics*, Glencoe, IL: Free Press.

—— [1883] (1996) *Investigations into the Method of the Social Sciences*, Grove City, PA: Libertarian Press.

Mestrovic, S. (1997) *Postemotional Society*, London: Sage.

Milbank, J. (1990) *Theology and Social Theory: Beyond Secular Reason*, Oxford: Blackwell.

Milbank, J., Pickstock, C. and Ward, G. (eds) (1998) *Radical Orthodoxy*, London: Routledge.

Mirowski, P. (1989) *More Heat than Light*, Cambridge: Cambridge University Press.

—— (2002) *Machine Dreams: Economics Becomes a Cyborg Science*, Cambridge: Cambridge University Press.

Mitchell, J. [1974] (1990) *Psychoanalysis and Feminism*, London: Penguin.

Mithen, S. (1997) 'Cognitive archaeology, evolutionary psychology and cultural transmission, with particular reference to religious ideas' in Barton, C.M. and Clark, G.A. (eds) *Rediscovering Darwin: Evolutionary Theory and Archaeological Explanation*, Arlington, VA: American Anthropological Association, pp. 67–86.

Mokyr, J. (2005) *The Gifts of Athena: Historical Origins of the Knowledge Economy*, Princeton, NJ: Princeton University Press.

Monod, J. (1972) *Chance and Necessity: Essays on the Natural Philosophy of Modern Biology*, London: Collins. (Originally published as *Le hasard et la nécessité*, Paris: Éditions du Seuil, 1970.)

Montero, M. (1997) 'Political Psychology: A Critical Perspective' in Fox and Prilleltensky (1997), pp. 233–44.

—— (2001) 'From Action and Reflection to Critical Psychology' in *Critical Psychology*, Issue 1, pp. 84–9.

Morss, J.R. (1996) *Growing Critical: Alternative Developmental Psychology*, London: Routledge.

—— (2000) 'Connecting with Difference: Being Critical in a Postmodern World' in Sloan (2000), pp. 103–11.

Nelson, R.R. and Winter, S. (1982) *An Evolutionary Theory of Economic Change*, Cambridge, MA: The Belknap Press, Harvard University Press.

Neisser, U. (1967) *Cognitive Psychology*, New York, NY: Appleton-Century-Crofts.

Nietzsche, F. [1873] (1976) '*From* On Truth and Lie in an Extra-Moral Sense' in *The Portable Nietzsche*, New York, NY: Viking, pp. 42–7.

—— [1883–8] (1968) *The Will to Power*, New York, NY: Vintage Books.

Nsamenang, B. (2000) 'Critical Psychology: A Sub-Saharan African Voice from Cameroon' in Sloan (2000), pp. 91–102.

Nye, R. (1995) 'At the Crossroads of Power and Knowledge: The Crowd and its Students' in Le Bon [1985] (1995), pp. 1–26.

O'Connor, K.V. (1997) 'Reconsidering the psychology of religion – Hermeneutical approaches in the contexts of research and debate' in Belzen, J.A. (ed.) *Hermeneutical Approaches in the Psychology of Religion*, Amsterdam: Rodopi, pp. 85–108.

Organisation for Economic Co-operation and Development (OECD) (1996) *The Knowledge-Based Economy*, Paris: OECD.

—— (1999) *The Knowledge-Based Economy: A Set of Facts and Figures*, Paris: OECD.

Oropeza, I.D. (2000) 'A Central American Voice' in Sloan (2000), pp. 125–35.

Pahnke, W.N. (1970) 'Drugs and Mysticism' in Aaronson, B. (ed.) *Psychedelics: The Uses and Implications of Hallucinogenic Drugs*, New York, NY: Doubleday, pp. 145–65.

Palmer, M. (1997) *Freud and Jung on Religion*, London: Routledge.

Parker, I. (1989) *The Crisis in Modern Social Psychology – and how to end it*, London: Routledge.

—— (1992) *Discourse Dynamics: Critical Analysis for Social and Individual Psychology*, London: Routledge.

—— (1997a) *Psychoanalytic Culture: Psychoanalytic Discourse in Western Society*, London: Sage.

—— (1997b) 'Discursive Psychology' in Fox and Prilleltensky (1997), pp. 284–98.

—— (1999) 'Critical Psychology: Critical Links' in *Radical Psychology*, Summer, 1(1). (Also published in *Annual Review of Critical Psychology*, vol. 1, pp. 3–18.)

—— (2001) 'Critical Psychology: Excitement and Danger' in *Critical Psychology*, Issue 1, pp. 125–7.

Persinger, M.A. (1987) *Neuropsychological Bases of God Beliefs*, New York, NY: Praeger.

Peters, M.A. (2001) *Poststructuralism, Marxism and Neoliberalism: Between Theory and Politics*, Lanham, MD: Rowman & Littlefield.

Peters, M.A. and Besley, A.C. (2006) *Building Knowledge Cultures: Education and Development in the Age of Knowledge Capitalism*, Lanham, MD: Rowman & Littlefield.

Piaget, J. (1926) *The Language and Thought of the Child*, London: Routledge.

Pinker, S. (1997) *How the Mind Works*, New York, NY: W.W. Norton & Company.

Piore, M.J. and Sabel, C.F. (1984) *The Second Industrial Divide: Possibilities for Prosperity*, New York, NY: Basic Books.

Poewe, K. (2006) *New Religions and the Nazis*, London: Routledge.

Polanyi, K. (1944) *The Great Transformation: The Political and Economic Origins of Our Time*, Boston, MA: Beacon Press.

Port, R.F. and Van Gelder, T. (eds) (1995) *Mind as Motion: Exploration in the Dynamics of Cognition*, Cambridge, MA: MIT Press/Bradford Books.

Pratt, J. [1920] (1924) *The Religious Consciousness: A Psychological Study*, New York, NY: Macmillan.

Prilleltensky, I. (2000) 'Bridging Agency, Theory and Action: Critical Links in Critical Psychology' in Sloan (2000), pp. 67–81.

Principe, W. (1983) 'Towards Defining Spirituality' in *Sciences Religieuses/Studies in Religion*, vol. 12, pp. 127–41.

Proudfoot, W. (1985) *Religious Experience*, Berkeley, CA: University of California Press.

Raphael, D.D. and Macfie, A.L. (1976) 'Introduction' in Smith [1759] (1976), pp. 1–52.

Rawls, J. (1971) *A Theory of Justice*, Oxford: Oxford University Press.

Reich, W. [1933] (1970) *The Mass Psychology of Fascism*, New York, NY: Farrar, Straus & Giroux.

—— [1945] (1980) *Character-Analysis*, New York, NY: Farrar, Straus & Giroux.

—— [1948] (1975) *Listen, Little Man!*, New York, NY: Penguin.

—— [1953] (1971) *The Murder of Christ*, New York, NY: Farrar, Straus & Giroux.

Rescher, N. (1989) *Cognitive Economy: The Economic Dimension of the Theory of Knowledge*, Pittsburgh, PA: University of Pittsburgh.

Richards, G. (1996) *Putting Psychology in its Place: An Introduction from a Critical Historical Perspective*, (2nd edn, 2002), London: Routledge.

—— (2000) 'Psychology and the Churches in Britain 1919–1939: Symptoms of Conversion', in *History of the Human Sciences*, 13(2), pp. 57–84.

Rieff, P. [1959] (1965) *Freud: The Mind of the Moralist*, London: Methuen.

—— [1966] (1987) *The Triumph of the Therapeutic*, Chicago. IL: University of Chicago Press.

Riesman, D. (1961) *The Lonely Crowd*, New Haven, CT: Yale University Press.

Roazen, P. (2000) *Political Theory and the Psychology of the Unconscious*, London: Open Gate Press.

Roberts, R. (2002) *Religion, Theology and the Human Sciences*, Cambridge: Cambridge University Press.

Robinson, P. [1969] (1990) *The Freudian Left: Wilhelm Reich, Geza Roheim, Herbert Marcuse*, Ithaca, NY: Cornell University Press.

Rose, N. (1989) *Governing the Soul: The Shaping of the Private Self*, London: Routledge.

—— (1996) 'Power and Subjectivity; Critical History and Psychology' in Graumann, C.F. and Gergen, K.J. (1966), pp. 103–24.

—— (1998) *Inventing Ourselves: Psychology, Power and Personhood*, Cambridge: Cambridge University Press.

Roudinesco, E. (1997) *Jacques Lacan*, Oxford: Polity Press.

Saad-Filho, A. and Johnston, D. (eds) (2005) *Neo-Liberalism: A Critical Reader*, London: Pluto Press.

Sampson, E.E. (1983) *Justice and the Critique of Pure Psychology*, New York, NY: Plenum Press.

—— (2000) 'Of Rainbows and Differences' in Sloan (2000), pp. 1–5.

Samuels, A. (1989) *The Plural Psyche*, London: Routledge.

—— (1993) *The Political Psyche*, London: Routledge.

—— (2001) *Politics and the Couch: Citizenship and the Internal Life*, London: Profile Books.

Sapsford, R. (1998) 'Domains of Analysis' in Sapsford *et al.* (1998), pp. 65–74.

Sapsford, R., Still, A., Wetherell, M., Miell, D. and Stevens, R. (1998) *Theory and Social Psychology*, London: Sage.

Sartre, J-P. (1948) *Existentialism and Humanism*, London: Methuen.

Schraube, E. (2000) 'Reflecting on Who We Are in a Technological World' in Sloan (2000), pp. 46–54.

Scholte, J.A. (2000) *Globalization: A Critical Introduction*, Basingstoke: Macmillan.

Sedgwick, P.H. (1999) *The Market Economy and Christian Ethics*, Cambridge University Press: Cambridge.

Seigel, J. (2005) *The Idea of the Self: Thought and Experience in Western Europe Since the Seventeenth Century*, Cambridge: Cambridge University Press.

Shamdasani, S. (2003) *Jung and the Making of Modern Psychology: The Dream of a Science*, Cambridge: Cambridge University Press.

——— (2005) 'Psychologies as ontology-making practices: William James and the Pluralities of Psychological Experience' in Carrette (2005a), pp. 27–44.

Sharf, R.H. (1998) 'Experience' in Taylor, M. (ed.) *Critical Terms for Religious Studies*, Chicago, IL: University of Chicago, pp. 94–116.

Sharpe, E. (1986) *Comparative Religion: A History*, London: Duckworth.

Shepherdson, C. (2003) 'Lacan and Philosophy' in Rabaté, J.-M. (ed.) *The Cambridge Companion to Lacan*, Cambridge: University of Cambridge, pp. 116–52.

Shotter, J. (1975) *Images of Man in Psychological Theory*, London: Methuen.

——— (1997) 'Cognition as a social practice: From computer power to word power' in Johnson, D.M. and Erneling, C.E. (eds) *The Future of Cognitive Revolution*, Oxford and New York, NY: Oxford University Press, pp. 314–17.

Shotter, J. and Gregen, K.J. (eds) (1989) *Texts of Identity*, London: Sage.

Segal, R. (1978) Review of *Rethinking Symbolism* by Dan Sperber, *Journal of the American Academy of Religion*, 46(4), p. 610.

Simmel, G. [1908a] (1971) 'The categories of Human Experience' in Levine, D.N. (ed.) *On Individuality and Social Forms: Selected Writings*, Chicago, IL: University of Chicago, pp. 36–40.

——— [1908b] (1971) 'Group Expansion and the Development of Individuality' in Levine, D.N. (ed.) *On Individuality and Social Forms: Selected Writings*, Chicago, IL: University of Chicago, pp. 251–93.

——— [1957] (1971) 'Freedom and the individual' in Levine, D.N. (ed.) *On Individuality and Social Forms: Selected Writings*, Chicago: University of Chicago, pp. 217–26.

Simons, J. (1995) *Foucault and the Political*, London: Routledge.

Sloan, T. (1996) *Damaged Life: The Crisis of the Modern Psyche*, London: Routledge.

——— (ed.) (2000) *Critical Psychology: Voices for Change*, London: Palgrave Macmillan.

Slone, D.J. (ed.) (2006) *Religion and Cognition: A Reader*, London: Equinox.

Smail, D. (1987) *Taking Care: An Alternative to Therapy*, London: Constable.

Smith, A. [1759] (1976) *The Theory of Moral Sentiments* (Raphael, D.D. and Macfie, A.L. (eds)) Oxford: Oxford University Press/Indianapolis, IN: Liberty Fund.

——— [1776] (1994) *The Wealth of Nations* (Cannan, E. (ed.)), Toronto: Random House.

Sperber, D. (1975) *Rethinking Symbolism*, Cambridge: Cambridge University Press.

——— (1985a) *On Anthropological Knowledge*, Cambridge: Cambridge University Press.

——— (1985b) 'Anthropology and Psychology: Towards an Epidemiology of Representations' in *Man*, 20(1), pp. 73–89.

——— (1996) *Explaining Culture: A Materialist Approach*, Oxford: Blackwell.

—— (1997) 'Individualisme méthodologique et cognitivisme' in Boudon, R., Chazel, F. and Bouvier, A. (eds) *Cognition et sciences sociales*, Paris: Presse Universitaires de France, pp. 123–36.

—— (ed.) (2000) *Metarepresentations: A Multidisciplinary Perspective*, Oxford: Oxford University Press.

Squire, C. (1989) *Significant Differences: Feminism in Psychology*, London: Routledge.

Starbuck, E.D. (1899) *The Psychology of Religion*, London: Walter.

Stavrakakis, Y. (1999) *Lacan and the Political*, London: Routledge.

Steinmueller, W.E. (2000) 'Will information and communication technologies improve the "codification" of knowledge?' in *Industrial and Corporate Change*, 9(2), pp. 361–76.

Still, A. (1998) 'Historical Origins of Social Psychology' in Sapsford *et al.* (1998), pp. 19–40.

Symington, N. (1991) *The Analytic Experience*, London: Free Association.

Szasz, T. [1970] (1997) *The Manufacture of Madness*, Syracuse, NY: Syracuse University Press.

Taylor, C. (1989) *Sources of the Self: The Making of Modern Identity*, Cambridge, MA: MIT.

—— (2004) *Modern Social Imaginaries*, Durham, NC: Duke University Press.

Taylor, E. (2005) 'Metaphysics and Consciousness in James's *Varieties*: A Centenary Lecture' in Carrette (2005a), pp. 11–26.

Teo, T. (2005) *The Critique of Psychology: From Kant to Postcolonial Theory*, New York, NY: Springer.

Throsby, D. (2001) *Economics and Culture*, Cambridge: Cambridge University Press.

Tillich, P. [1952] (1980) *The Courage To Be*, Glasgow: Collins.

Tolman, C.W. (1994) *Psychology, Society and Subjectivity*, London: Routledge.

Turing, A.M. [1950] (1964) 'Computing Machinery and Intelligence' in Anderson, A.R. (ed.) *Minds and Machines*, Englemood Cliffs, NJ: Prentice-Hall, pp. 4–30.

Turner, V. (1974) *Dramas, Fields, and Metaphors: Symbolic Action in Human Society*, Ithaca, NY: Cornell University Press.

Turkle, S. [1978] (1992) *Psychoanalytic Politics: Jacques Lacan and Freud's French Revolution*, 2nd edn, London: Free Association.

—— [1984] (2005) *The Second Self: Computers and the Human Spirit*, Cambridge, MA: MIT Press.

Ussher, J. (1989) *The Psychology of the Female Body*, London: Routledge.

—— (2000) 'Critical Psychology in the Mainstream: A Struggle for Survival' in Sloan (2000), pp. 6–20.

Valente, J. (2003) 'Lacan's Marxism, Marxism's Lacan (from Žižek to Althusser)' in Rabaté, J.-M. (ed.) *The Cambridge Companion to Lacan*, Cambridge: University of Cambridge, pp. 153–72.

Vitz, P. [1977] (1994) *Psychology as Religion: The Cult of Self-Worship* (revised edition), Grand Rapids, MI: Eerdmans.

Walkerdine, V. (1988) *The Mastery of Reason: Cognitive Development and the Production of Rationality*, London: Routledge.

—— (2001) 'Editorial' in *Critical Psychology: The International Journal of Critical Psychology*, Issue 1, pp. 9–15.

—— (ed.) (2002) *Challenging Subjects: Critical Psychology for a New Millennium*, New York, NY: Palgrave.

Waterman, A.M.C. (2004) *Political Economy and Christian Theology Since the Enlightenment: Essays in Intellectual History*, London: Palgrave Macmillan.

Watson, P. (1993) 'Apologetics and Ethnocentrism: Psychology and Religion within an Ideological Surround' in *International Journal for the Psychology of Religion*, 3(1), pp. 1–20.

Watts, F. (2002) *Theology and Psychology*, Aldershot: Ashgate.

Weber, M. [1904–5] (2001) *The Protestant Ethic and the Spirit of Capitalism*, London: Routledge.

—— (1947) *The Theory of Social and Economic Organization*, Oxford: Oxford University Press.

Westland, G. (1978) *Current Crises of Psychology*, London: Heinemann.

Wetherell, M., McGhee, P. and Stevens, R. (1998) 'Defining Social Psychology' in Sapsford *et al.* (1998), pp. 5–18.

Wharton, A.S. (1993) 'The Affective Consequences of Service Work: Managing Emotions on the Job' in *Work and Occupations*, 20(2), pp. 205–32.

Whitehouse, H. (1995) *Inside the Cult: Religious Innovation and Transmission in Papua New Guinea*, Oxford: Oxford University Press.

—— (2000) *Arguments and Icons: Divergent Modes of Religiosity*, Oxford: Oxford University Press.

—— (2001) 'Transmissive frequency, ritual, and exegesis' in *Journal of Cognition and Culture*, 1(2), pp. 167–81.

—— (2002) 'Modes of Religiosity: Towards a Cognitive Explanation of the Sociopolitical Dynamics of Religion' in *Method and Theory in the Study of Religion*, 14(3/4), pp. 293–315.

—— (2004) 'Modes of Religiosity and the Cognitive Science of Religion' in *Method and Theory in the Study of Religion*, 16(3), pp. 321–35.

—— (2005a) *Modes of Religiosity: A Cognitive Theory of Religious Transmission*, Walnut Creek, CA: Altamira Press.

—— (2005b) 'The Cognitive Foundations of Religiosity' in Whitehouse H. and McCauley R.M. (eds) (2005), pp. 207–32.

Whitehouse, H. and McCauley, R.M. (2005) *Mind and Religion: Psychological and Cognitive Foundations of Religiosity*, Walnut Creek, CA: AltaMira Press.

Williams, M. (2000) *Science and Social Science: An Introduction*, London: Routledge.

Williams, R. (1976) *Keywords: A Vocabulary of Culture and Society*, London: Fontana.

Williams, S.J. (2001) *Emotion and Social Theory*, London: Sage.

Wilson, R.A. (2004) *Boundaries of the Mind: The Individual in the Fragile Sciences*, Cambridge: Cambridge University Press.

Winnicott, D. [1971] (2005) *Playing and Reality*, London: Routledge.

World Bank (1998) *World Development Report: Knowledge for Development*, Oxford: Oxford University Press.

Wulff, D. (1992) 'Reality, Illusion, or Metaphor? Reflection on the Conduct and Object of the Psychology of Religion' in *Journal of the Psychology of Religion*, vol. 1, pp. 25–51.

—— (1997) *Psychology of Religion: Classic and Contemporary*, New York, NY: John Wiley & Sons.

Wyschogrod, E., Crownfield, D. and Raschke, C.A. (1989) *Lacan and Theological Discourse*, New York, NY: SUNY Press.

Zaleski, C. (1993/4) 'Speaking of William James to the Cultured Among his Despisers' in *Journal of the Psychology of Religion*, vol. 2/3, pp. 127–70.

Žižek, S. (1991) *Looking Awry: An Introduction to Jacques Lacan through Popular Culture*, Cambridge, MA: MIT Press.

Zuidhof, P.-W. (2002) 'Economies of Freud' (unpublished paper: www.fhk.eur.nlpersonal/zuidhof/).

Index

eBooks – at www.eBookstore.tandf.co.uk

A library at your fingertips!

eBooks are electronic versions of printed books. You can store them on your PC/laptop or browse them online.

They have advantages for anyone needing rapid access to a wide variety of published, copyright information.

eBooks can help your research by enabling you to bookmark chapters, annotate text and use instant searches to find specific words or phrases. Several eBook files would fit on even a small laptop or PDA.

NEW: Save money by eSubscribing: cheap, online access to any eBook for as long as you need it.

Annual subscription packages

We now offer special low-cost bulk subscriptions to packages of eBooks in certain subject areas. These are available to libraries or to individuals.

For more information please contact webmaster.ebooks@tandf.co.uk

We're continually developing the eBook concept, so keep up to date by visiting the website.

www.eBookstore.tandf.co.uk